LAND OF TWEED

Land of Tweed

by

DAWN MACLEOD

WILLIAM BLACKWOOD
Edinburgh

First published in 1983 by
William Blackwood & Sons Limited
162 Leith Walk
Edinburgh EH6 5DX

British Library Cataloguing in Publication Data

MacLeod, Dawn
Land of Tweed.
1. Borders (Scotland) – Description and travel –
1981-
I. Title
914.13'704858   DA880.B72

ISBN 0-85158-161-7

Printed at the Press of the Publisher

Acknowledgements

The author acknowledges with gratitude the Foreword contributed by His Grace The Duke of Buccleuch and Queensberry, K.T.

She thanks all owners of castles, great houses and grounds, together with their curators and factors, for supplying material and checking scripts; also many other local residents who discussed life and work in the Borders.

The help and encouragement of Lord Horder, who provided practical assistance on a number of exploratory tours, and of her husband, Alfred Wilson, who patiently examined scripts and proofs, has been invaluable.

Dedication

TO THE MEMORY OF A DEAR FRIEND AND NEIGHBOUR HELEN
LAURIE (NEE TURNBULL HOGG) WHO MAINTAINED TO THE END
HER PRIDE IN HAVING BEEN BORN A SOUTER OF SELKIRK

Contents

List of Illustrations

A map of the Borders appears on pages 10 and 11

The author thanks the following for permission to reproduce their photographs: Sidney Clarke 24, 27, 35; *Country Life* 31; Cumberland Newspapers 2; Department of the Environment 5, 9, 10, 11, 30; Inglis Stevens 12; Hector Innes 7, 8, 17, 21, 25, 32; Lord Horder 26, 28, 29; Lilywhite 23; National Galleries of Scotland 22; National Trust for Scotland 20; Neil Potts 6; *Radio Times* 13; Tweeddale Press 3, 4, 14, 15, 16, 18, 33, 36; *Scotsman* Publications 10; *Scots Magazine* 34.

Foreword

Many visitors to Britain seem to think that Scotland only begins at some imaginary line joining Edinburgh and Glasgow. They either fly or train to the Capital and, spellbound by the magic of Queen Victoria and Balmoral, they hurry North to the Highlands, with hardly a backward glance. Even those who drive up the motorways, that disgorge them on to the A1 or the A7, or the A68 or the A74 or the A76, dash through the Borders, as if it were a vacuum, without looking to right or left.

Yet as readers of this book will see, what a mistake they make! Hardly any part of the British Isles can boast of such a high concentration of attractions – beautiful 800 year old Abbeys, treasure laden historic houses, and 'the Scott Country' in all its scenic beauty, as immortalised by Sir Walter Scott of Abbotsford and James Hogg, the Ettrick Shepherd. 'The Borders', between the Cheviots and Edinburgh, contains the Tweed Valley, the home of some of the most famous names in Tweeds and Knitwear. There is a fine network of relatively uncrowded roads, excellent accommodation of all types, together with a climate, whose moderate rainfall and high average of sunshine are ideal for the tourist.

I am sure that those who are fortunate enough to read this book, as seeing through a window on to a fascinating new landscape, will be the first to confirm that the Borders are on no account to be missed, for Scotland begins with 'the Scott Country'.

The Duke of Buccleuch and Queensberry, K.T.

Preface

Unlike many books about the Borders, this one contains more of life than death. Those centuries of bloody strife, religious intolerance and cattle-reiving have given place here to the vigorous contemporary affairs of Border people. It is intended mainly for incomers and tourists, although some old residents say that it depicts a good deal that is new to them, and exiled Scots are always glad to refresh their memories of home.

Attempts at delineating the precise area covered by the term 'Scottish Borders' sometimes lead to argument. To give one example, those who have no connection with Peebles do not regard it as a true Border town, while its inhabitants assert vehemently that it is. The actual Border line (said to be sixty miles as the crow flies and 110 miles as man walks) has been marked and mapped, and is a controversial boundary only to those Scots who think that England should withdraw south of the River Tweed, right down to its mouth, putting Berwick-upon-Tweed once again into Scotland. Most Berwickers prefer to stay as they are, at the northern tip of Northumberland.

The 'Border Country' is another matter. It is a large, indefinable and yet distinct conception which needs to be felt rather than drawn out on a map. Then there is the Borders Region – a newly-hatched affair brought into being under the scheme known as the 'Regionalisation of Local Government in Scotland', dated May 1975. I have chosen to deal mainly with its four districts – no longer counties – of Berwickshire, Roxburgh, Ettrick and Lauderdale, and Tweeddale, with a few excursions into Eskdale, East Lothian and into England at Berwick-upon-Tweed.

The inhabited great houses, castles and grounds described in chapters 6 and 7 are open to the public in the tourist season, with the exception of Bemersyde. Uninhabited castles, towers, and abbeys classified as ancient monuments in the care of the Department of the Environment are open at certain times throughout the year. Smailholm Tower is an exception, having been restored recently and given a custodian who is currently not employed in winter months. Autumn in the Borders is often blessed with good weather, with wooded landscapes showing their richest colour, and so there is a tendency to keep inhabited houses open well into October.

Where such wealth and variety of material offers itself, compression is inevitable for a book of reasonable size and price. Selection of a personal nature has therefore been made. I am aware that many other places may claim equal merit. It is hoped that this taste of the Scottish Borders and Border people will encourage newcomers to seek out and savour more for themselves. Everyone who samples this lively and lovely part of Scotland will assuredly want to return.

I hope that those who may not be free to travel – except in spirit – will remember the gist of what they find here, long after the pages have been turned. A mural decoration of the sixteenth century, now preserved in a room above the library at Berwick-upon-Tweed, puts the idea in four lines of black-letter:

WYSDOME & SCIENCE
WHICH ARE PURE BY KYNDE
SHUDE NOT BE WRIT IN BOOKES
BUT IN MYNDE

Dawn MacLeod

1

Approaches

Travellers from England should, if possible, approach the Scottish Border country by way of Redesdale Forest and Carter Bar. The 14,000 acres of this Northumbrian forest are puny when compared with 75,000 acres of the great Kielder Forest farther west; but there are enough trees here to blanket the A68 for some five miles as the road makes a long ascent from Otterburn past Catcleugh Reservoir to the summit – where, at 1,370 feet above sea level, it passes into Scotland. Even at this remote edge of Northumberland, Redesdale's sheltering trees, meandering river, wayside villages and hamlets, and unbeautiful army camps, somehow manage between them to typify the English love of order and cosiness, forming a powerful contrast to the vast, unclothed sweep of hill and moor which springs upon the eye when Carter Bar is reached. *Scotland* says the notice-board, and the stranger automatically takes a deep breath and braces himself to meet the greater sternness of Caledonia.

For the returning exile, this moment of arrival at the Scottish Border brings exhilaration, at times accompanied by swiftly dried tears as he regrets his years of banishment. To such as he, the country, even in its grimmest mid-winter aspect, generates an air of kindliness and warmth begotten of those who live in isolated croft, village and built-up city: the Scots folk who always seem to keep a bright fire on the hearth and a humble cup (or grander glass) of refreshment at hand for the visitor. Let not the stranger feel apprehensive. If he is honest and friendly he will soon be made to understand that he is welcome to make himself at home here.

Of the many journeys I have made into Scotland by Carter Bar from south of the Border, one stands out in a kind of brilliant spotlight, unforgettable. It was an experience woven from several strands, each perfect in its own way. The season had reached that glorious week when spring begins to feel like summer. The weather was ideal, warm without being stuffy, clear and sunny but with just sufficient cloud shadow to make the landscape into a moving picture of constant change while we stood to watch; the company – that of a gallant old Scots warrior – proved congenial; to crown the day, we were greeted by a most welcome sound, which I had waited and listened for expectantly all the way home after our Mediterranean holiday – the elusive, haunting voice of the cuckoo.

My friend and I had watched migrating birds, coming in exhausted from Africa, landing to rest on beaches along the Cote d'Azur from Nice to Marseilles. As the car turned inland and covered the great open spaces of central France, more of these returned migrants were seen and heard in every hedge and field until we reached Calais. Once we were across the Channel, and had left Dover behind us, we thought to hear the cuckoo in some Kentish orchard; but when the engine was switched off, sometimes for more than an hour as we lazed and ate sandwiches under the trees, no echoes came to rouse us. In Sussex, Hampshire, Berkshire, Buckingham, Northampton, Lincolnshire, Yorkshire, Durham and Northumberland the country was silent, so far as cuckoos were concerned.

By the time we reached Carter Bar the month of May was in. In fact it happened to be my birthday. My companion had not been reminded of this anniversary; no presents or cards reached me; but here, breaking the quiet of the hills in startling volume, the cuckoo broadcast a greeting. To work out why some human beings should be moved by so absurd a cry, and that produced by one of the most barbaric of birds, would take a lifetime of research. Poets have felt it in the deep heart's core, and there is additional pleasure in a shared emotion, however inexplicable.

Another, less frequented, road for motorists coming from England is the route from Hexham to Chollerford on the Roman Wall, along the North Tyne on B6320 to Bellingham (pronounced 'Bellinjam') and thence by Tarset and Falstone through the immense Kielder Forest to Saughtree, where they may choose to go north on B6357 to Bonchester Bridge and there branch off either to Jedburgh or to Hawick; south-west to Canonbie and Dumfries; or north-west by Langholm to Roxburgh or on to Selkirk and the lovely, lonely St. Mary's Loch. Whatever his goal may be, the traveller is likely to take an interest in the fact that he has driven through part of the largest Forestry Commission property in the

British Isles. The whole Border Forest Park covers some 145,000 acres and comprises Kielder, Redesdale and Kershope Forests on the English side of the Border, with Wauchope and Newcastleton in Scotland.

Near Saughtree lies the remote demesne of Thorlieshope, sometimes known as Charlieshope, because it has come to be regarded as the origin of the home ascribed by Sir Walter Scott to Dandie Dinmont, who bred those immortal terriers Auld Mustard and Auld Pepper; Young Pepper and Young Mustard; Little Pepper and Little Mustard. Dandie Dinmont's own name is perpetuated in the breed of dog he fancied – 'A race', as Scott wrote, 'in the highest estimation at this day, not only for vermin-killing but for intelligence and fidelity'. But in his notes to the book, the author of *Guy Mannering* states that James Davidson of Hyndlee bred the famous 'cruet' dogs, and that Dandie Dinmont was a composite character. Scott certainly explored the remote country round about Saughtree, and probably the name of Charlieshope came into his mind from a memory of Thorlieshope.

At the western edge of the Border country, between Cumberland and Dumfries, stands the Gretna Green Forge and gateway to Scotland. To me, this is too much of a baited trap for tourists; but if you are one who always likes to do the 'done thing', this is obviously your route. For those who prefer the less hackneyed, there is an alternative way by Longtown and Canonbie. Given plenty of time, the road B6318 through Greenhead and Gilsland – with a side-glance at *Camboglanna* on the Roman Wall – takes one meandering delightfully around the north-east tip of Cumberland (now part of Cumbria) under Bewcastle Fell, and eventually across both the old railway and the Border near the defunct station of Canonbie. What a fascinating line that must have been! I regret never having made use of it. Until recent years such services were expected to remain permanently available for our benefit at any time we chose.

As yet no consideration has been given to the pedestrian. The most spectacular and strenuous walk from England into Scotland is by the Pennine Way, the length being adjustable. If you decide to start from the beginning, at Edale in Derbyshire, it will cause you to trudge over more than 250 miles of the roughest going in Britain. For the less ambitious, the walk may be cut to about forty-five miles by starting out from the large village of Bellingham in Northumberland. The last section, being the most exposed of all, is no place for the unfit or the timorous. To shorten it still more, it is easy to drive up the A68 to Byrness in Redesdale: a point from which the Way takes the walker by Raven's Knowe and the Border Fence to Kirk Yetholm in Roxburgh, a hard walk of some twenty-seven miles. Byrness has another attraction: a forest drive linking the A68 to the North Tyne and Kielder Castle. The Forestry Commission opened this drive in the summer of 1973.

For the first few miles, the Pennine Way northwards out of Byrness skirts the boundary of the Redesdale All Arms Range, based on the camp at Rochester, and warning notices posted by the War Department are much in evidence. Missiles which fly around when the red flags are hoisted, and the helicopters often to be seen and heard on these occasions, provide appropriately warlike symbols to link our modern army with the deserted camps at Chew Green. The great Roman road, Dere Street, runs past this point, and a new route constructed by the army in recent years follows the old 'Gamel's Path' to Chew Green and then into Coquetdale. The walker must now decide whether to continue along the Border fence for about twenty desolate miles until the Pennine Way reaches Burnhead and a friendly little road along Halterburn and down into Kirk Yetholm, or (if the heart or the weather fails), to leave the Border beyond Chew Green taking what remains of Dere Street for the three-mile descent to Tow Ford, and thence along four miles of road to Hownam in Roxburgh. As there is no bus service, it is necessary to make provision here for a car.

In theory it should be possible to find one's way without trouble on either of these courses with the aid of compass and Ordnance Survey maps; but the newcomer will be well advised to arm himself also with a copy of A. Wainwright's *Pennine Way Companion*, a detailed pocket-sized guide to the whole of the Way. It has been carefully compiled by a team of seasoned walkers, who noted every detail likely to help those who would follow in their tracks. They are forthright in warning pedestrians that this marathon is not suitable for the inexperienced or the delicate – especially the last section between Byrness and Yetholm. These cautionary paragraphs were proved to be well founded when, in the autumn of 1973, a student who had overtaxed his strength collapsed in the Cheviots during a wintry squall, and died before his companion was able to summon help.

To set against this grim story, I heard recently of a man in his seventies who succeeded in walking from Edale to Kirk Yetholm without suffering any ill-effects. He and his young Australian friend had to face a high wind in the Cheviots, and when the girl, exhausted by the effort, lay down in the grass to recover, she was rolled over and over by the gale like a helpless log. During the last weeks of September and early October, weather changes in this part of the country are often sudden and violent. We Border residents accept the fact that we may be sunning ourselves in light clothes one day, and heaping fuel on the fire and woollies on our persons next morning. Visitors from London and the south of England seldom experience such brusque changes at home, and in consequence they are apt to underrate the hazards of these northern hills.

For the pedestrian who likes to amble rather than tramp, there is a painless method of passing from England to Scotland on foot, by way of the Union Chain Bridge, about a mile down river from the Tweedside village of Horncliffe in Northumberland. On that structure, the first 'tension bridge' to be erected in Britain – its design was patented by Captain Samuel Brown RN of Eyemouth in 1817 (see chapter 5) – you may safely loiter, unmolested by more than two cars an hour, to gaze at the great river. It reaches the sea at Berwick-upon-Tweed, some seven miles off, and at this secluded spot you may watch salmon fishers in their distinctive high-prowed boats, known as cobles; admire the well-wooded banks; and listen to the songs and calls of both land and sea birds. When you have detached yourself from these pleasant sights and sounds, and reached the northern shore of Tweed, you will find yourself in Scotland, just over a mile from the A699 road into Berwick.

If you then pick up a car or bus going east, it will soon take you to Gainslaw, where again the Border is crossed – this time back into Northumberland. Going by car from Horncliffe, it is possible to cross the Border twice in under ten minutes. Life at this eastern end of the Border country provides plenty of such minor excitements, which are seldom mentioned but never quite ignored. In the ordinary course of daily affairs it is frequently convenient to buy one's postage stamps in Scotland one week and in England the next, causing observant recipients of letters to ask why stamps sent from Berwickshire bear the lion rampant on some occasions and not others. The services of Banks as cashers of cheques are utilised without fear or favour in both countries and so one's wallet usually contains a mixture of Scottish and English bank notes.

When I remarked to a friend that the proximity of the Border added a little extra zest to life without causing any trouble, she replied with a show of chagrin that this was not always true. A consignment of some rare breed of goose, sent to her order by an English farmer, had been stopped at the Border because the Scottish Department of Agriculture had imposed a ban on the import of poultry from England. 'The Border is always *there*,' she said darkly. 'If the Scottish Nationalists were to gain power and drive a wedge between the two countries, it could make life very tiresome.' No doubt many Scots would think that gains on swings of independence might outweigh losses on the roundabouts of union with the Sassenach. Meantime we enjoy perfect freedom to skip to and fro across the Border, 'doing our shopping' in England or 'getting the messages' in Scotland, just as we please, so long as we do not put live birds on the list.

In the seventh century AD an importation which crossed the eastern Border unhindered, with profound effect, was the Christian faith. On this side of the land it came from Lindisfarne, from a daughter-house of Columba's church on Iona, which originated with the mission of Aidan in 634. The long southward journey of Aidan from Iona in response to a request made by the Christian King Oswald of Northumbria, resulted not only in the establishment of a great centre of the faith and of learning on what came to be called Holy Island, but led to bands of missionaries going back north over the Border to evangelise the country of Tweed, Ettrick and Yarrow. (I speak of the Border as it is now fixed. In Aidan's day the territory between Tweed and Forth belonged to Northumbria.) The best-loved name associated with Lindisfarne is that of Saint Cuthbert – a Borderer who, as a young man, saw in a vision Aidan's soul being transported to heaven. He went immediately to the Prior of Melrose – Boisil, who gave his name to St. Boswells – and offered his life to religious service. Later he became Prior of Melrose and then of Lindisfarne.

I believe the spread of Christianity to be the most important approach of all. There can be few children of Scottish birth who have not heard the story of the monk Columba and his arrival on the island of Iona in the West Highlands. The beautiful strand where he and his twelve companions are believed to have landed, after their sea passage from Ireland in a frail craft of wicker, is still known as the Bay of the Coracle.

In our time, other means of approach to the Borders include the aeroplane – although commercial flights all begin and end outside the actual Border counties. Only helicopters and small private aircraft are provided with landing strips here and there in the country south of urban Edinburgh and Glasgow. While on a transatlantic jet flight from Toronto to Prestwick, which arrived off Scotland on a morning of unusual brilliance and clarity, I was able to look down on Britain as though surveying a map laid out below. On the descent towards the Scottish coast, I thought I could identify both northern Ireland and the small island off the Ross of Mull where Saint Columba founded his community in 563 AD. Whether this experience was a matter of of eyesight or inward vision I cannot now say with certainty. Other travellers have considered it impossible to pick out Iona before landing at Prestwick. I believed at the time that I had done so. In any case the idea left its mark, turning my attention from the huge and impressive piece of engineering which had safely ferried us over the Atlantic in a few hours, to contemplation of the greater, sustained flights of the human spirit, as exemplified by that remote little Isle of Iona.

Our approach to places is already conditioned by personal interests, acquired knowledge, mental and spiritual gifts which, whether we are aware of it or not, take a considerable share in our enjoyment of travel. Each new experience in its turn influences the personality and becomes part of us. Walter de la Mare expressed a parallel idea in neat verse:

> It's a very odd thing –
> As odd as can be –
> That whatever Miss T. eats
> Turns into Miss T.

If the relaxed summertime pleasure of cliff, hilltop, riverside or woodland picnic is sought, the Borders will provide you with a change of scene for every day of the vacation, free of long drives, traffic jams, or frustrating searches for vacant sites. Only the coastal beaches, in good weather, become thickly populated. When inertia begins to pall, the variety of active pursuits which are available in this part of the country surpasses anything to be found in southern English areas of comparable size. To enumerate them all would be tedious. Tourist Boards and local papers issue booklets and one called *The Borders*, obtained from the Tweeddale Press Group, covers a lot of ground. Golf and fishing are more plentiful and cheaper than in England, unless the angler has set his sights on the costly salmon. Motor rallies in the district of Berwickshire, which bred the famous Jim Clark; the speedway near Berwick-upon-Tweed; skin diving off the coast from St Abbs to Eyemouth, and curling at Kelso are some of the less common occupations – the latter in winter months.

With a view to filling intellectual gaps in one's approach to the Borders, it is useful to study the *History of the Berwickshire Naturalists' Club*, published annually for the benefit of members and other interested parties. These little green books are issued by one of the oldest antiquarian societies in the country, founded by Dr George Johnston in 1831. For desert island reading, I can think of no better choice than a bound volume of all 152 parts, although it would need a crane to lift it. This club caters for such a multiplicity of interests that even the most dejected castaway could not fail to be stimulated by its proceedings.

In 1931, the centenary year, the Berwickshire 'Nats.' as they style themselves in private, put up a fine memorial to their founder inside the eighteenth century 'Marchmont' curtain walls of Hume Castle. This curious relic of a fine old Border fortress, which Cromwell destroyed, is poised on a crag over 600 feet above sea level, overlooking the rich agricultural plain of 'The Merse' and its encircling hills. The memorial takes the form of an engraved direction-finder, a large circular dial fixed to a pedestal, with pointers to all the hills, castles, abbeys, towns and other features of interest in the district. Lest individual hilltops are not sufficiently identifiable from this, the engraver has skilfully etched their portraits to coincide with names round the outer edge of the dial. The pedestal is inscribed with a well-balanced quotation from the writings of the founder: 'I have taught myself to take note of and pleasure in those works with which the Creator has crowded and adorned the paths I daily walk.' From recent accounts of the *macro-lepidoptera* of Berwickshire, plants of *Daphne laureola*, *Reseda lutea*, and Oxford Ragwort at Chirnside, and the rare appearance of a wryneck in the garden of Swinton House, to studies of herb gardens, witchcraft, and the postal history of the area, it is clear that the Nats. are still teaching themselves to follow his example.

Those who walk up the steep village street of Hume will find, on the left-hand side, a notice-board which gives the name and address of the custodian. From this near-by cottage the keys are handed over on loan for a small fee, and the visitor is free to explore the place for as long as he pleases. It is as well to refrain from making this expedition until a clear, bright day of good visibility, for one such bird's eye view of the eastern Border country is worth many hours of map study.

For many of us, a historical approach to the Borders is closely linked to a literary one, because Sir Walter Scott's Waverley novels appealed to our imaginations in youth. They are destined to provide a mine of television material for children of today. In *The Bride of Lammermoor* Scott takes us to the sea-coast south of Dunbar, and in *Guy Mannering* to the wild hills of Liddesdale and as far west as Galloway, while his *Minstrelsy of the Scottish Borders* covers the whole area. There is also *The Black Dwarf*, with its famous reference to 'long sheep and short sheep' – Cheviots being known as 'long' and the original black-faced breed as 'short'. There is a well-known story of Scott in the company of sheep-farmers, asking solemnly how long a sheep had to be in order to be classed as a long sheep. 'It's the woo', Sir, it's the woo' that makes the difference. The lang sheep ha'e the short woo', and the short sheep ha'e the lang thing, and these are just kind o' names we gi'e them like.' Which, as Scott said to a friend, made a perfect sheepfold of his understanding.

In youth, my physical approach to Scotland was invariably made by train, and whether we travelled up the west coast to Carlisle and thence to the Highlands by way of Carstairs, Perth and Inverness, or chose the east coast route by Berwick-upon-Tweed and Edinburgh, those old steam trains seemed always to beat out the refrain of *Sir Walter Scott, Waverley, Waverley, Waverley*, as we approached the Border. On night journeys I would lift the sleeper blind and gaze out in the hope of seeing a beacon fire near some stout Border watchtower; but all I saw was a trail of sparks from the engine.

Between those two main arteries of rail transport lies hidden Scott's romantic dream in stone – the house of Abbotsford – cosily placed below the junction of Tweed and Ettrick.

When Sir Walter in 1799 was appointed Sheriff of Selkirk – or more exactly, of Ettrick Forest – he obtained a lease of his cousin's house, Ashiesteel – 'A decent farmhouse overhanging the Tweed, and situated in wild pastoral country', he wrote. The position suited his new duties, and here he first became integrated into Border life and custom. When his cousin later required the house, Scott was inspired to plan his own Border residence, to be named Abbotsford. Selkirk's old Courtroom may still be seen in the market-place,

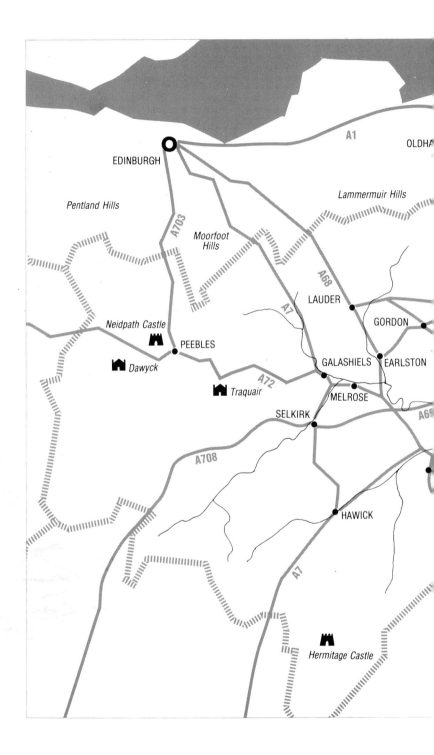

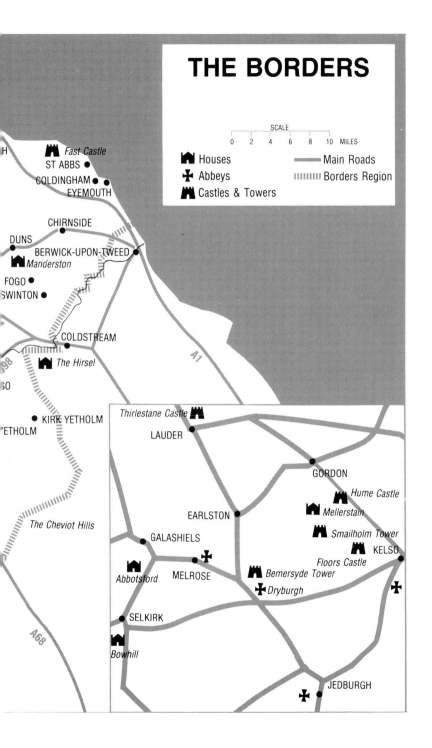

THE BORDERS

SCALE

0 2 4 6 8 10 MILES

🏰 Houses — Main Roads

✚ Abbeys ⅲⅲⅲ Borders Region

🏰 Castles & Towers

H

🏰 *Fast Castle*
ST ABBS ●
COLDINGHAM ● ●
EYEMOUTH

CHIRNSIDE ●
DUNS ●
BERWICK-UPON-TWEED ●
🏰 *Manderston*

FOGO ●
SWINTON ●

COLDSTREAM
🏰 *The Hirsel*

398

60

● KIRK YETHOLM
ETHOLM

A1

The Cheviot Hills

A68

Thirlestane Castle 🏰
LAUDER ●

● GORDON

🏰 *Hume Castle*
🏰 *Mellerstain*

EARLSTON ●

🏰 *Smailholm Tower*

GALASHIELS ●

🏰 KELSO ●

🏰 *Abbotsford*

● ✚
MELROSE

🏰 *Bemersyde Tower*
Floors Castle

✚ *Dryburgh*

✚

● SELKIRK

🏰 *Bowhill*

✚ ● JEDBURGH

with Sir Walter's bench and the chair he used, his robing-room and (sometimes) the Royal Burgh's silver cup, which he himself designed. The Courtroom is open to the public during summer months.

There is no doubt that we, as a family, knew about all these places; yet in those unmotorised days we never penetrated to the central Borders or stopped at any point except when the train halted at railway stations to set down and pick up passengers. Even in this age of motoring, most visitors to Scotland rush through Berwick, Roxburgh and Peeblesshire obsessed by thought of the Highlands, looking neither to right nor left until their distant goal is reached.

But it may be that the tide is just about to turn. In late summer we met near Peebles a London couple whose intention had been to spend one night there before continuing their journey to Aviemore and Ullapool. What they saw of the Borders on arrival so pleased them that they asked if they could keep their room for two weeks – the entire holiday, having found the proprietors of overcrowded hotels further north willing to cancel the original bookings. Peebles, we heard, has had several experiences of this kind with guests who decided to go no further.

Sir Walter Scott's first approach to the Borders was caused by misfortune. Some eighteen months after his birth in Edinburgh in 1771, he contracted what was described as a fever (probably infantile paralysis) which left him without power in his right leg. The maternal grandfather suggested that the crippled infant be conveyed to the other grandparents at their farm of Sandyknowe near Smailholm in Roxburghshire, where it was hoped the invigorating air and good country food might bring about a cure.

Sandyknowe, which in Scott's boyhood was a single-storey house roofed with a thatch, still stands, although much altered and enlarged. In later years the author said that here, at the age of about three, he had first become conscious of his own existence. The moment of enlightenment occurred in the small parlour, where grandfather Robert Scott received an important visitor, Sir George MacDougal of Makerstoun. The military gentleman, dressed in an embroidered scarlet waistcoat and a light-coloured coat, with his white hair tied in soldierly style beneath a cocked hat, put himself about to kneel on the floor of the parlour and trail his gold watch over the carpet, inducing little Walter to crawl after the glittering lure. Probably the boy was not much older when, on a day of gathering storm, he was found lying in the grass outside the dwelling, clapping his hands at every flash of lightning and crying 'Bonny! Bonny!'

Another literary approach to the Border country may be made through the works of the poet James Hogg, the self-styled 'Ettrick Shepherd', who was born at Ettrickhall in 1770. His beloved farm of Eltrieve, which in middle life he obtained free of rent from the Duke of Buccleuch, lies on the route B709 from Tushielaw to Gordon Arms, to the east of St Mary's Loch. He came from a long line of shepherds and foresters, people skilled in magic and renowned for their feyness. The poet's grandfather was reputed to be the last man in Ettrick Forest to hold converse with the fairies. Hogg's mother remembered a large number of traditional Border ballads, which she passed on to her children, and in her old age she recited these to Walter Scott, who had them printed in *Minstrelsy of the Scottish Borders*. With the forthright good sense and taste still found among simple folk in these parts, she reproved Scott for polishing and publishing the material. 'They were made for singin', and no for readin'; but ye hae broken the chairm noo, and they'll never be sung mair.'

At the tender age of seven her son went to work at herding in summertime, his wages being a pair of shoes and a ewe-lamb. For two winters he managed to attend a school, but his scholastic attainments in youth were understandably limited. Inspired at the age of thirty by the poetry of Burns, he set himself to write, seated outdoors on a rock after his flock had been tended. A competent shepherd, he published an essay on sheep which brought greater financial reward than the poems, now so well-known, produced for the author in his life-time.

Hogg knew his sheep: 'animals having little character save that of natural affection', and he understood and loved the indispensable sheepdogs without whom the hill shepherd could not do his work. 'The most docile and affectionate of all the animal creation', Hogg called them, and he would share his food with the dogs and a corner of his plaid in dour weather. As a result, he generally owned the best specimens in all the Border sheep country. One animal called Sirrah had been bought for a guinea from a shiftless drover. The dog was ill-used and in very poor condition, but soon proved to be highly intelligent and anxious to please his new master. 'When hard pressed in accomplishing the task he was put to, he had expedients that bespoke a great share of the reasoning faculty.' Sirrah was strongly attracted by music, with particular liking for the

An old-time Border shepherd wearing a plaid of tweed

metrical psalms on Sundays. Unfortunately he felt compelled to join in, and having what Hogg described as 'an outrageous ear', his efforts were not welcome.

Hogg's long poem *The Queen's Wake*, issued when he was forty-three, contains the famous lines about Kilmeny. The story bears some resemblance to the older one of Thomas the Rhymer – Thomas Learmonth, 'True Thomas', a thirteenth-century laird of Ercildoune (Earlston), who went away with the Fairy Queen for seven years – or so he made people believe.

> True Thomas lay on Huntlie bank,
> a ferlie* he spied with his ee;
> And there he saw a ladye bright
> Come riding down by the Eildon Tree.
> *marvel

But Hogg's young girl, Kilmeny, goes in search of an entirely different place, a kind of lost paradise. It proved to be her spiritual home, 'a land where sin had never been', and once she had seen it she could not bear earthly life any more.

The poet's output was large and varied. His extraordinary novel, *The Confessions of a Justified Sinner*, was written far in advance of its time. André Gide, reviewing a modern edition, said that he read it with stupefaction and with admiration that increased with every page. Befriended by Sir Walter Scott, by Professor John Wilson (Christopher North), by Allan Cunningham and by the scholarly John Leyden, Hogg developed no mean opinion of his own worth as a writer. Yet shepherd and farmer he remained to the end, declining Scott's invitation to London for the Coronation of George IV with the excuse that he could not miss St Boswells Fair. One remembers the story of an old Border shepherd who, when he lay dying in pious hope of eternal life, gave his idea of paradise as 'Bourhope at a reasonable rental forever'. Possibly the heaven of James Hogg also had the appearance of a Border sheep farm.

There is a monument to him outside Ettrick Church, and another near Tibbie Shiel's Inn at St Mary's Loch. When I visited Langholm for the Common Riding ceremonies, I learned – in addition to the pithy Scots language of the Fair-cryer – some surprising facts about the latter sculpture. The stone, a block weighing six tons, came from a quarry at Whita Hill above Langholm. At that time they had no mechanical equipment, and the first day's work with horses resulted in progress downhill of only

A fair-cryer at Langholm

a hundred yards. Next morning the team decided to abandon the horses, and with a large gang of voluntary assistants they manhandled the block of stone down the steep hillside and Kirkwynd into the market place. Once on a level road, they were able to load it into a wagon and draw it over to Hawick, to be carved into the imposing likeness of Hogg which now stands facing the Loch of the Lowes, a short distance from St Mary's Loch.

Approaches to the Border country from central Scotland have not yet been considered. Starting on the west, the main routes are from Ayr by Dalmellington and Dumfries, and from Kilmarnock through Cumnock and thence either by the dignified ducal town of Thornhill on the main road, or through the hills past Leadhills to the neighbourhood of Moffat. On a recent drive from Ayrshire to Peebles we made a slick getaway off the busy Moffat road (A74) by means of the invitingly named Greenhill Stairs. From this spectacular short cut across the grassy hills there is a splendid prospect of Annandale far below. We then had to double back on the A701, stopping after about five miles, just short of the point where the counties of Lanark, Dumfries and Peeblesshire meet, to look down on the gloomy hollow known as the Devil's Beef Tub. Cattle thieves used to secrete their spoils in this hidden glen, and Sir Walter Scott in *Redgauntlet* retold one of the many legends that cling to the place.

A story of his own time describes the devotion to duty of the guard and driver of a mail coach who, in 1831, insisted upon continuing their scheduled journey from Moffat over this exposed hill road on a February evening of terrific blizzard. When the coach stuck fast in the snow, the guard and driver struggled forward on foot carrying the mailbags, but they were soon overwhelmed. Only the terrified horses survived, reaching an isolated farmhouse at Corehead in the Devil's Beef Tub, to startle the sleeping inmates long after nightfall. The bodies of the two men, buried in a deep drift, were not found for five days.

Sir Walter Scott in his *Journal* made a note of the exceptionally severe weather experienced in Edinburgh at that time. Between January 31 and February 9 he wrote: 'The snow became impassable, and in Edinburgh I remain immovably fixed for ten days.' Half a mile from the Devil's Beef Tub, beside the present road where it crosses a burn, the small round tower-like monument erected to commemorate the victims of the mailcoach disaster bears these words:

NEAR THE HEAD OF THIS BURN
ON 1ST FEBRUARY 1831
JAMES McGEORGE, GUARD
and JOHN GOODFELLOW, DRIVER
of the DUMFRIES to EDINBURGH MAIL
LOST THEIR LIVES IN THE SNOW
AFTER CARRYING THE BAGS THUS FAR.

ERECTED 1931

A guard's horn, carved in low relief, ornaments the stone.

Not far off, on the edge of the Beef Tub, a stone obelisk serves as a reminder of a martyr of the Covenanting Times. John Hunter, a Tweedsmuir youth, was on his way to visit a sick friend at Corehead when a party of dragoons rode him down and shot him. He lies buried in the kirkyard at Tweedsmuir, and his tombstone was one of those cleaned by Scott's 'Old Mortality'.

From the Devil's Beef Tub is but a short drive into Peeblesshire (now Tweeddale) to the source of that great Border river, the Tweed. Moray McLaren in *The Shell Guide to Scotland* does not agree that Tweed rises in Peebles; he states that it runs from Lanarkshire to Berwick, and quotes the old saying 'Anna, Tweed and Clyde rise oot o' ae hillside'. The three original counties of Peebles, Lanark and Dumfries march with one another very close to Tweed's Well, which is marked as the source: but that well is (or was) in Peeblesshire. Here is a piece of exploration for the Scouts or other youth groups to work on.

Tweed's Well lies in a valley below the road to the west, and from this bubbling spring the river may be closely followed by car throughout its lovely course, via Peebles, Innerleithen, Melrose, Kelso and Coldstream to Tweedmouth on the east coast. The small church of Tweedsmuir lies less than five miles from Tweed's Well, on the east bank and near to that enchanting minor road through the hills which runs past Talla Reservoir and along Megget Water to Cramalt, where a few stones mark the old royal hunting lodge of Scottish kings. Mary Queen of Scots was here with Darnley in 1566. From this romantic, wild retreat the road winds down to St Mary's Loch at Cappercleuch, where it joins the main route from Gordon Arms to Moffat.

All this countryside is associated with that well-loved writer of our own time, John Buchan, who took the name of Tweedsmuir when he accepted a peerage. The son of a Free Kirk minister and born in the city of Perth, Buchan spent most of his holidays in Tweeddale during childhood and youth. His mother's family, the Mastertons, had been sheep-farmers for generations, and her three sons and one daughter all regarded the farm at Broughton as 'home'. John Buchan developed a great and lasting affection for the hill shepherds – 'men of the long stride and clear eye, a great race' – and spent much time in their company. One summer night in boyhood he stayed abroad with a shepherd of Redeswirehead, lying out in the heather. They talked quietly for a time; sunset glowed and faded; the dark sent the lad to sleep. A gunshot woke him with a start. The shepherd had shot and killed a vixen which had been taking too many lambs. This man could tell the time within a quarter of an hour by the sky, and could 'walk by night in a snowstorm to any place in Tweeddale'. A good-living, God-fearing person, sober, diligent, and a master of his craft. What better friend could the youth have found anywhere?

The character of the Border shepherd and hill-farmer seems to epitomise all that is best in the human occupants of this region.

The following extract from a book of reminiscences dated 1894 portrays vividly a farmer of the Lammermuirs over a hundred years ago; another sturdy character worth remembering.

> Mr James Dods was a man of primitive manners and much simplicity of character, who knew little of the world beyond what he saw of it within the range of his native hills.

On one occasion he made a journey on horseback from his farm, Belton Dods, to Belton House, the seat of his landlord, Mr James Hay of Belton, for the purpose of paying his rent. On that memorable day he was dressed in his best suit of clothes – a sky-blue coat, waistcoat, breeches, a pair of grey stocking-hose reaching from above the knee to his shoes, which they partly covered in the manner of modern gaiters. On his head he wore a flat lowland blue bonnet. His riding gear was no less primitive than his dress. A pair of sods served him for a saddle, to each of which were attached straw ropes for supporting his legs in the manner of stirrups, and he guided his stout nag by means of a pair of "branks" (scold's bridle). Thus equipped he proceeded on his journey, accompanied by two noble collies.

Arriving at Belton House, Mr Dods inquired of a groom if a man 'could get his beast put up for a blink'. 'Put up your beast! Do you take this for an inn?' But Mr Hay had witnessed the arrival of his tenant from a window of the house. Throwing up the sash he ordered the servant to put up Mr Dod's horse in the stable and to see it properly attended to. The man went off to do his master's bidding, and Dods was ushered with due formality into the presence of his laird, accompanied by the two dogs. After the usual salutations he drew from his pocket a napkin, in the corner of which the amount of the rent in hard cash was carefully tied, and handed it to Mr Hay, observing that he would find it 'a' richt, for the gudewife had tauld it a' ower yestreen mair than yince'.

With money matters settled, Mr Dods was introduced to Mrs Hay, who had expressed a wish to see him. The tenant was then invited to dine. After many excuses, saying that it would be 'ower muckle fash' to his hosts, and so on, Mr Dods finally consented. It was a strange scene, for Mr Dods was too happily ignorant of manners and customs other than his own to be ill at ease. He was delighted with the honour done him, and unconscious of the breaches of decorum he committed, and so able to quote wise saws and crack jokes with unfeigned enjoyment, and to the great amusement of the Hays.

One of his blunders must have given rise to some anxiety, on the part of Mrs Hay in particular.

When he had picked some bones with his teeth, he threw them over his shoulder on to the carpet for the benefit of the collies that stood behind his chair. In vain his hostess suggested that the dogs would be fed afterwards by the servants. Mr Dods understood not her polite hints, and replied 'Nae trouble ava', madam. I just dae sic like at hame, the faithfu' creatures like a bit frae my hand best', and over went another bone. At last he actually set down the plate with greasy contents on the floor for the 'dougs', never once dreaming of the damage he was doing to Mrs Hay's Brussels carpet.

But with all his deviations from the rules of the table, the dinner passed off to the mutual satisfaction of the entertainers and the entertained, and after drinking wine with his laird, Mr Dods made a grateful adieu, mounted his horse, and rode home to 'Benty Dods' with glee equal to that of Tam O'Shanter when he had witnessed the dance of the witches at Alloway Kirk.

A young Border shepherd

Coming down to the present day, I have met in Berwickshire a young couple who descended to the Merse from a remote Lammermuir farm 'to better themselves', as they supposed. After a few years of life in a big village within reach of several towns, they began to wonder if they had sold their birthright of freedom, peace, clean air, and country pursuits for the children, in exchange for a mess of polluted pottage which modern civilisation provides. The wife (now postmistress) told me that when her husband worked as a hill shepherd she had always felt so proud of him. Going off to care for his flock in all weathers, his dogs circling about him, he seemed to her not only a good, skilled craftsman, but somehow linked to the Good Shepherd of her Bible, and thus engaged in a specially hallowed occupation, which the better-paid work in engineering could not match. Although she and her contemporaries may not spend much time in church, they are still influenced by deep-rooted Scottish piety that will not easily die.

We have stepped aside from road approaches to take in some facets of Border character, and must now resume the survey of routes coming down from the north. The way from Edinburgh between the Pentland and Moorfoot Hills to Peebles is the shortest route from a Scottish city to a Border town. That is, if Peebles is to be regarded as truly part of the Border country, which I doubt. An attractive, clean, well-ordered place, it has a relaxed atmosphere and seems to be looking steadily northwards to Edinburgh, forgetting or ignoring the old enemy to the south: a slant of mind which one feels to be reversed in all other sizeable Border settlements, long buried though the enmity is. Perhaps the involvement of Peebles with Edinburgh is due to the excellent and direct road – a mere twenty-three miles – which in a modern car puts the capital within commuting distance. The next main route, a little farther east, is the A7 from Edinburgh to Galashiels. It links the city to 'Gala', Selkirk, Hawick and Langholm, and gives – in seventy miles or so – the most concentrated view of the Border counties available to a motorist with but a few hours to spend. And yet, how much he would inevitably miss!

Many travellers from the north going by road to 'The Merse' of Berwickshire take one of two routes, known locally as 'Soutra' and 'Cranshaws'. Both are hilly, tricky in parts when roads are frost-bound, sometimes wrapped in 'haar' off the North Sea, but in good weather full of variety and charm. The first goes through Pathhead and down Lauderdale, the second, lovelier and more lonely, by Gifford to the heart of Lammermuir. Crossing the new-born Whiteadder Water, which eventually joins the Tweed outside Berwick, and passing Cranshaws Reservoir, the main road descends to Duns or Chirnside. Even more remote is a little road which branches off about six miles south of Gifford for Longforma-cus, ultimately joining the Duns to Greenlaw road at Clockmill. Spartleton Edge, Duddy Bank, Durrington Great Law; far out in the folds of the Lammermuirs it is easy to visualise that man with his sheep, and his young wife thinking that he looked like a picture of the Good Shepherd. Even Mr James Dods might suddenly appear from his hidden nest at Belton Dods under the witches' cairn, and were he to approach us mounted on a home-made saddle with straw ropes for stirrups, guiding his nag with a scold's bridle, he would fit the timeless moorland so well that we interlopers would hardly dare to raise a laugh.

The amazing thing about those silent, seemingly remote Lammermuir hills is that they are at no point above ten or twelve miles as the crow flies from a main road. One of the busiest, the A1, runs up the east coast from Newcastle through Berwick-upon-Tweed to Edinburgh. Although much of Berwickshire's shoreline is of considerable interest and charm, the coast road is not as a rule chosen by private motorists who live in the area. It is very much a lorry route, and in places not designed for passing convoys of those juggernauts. But, unless you are coming from the west, it is necessary to take some part of the A1 in order to reach Berwick. No longer inside Scotland, the fine old walled town has been Scottish and may become Scottish again, who knows? In any case it is impossible to omit a description of it.

2

Berwick-upon-Tweed

The Borough and Town of Berwick-upon-Tweed cannot fail to attract those who will spare time to look beyond its shop windows and Bingo hall. It has greater fascination, coupled with a more violent past, than any other town in the kingdom. The first on my list of grim memories, a long list of battles, is at the same time a contributory factor to present charm; but details of the savage tug-of-war which bedevilled the place for centuries before the Union of Crowns with King James VI of Scotland I of England in 1603, when it ceased to be a bone of contention between Scot and Sassenach, may I think be left inside the covers of history books. So many writers have dwelt on the sufferings of Berwick that the name has acquired a patina of gloom. The effect of constant siege and the need for defences, as these have coloured the structure and life of the present-day town, are of greater concern to us now than accounts of bloody strife in the past.

The second ill-favoured memory, which every visitor to Berwick must carry away, relates to the unending flow of heavy traffic on the main east coast route from Newcastle to Edinburgh (the A1 or Great North Road) – a matter which has lately given rise to battles carried out with words instead of weapons. To stand at the corner of Golden Square and Marygate, where long vehicles roar from the Royal Tweed Bridge of 1928 right into the heart of the shopping centre, before turning north-west through the Scots Gate and up Castlegate, is to wonder whether the internal combustion engine has ever been so powerfully and hideously out of place as it is here. The congestion is, in part, due to those massive defences which encircle the town like a tight corset, and which some people have wished to see breached in order to make more room for traffic. The fortifications are of such outstanding merit, and in so good a state of preservation, that overwhelming protests have been showered on those who would destroy any part of them. Berwick waits for the obvious and overdue solution, the construction of a by-pass which will remove heavy through traffic from the town centre.

Unlike crafty shopkeepers, we have put the worst fruit on top and kept the choicest hidden. If Berwick is polluted by fumes and noise at its heart, it also provides a finer network of escape-routes for pedestrians than any other town of comparable size. These walks are not due to any gimmicks of town-planning, to the insertion of 'precincts' or other ideas of tempering the traffic invasion to ease the lot of shoppers. They are in fact a side-effect of military ideas of past centuries, which engineered great ramparts to enclose the town. Luckily for us today, they are unsuited to motor vehicles.

Starting at the railway station – a Victorian intruder squatting on the site of the great hall of Berwick Castle, whose remaining walls were razed to make way for the old LNER which preceded British Rail – we may easily find a path behind the telephone kiosk which takes us into a little garden at a lower level. Thence, by a flight of steps, it is possible to descend to a long flat promenade along the northern bank of the River Tweed, a sheltered walk where it is often possible to sun oneself even in winter, sheltered from the colder winds by the walled town up above. A walk down Castlegate, or along the river past the Royal Border Bridge and up to Meg's Mount, leads to Scots Gate and the next escape-route from traffic. This 'Gate' really is a gateway, three-arched and dating from the early nineteenth century, when it replaced a single arch. It straddles the meeting of Castlegate and Marygate, which are roads and should really be spelled 'gait'. It is a relief to 'gang one's ain gait' out of traffic here, by slipping upstairs at the north side of Scots Gate and so to the ramparts. Treading this other world of freedom and mown turf induces a superior, almost god-like state of mind 'Up above the world so high'. If you have an hour to spare, and enjoy windy walks, you may go right round the town at this level.

Clockwise from Scots Gate, the next bolt-hole from Berwick's streets is the Cowport off Wallace Green, the only surviving gateway in the Elizabethan ramparts. It is a vaulted tunnel, slightly angled where it was defended by a portcullis, with a wooden gate dating from 1750, and a little guard-house inside dated 1755. From this point traffic-free walks may be taken to golf course, beach, bathing pool, children's playground and rose garden – something for everyone in fact.

The King's Own Scottish Borderers on parade in Coldstream

Beside Wallace Green (where, it is said, part of Sir William Wallace's corpse was buried), are the imposing Ravensdowne Barracks designed in 1717, possibly by Vanbrugh, with a fine central gateway decorated with the arms of George I. Those interested in heraldry will like to know that the arms are quartered: 1. England and Scotland; 2. France; 3. Ireland; 4. Hanover (with its white horse and the electoral bonnet.) The French arms were retained on the British royal arms until the title of King of France was discontinued in 1801. The arms of Hanover, introduced by George I as Elector of Hanover, were kept until Victoria became Queen of Great Britain in 1837, when the Hanoverian throne passed to the nearest male heir. Until 1806 the ruler of Hanover was one of the German princes who formally elected the Holy Roman Emperor: hence the electoral bonnet on the arms.

The King's Own Scottish Borderers regimental museum inside the gates consists of four very well arranged rooms in a fine old building and is worth a visit. At the top of the stairs an imposing

25

wall chart details regimental history from its inception as Leven's (The Edinburgh) Regiment in 1689, to its assumption of the current name in 1887, up to 1952 when the 1st Battalion returned from Korea. It shows, among many notable incidents, that detachments in the late eighteenth century were employed as marines. After the return of HMS *St. George* to England in 1797, one detachment marched from Portsmouth to Plymouth. This march probably took place with particular smartness, seeing that men stood to gain 'Very big Prize Money'.

Of the many heroes commemorated, perhaps the best-known is Piper Laidlaw. His bravery at Loos was recognised by bestowal of the first Victoria Cross to be awarded a Borderer in the Great War of 1914-18. Among many old uniforms on show in the museum are Victorian shakos and helmets of the oddest shapes, fascinating curios to modern eyes. There are also reminders of Laurence Sterne's book *Tristram Shandy*, the eighteenth-century classic whose hero, Uncle Toby, was a retired captain of Leven's regiment wounded at Namur in 1695. With Corporal Trim of the same regiment (wounded two years earlier,) Uncle Toby used to follow Marlborough's campaigns in his garden. There is an illustration of the two old soldiers acting out the Siege of Namur.

After being side-tracked by the barracks, I will resume the perambulation of Berwick's walls. If we walk past the Town Hall and along Woolmarket, leaving the grand modern post-office behind on our left, there is a narrow passage ahead from Ravensdowne which emerges on the ramparts near 'Lion House', a three-storey stone building, with a magnificent outlook to the sea, and a couple of sentimentally-silly-looking lions guarding it. (For some years the house was in derelict condition, but the Berwick-upon-Tweed Preservation Trust has now restored it.) At this section of the defences there are many paths to choose from, and so wide an expanse of well-kept grass to walk about on that a full decription would be tedious. Had we continued the circuit direct from Scots Gate to Cowport and thence to 'Lion House' in a clockwise progression, we should by now have followed rather more than half the line of the inner ramparts. There are also remnants of older defences still to be explored beyond the walls to the north-east, which will be mentioned again later.

Assuming the Town Hall to be the hub of a wheel, we may now take the next 'spoke' down Hide Hill to the King's Arms Hotel, an old coaching inn with memories of Charles Dickens and an atmosphere still hospitably relaxed in Pickwickian style. From the corner below it a narrow street leads past a big motor showroom and garages, and after a few twists we reach the goal. It is known as the Ness Gate, and through its comparatively modern arch there is a surprising glimpse of tumbling waves, breakwater and lighthouse; an unexpected seascape viewed from more or less sea-level, whereas hitherto the sea has been looked at from the top of the town's defences. It is also possible to climb some steps here to the ramparts, and in front of the Ness Gate a small grassy garden with a few seats is pleasant to dawdle in during summer months.

Having returned to the corner below the King's Arms, we may go a little farther downhill, past the Playhouse Cinema and the Swimming Baths. Beside the seventeenth-century Shore Gate, with its massive studded wooden doors, is a narrow flight of steps which carries us up in front of the Gate House – and suddenly we have the pleasure of coming out on the medieval walls above the shipyard, with an imposing view of Berwick's three bridges. Never was anything so like a theatrical set as the old, odd, corners of this fascinating town. The Quay Walls here are graced by some of the best houses in Berwick, including the fine eighteenth-century Custom House, originally built for use as a dispensary. It was the first public health institution in the town.

Looking up river from this point, the bridge nearest to us is the oldest structure. It dates from the years 1610 to 1634; it is 1,164 feet long and has fifteen arches, each with a bay above it for the safety of pedestrians. The carriage way is only seventeen feet wide, and this bridge is unique in my experience by having a single-line traffic for foot passengers, who are exhorted to keep to the right-hand narrow pavement. There is just room for cars to pass on the roadway, but walkers who see a large car or van approaching will usually scurry to the nearest bay for refuge lest elbows or shins are grazed. In 1672 a French visitor, Monsieur Jorvin, wrote a glowing account of this bridge. After forty years it still ranked as a novel and wonderful sight. 'There is not a stone bridge in all England longer or better built than that of Berwick, which has fifteen large and wonderfully wrought arches; it is considered as one of the most remarkable curiosities in the kingdom.'

A popular and possibly invented story behind the inception of the great work is slightly unkind to the memory of that strange son of Mary Queen of Scots, James VI of Scotland and I of England. Known as 'the wisest fool in Christendom', he was clever enough to set out for England in 1603 directly the news of Queen Elizabeth's death reached him. He travelled through Berwick, and the ancient wooden bridge – which in those days was the sole crossing of the Tweed available in its lower reaches – so shook and rattled under the royal cavalcade that poor James is supposed to have lost his nerve. He dismounted in a hurry and prayed to God to deliver him from the raging waters below. His henchmen tried to convince him that there was no plot to cause collapse of the bridge, and ended by almost carrying the terrified monarch to the further shore, where he fell on his knees and kissed the ground. He then declared that the first work of his reign must be the construction of a solid stone bridge to unite his two kingdoms at this spot. Solid it is. For three centuries it carried all the traffic from the Great North Road into Scotland, and it looks good for another century or two.

The Tweed in flood can be menacing, and the inordinate time taken over the construction of this bridge – more than 24 years – was due in part to delays caused by a series of storms and spates, in one of which the old timber bridge was swept away and a section of the new stonework damaged. Perhaps James VI in 1603 had had a flash of prevision, after all. The sixth stone pier of his bridge, counting from the Berwick side, marks the ancient boundary between the town and the County Palatine of Durham; it has a higher parapet, and this is the place where sods were formerly placed to guide officials in the execution of their warrants. The Bridge (or 'English') Gate, demolished in 1825, was one of four town gates to be closed at curfew and guarded during the night watches. A pair of stout wooden palisades was used for extra protection upon the bridge itself. Berwick is still reminded of these precautions at eight o'clock in the evening, when curfew sounds from the Town Hall belfry.

The original sundial on the downstream parapet fell into decay, and was replaced in the nineteenth century. All that remains is a square stone pillar at the north end of the bridge, from which the dial has been removed. One fine afternoon I walked across the right-hand side and back on the opposite pavement, dreaming of the huge excitement which must have been felt by Berwickers when, in 1634, the splendid new bridge was opened for their use. As I drew near to the sundial pillar, wondering what sort of ceremony had been held, and what hour the dial told then, two middle-aged ladies in front of me were deep in conversation. Owing to the need to walk in single file, the leader had to speak rather loudly over her shoulder to her companion. My vision of the past could not survive the theme of their debate, which concerned the merits and demerits of the latest model washing-machine.

The next bridge upstream, the Royal Tweed Bridge, was completed in 1928 and opened by the Prince of Wales (later King Edward VIII). This concrete structure of four spans, the largest being 361 feet, is, like so much twentieth-century work, strong and practical but without elegance or charm. It is 1,405 feet long and carries the A1 road into Berwick from the south, causing the unsuitable congestion and noise which has already been mentioned. A little farther upstream is the third and most spectacular of the town's three bridges, the Royal Border Bridge designed by Robert Stephenson (son of the inventor of the steam locomotive), to carry the railway linking London to Edinburgh. It was opened by Queen Victoria in 1850, but may have been completed earlier than that, for a print dated 1848 shows a train puffing across the 'North British Railway Viaduct'. It has twenty-eight arches, is 720 yards long, and stands some 126 feet above the water. The cost of this fine bridge was a mere £253,000.

The association with Queen Victoria accounts for the title 'Royal'; but nobody has yet explained why it should be called 'Border Bridge', seeing that at this point the Tweed does not constitute the Border – which leaves the river at Gainslaw, a few miles farther west. During many years of rail travel up this coast to Edinburgh and beyond, I regularly saluted Scotland at the centre of Stephenson's bridge, and was only made aware of the error when Wendy Wood, in her militant Scots nationalism, removed the *England* sign from Lamberton Toll, three miles north of Berwick, and dumped it in the middle of the 1928 Tweed road bridge. It did not remain there for long; but the furore caused by this bold act apprised many people besides myself of the fact that Berwick-upon-Tweed is not in Scotland. Another misconception which I shared with many travellers from England was the belief that a fine tower visible from the carriage windows must be Berwick's church belfry, when in fact it is the tower of the Town Hall.

The story goes that a similar mistake has been made inside the town by newly-arrived soldiers, who marched to the Town Hall on Sunday church parade, and even by a visiting minister who went to the Hall to preach and was furious at finding himself locked out of the 'church' on Sunday morning! I was not altogether wrong in taking the tower for Berwick's belfry. The Parish Church at Wallace

29

The fortifications at Berwick-upon-Tweed

Green, built between 1649 and 1652 during the Protectorate, has no belfry of its own, and until the death of an old bell ringer some years ago parishioners were summoned to services by the Town Hall bells. No doubt this division of labour helped to confuse the soldiers and the visiting preacher. Oliver Cromwell, who would not permit a belfry at the church, is really to blame.

Robert Stephenson's description of his new railway-station as 'the final act of union' still seems to carry overtones more of hope than achievement, so far as Berwick-upon-Tweed is concerned. The recent Maud and Wheatley Commissions have left the town in unsplendid isolation, separated from Berwickshire and more or less marooned in a remote corner of Northumberland. In practice it serves as shopping centre and gathering-place for people living in a wide area of surrounding country, English and Scots, many of whom would have preferred to see Berwick elevated to the position of administrative base for an eastern Borders region, without restrictive barriers based on quarrels of long ago. Already it is conceded that residents inside Scotland may use the X-ray facilities at Berwick Infirmary, thus saving many a long journey to Edinburgh or to Peel Hospital beyond Galashiels. It would be equally convenient to have social services, planning, income-tax and other officials available in Berwick to all local residents.

We have strayed, by way of bridges and a railway-station, some distance from the outer defences of the town, which were touched on earlier. In 1292 Edward I of England ('Longshanks'), declared John Baliol King of Scotland, a ceremony which took place in the great hall of Berwick Castle. When the remains of that hall were removed for the construction of the station, Baliol's success was commemorated by a plaque of handsome design hung above the stairs leading down to the platforms. It bears these words:

This station stands on the site of the great hall of Berwick Castle. Here on the 17th November 1292 the claim of Robert Bruce to the crown of Scotland was declined and the decision in favour of John Baliol was given by King Edward I, before the full Parliament of England and a large gathering of the nobility and populace of both England and Scotland.

The kingdom of John Baliol contained the prosperous royal burgh of Berwick-upon-Tweed, which then lacked any significant defences, except for its castle on the north-west overlooking the Tweed. Friction between Edward 'Longshanks' and his puppet

(Baliol) developed before long into a full-scale conflict. Berwick was captured by the English in 1296, and as a result of Edward's punitive savagery Baliol was induced to abdicate and many of his nobles submitted. The instrument of Scottish humiliation, known as Ragman Roll, contained the signatures of all those who, under pressure, took the oath of fealty to the English king. The word 'rigmarole' is said to derive from this long and unrealistic document – one that had very little meaning. Maybe King Edward too doubted its validity, and this caused him to lose no time in fortifying Berwick. At first the defences consisted of a ditch, bank and wooden palisade. A little later, between 1297 and 1298, construction of a stone wall was begun to replace the original barrier.

The famous stepped 'white wall' from the castle down to the Tweed, still partially surviving, is thought to date from the same period. Near to it is the modern walk leading down the escarpment from station approach to river, appropriately named 'Breakneck Stairs'. The old stepped wall does not now give an impression of whiteness; but a house in Railway Street, which has recently had its frontage cleaned, has become very pale in hue and glistens in sunlight. In all probability the castle wall is built of stone from the same quarry and looked equally white when it was new. To stand near it on a winter afternoon as the sunset reflects fierily behind Tweedmouth, and watch a long London train with enormous diesel engine drawing out of Berwick across Stephenson's viaduct, while below the salmon fishers in their archaic-looking cobles pursue the trade as their forbears have done for over a thousand years, is to glimpse in a few moments a pageant of human history that can be matched nowhere else in Britain, and a picture worthy of Turner's brush.

We cannot let such peaceful visions blind us to the fact that much of man's story has contained episodes of brutal violence, nor dare we forget that savagery is still with us today. Whether the cruelties of Edward I – he had thousands of men, women and children butchered at Berwick, and confined Isobel, Countess of Buchan in a cage of iron and wickerwork suspended on the castle wall in public view for no less than four years – were worse than the random killing and maiming of uninvolved citizens without warning by letter-bomb and other hideous devices in our own time, is a matter of opinion. Queen Victoria, had she been able to look backward and forward on that day in 1850 when she opened

Stephenson's bridge, might have been still more upset by the horrors of our time than by those of the Middle Ages. Even in her own reign the armed forces of the crown took severe punitive measures against inhabitants of distant parts of the Empire, which she doubtless thought essential for the safety of her realm.

For the greater protection of the town of Berwick, Edward I and his son Edward II strengthened the wall, which at that period ran from the castle in an easterly direction, on a line paralleled by the present Northumberland Avenue. It went to the Bell Tower, to Lord's Mount, and then nearly at right-angles south-east to the Brass Bastion, which is the most northerly point of the later Elizabethan walls already described. The present octagonal Bell Tower is not one of the original towers, but an Elizabethan replacement; while Lord's Mount, at the north-east angle of the medieval walls, was projected by Henry VIII in 1532 and brought into use in 1555. Recent excavation work has revealed much of the structure. Perhaps sufficient has been said to show that Berwick is rich in old fortifications, enough to keep anyone who cares for such things happily occupied for many weeks. The official guide-book, *The Fortifications of Berwick-upon-Tweed* by Iain Macivor, may be obtained from Her Majesty's Stationery Office or from Berwick booksellers.

Dr John Fuller, who published his *History of Berwick-upon-Tweed* in 1799, states that the circumference

> within the present walls is one mile, one quarter and 272 yards, but taking the ad-measurement in the site of the old walls, which will include the suburb of Castle-gate, the circumference will be found to extend to two miles and 282 yards. . . . The figure of Berwick, which is somewhat circular, approaches however nearer to that of an oval than that of a complete circle.

The doctor thinks that the principal street is 'shamefully cramped' by the Town Hall being placed injudiciously in the middle of it. In his day there was a second obstruction higher up, near Scots Gate, a building known as Main Guard. This eighteenth-century guard-house was dismantled in 1815 and has been re-erected on the road down to Palace Green. There are critics today who would like to see the Town Hall demolished to make way for faster traffic; but the majority of residents, backed by the Preservation Trust, is unlikely to allow this vandalism. Most pedestrians take the view that the Town Hall at the lower end and Scots Gate higher up the main shopping thoroughfare are obstructions of benefit to them because they prevent unsuitable speed on the part of motorists.

The Town Hall stands on the site of two earlier tolbooths, and dates from the second half of the eighteenth century. It is unusually narrow for its height, seemingly squeezed upwards to fit the confined space. The architects were a London firm, Samuel and John Worrall, who engaged contractors named Pattison and Dods. The last-named inscribed his name above the door as 'J. Dods – Architect', thus perpetuating himself in many people's eyes as the designer of Berwick's Town Hall. It has a grand portico with four Tuscan columns supporting a pediment engraved with the arms of the town, and a steeple, 150 feet high, which closely resembles that of St Martin-in-the-Fields, in London's Trafalgar Square. The belfry contains eight bells, one of which sounds curfew every night at eight o'clock, with the exception of Sunday. A hundred years ago the building served as Council meeting-chamber, Mayor's parlour, Sheriff court, police station, gaol and butter market. The cells may still be seen, and visitors are shown over the present Council chamber and the disused prison and belfry on application to the custodian, if twenty-four hours' notice is given.

Dr Fuller remarks that:

Were this elegant piece of architecture placed in a situation where it might appear to greater advantage, it would vie with almost any other in the kingdom.

In addition to the prison cells, he mentions that some apartments are let out by the corporation to tradesmen.

The eastern part of the ground floor is formed into a piazza, which is allotted for poultry, meal, egg and butter markets; also for the hiring of servants. It is called The Exchange, and measures 46 feet 9 inches in length, 36 feet 8 inches in width and 13 feet in height. The middle storey consists of two halls, a committee room, two smaller apartments and a large staircase leading to the uppermost floor. The first or outer hall is sixty feet long, thirty-one feet broad and seventeen feet high. In this hall the Mayor and Members of Parliament are elected; civil and criminal courts held, also Guild meetings. The inner hall is exceedingly well lit, having four windows fronting the south, and a large Venetian one in the east end of the hall. The Assemblies were formerly held here, and the Mayor's dinners and other great entertainments were given in it.

Dr Fuller refers to the upper flat, occupied as a common gaol, which he believes to be perhaps the most healthy and pleasant one in the kingdom. This is owing to its many large windows, from which the prisoners enjoy several excellent views of the town, the German Ocean, Bambro' Castle and Holy Island. There is a long gallery which they are allowed to perambulate. Tradesmen when confined [for debt] have a liberty to work in this gaol. We have even heard of some who retrieved their fortunes in it.

Having visited this grim establishment, I would not consider 'pleasant' a suitable adjective, and think the worthy doctor must have had a full stomach and a sluggish imagination to describe it in this way.

The building is certainly worth seeing, even though the old gaol, still unchanged but mercifully not in use, may induce a nightmare later on. Bare, cold cells, with heavy leg-irons still bolted to the walls, the bolts being padlocked on the outside; rings in the roof-beams where men were hung up by the wrists, able only to take their weight off stretched arms by standing on tiptoe – hence the phrase 'keep on your toes'; other rings in the walls, where men were spread-eagled to be birched, and metal hot-water bottles, shaped to waist and flank, which were applied to the lacerated flesh: hideous instruments of torture known as 'kidney bottles'; these and more make for disgust and horror in the modern mind.

Also shown is the 'condemned cell' of this, the oldest gaol still standing in Britain. The last prisoner to be hanged at Berwick was confined here before her execution in 1823. Grace Griffin, sentenced to death for the murder of her husband, sat or lay in semi-darkness on this plank bed, without mattress or cover, listening to the debtors on the other side of the partition as they worked on the construction of her coffin. In this receptacle she was obliged to sit while being taken in a horse-drawn cart to Gallows Hill, situated west of the present railway station. Local tradition says that this woman, who had protested her innocence throughout the trial, was accompanied on her last dreadful journey by a white dove, which flew down to perch on her shoulder.

While picturing these past horrors, the mind receives a sudden gleam of relief on seeing a series of drawings, of a refined and delicate nature, scratched on the wooden panelling of certain cells by prisoners. Nearly all of them depict sailing vessels. As Berwick used to be one of the most important seaports in the kingdom, most of those confined to its gaol were mariners. From the windows and the parapet used for exercise by certain classes of prisoner, a panoramic view of the rooftops can be seen. Some old buildings are still covered in the red pantiles which used to be brought in as ballast from the Low Countries where they were manufactured. An interesting feature of this form of roofing is that often the lowest courses, five or six rows, are of slate. We were told that this construction was devised to shed heavy snowfalls. With pantiles laid down to the gutter level, lower courses were likely to be choked, for the snow did not slide off them so readily as from the smooth slates.

The belfry, separated from the prison by immense double doors, contains a trapdoor in the floor, made for the purpose of lowering bells when these required attention. It was found useful also when drunk and incapable prisoners had to be confined in the cells. They were hauled up on a rope through the floor instead of being propelled along passages and up steep stairs. The belfry has its own separate access of wooden ladder-like steps, designed to keep the ringers away from the prison.

Single bells, in addition to ringing curfew at eight o'clock on weekday evenings, are used when the Freedom of Berwick is conferred, and the 'Pancake Bell' sounds over the town from 11.45 until noon on Shrove Tuesday. In the past it was customary to toll the 'Dead Bell' on the occasion of a death in Berwick. The fee paid by relatives covered a notice on the front door of the Town Hall, so that those who heard the bell could send messengers to find out which citizen had died. The more affluent families paid one guinea for this service, and were given a larger bell than the poor, who could only find half that sum.

Eight one-pint beer mugs in the belfry are still filled by the Mayor on special occasions. The ringers are encouraged to keep strict time by a notice which reads:

> Keep stock of time
> And goe not out
> Or elles you forfeit
> Out of doubt
> A jugge of beer.

The induction of a vicar at the Parish Church formerly involved new incumbents in a rush from ceremony to Town Hall, to ring themselves in, an ordeal which has now been discontinued.

From ghastly gaol and bare belfry the visitor descends to the comforts of Council Chamber, Mayor's Parlour and Assembly Hall. In the parlour may be seen many treasures, including a letter sent by Nelson in 1800 after receiving the Freedom of Berwick. The Mayor's unique purple robe hangs here, a garb which, together with the ancient office, has been retained by special permission of Queen Elizabeth II following re-organisation of local government, which has led to abolition of civic dignitaries in many other places. The handsome buff breeches, tails and top-hats worn by the mace-bearer and halberdiers (bearers of splendid halberds, the oldest in Britain, dating from 1685), will continue to grace the streets in mayoral processions.

Space has been devoted to the Town Hall, for it is the core and essential, dominating feature of Berwick, at first sight out-doing even the unique walls. Less noticeable is the parish church of the Holy Trinity, constructed of stone taken from the old castle, and one of the only two churches in England dating from the Commonwealth. Another piece of stonework which should on no account be missed is the pier, erected between 1810 and 1821 at a cost of about £61,000. This splendid bulwark against the sea is also a popular and unusual promenade, 960 yards long and a place of invigorating breezes and salt spray. It is guaranteed to rejuvenate tired city dwellers in record time. It is also a good look-out place from which to watch the salmon cobles, fishermen and seals which take their toll of fish. At low tide the shore has a large population of sea-birds, waders, swans and even rooks and wagtails in search of edible morsels. The pier terminates in an electrically-operated light, flashing every five seconds and visible for twelve miles.

Berwick has a chartered right to hold twice-weekly markets, on Wednesdays and Saturdays. The street from the Town Hall up to the corner of Golden Square, where the A1 joins Marygate, is lined on one side with the stalls of traders, centres of animated business all day, come wind and weather. Both sellers and customers are hardy folk. Some people consider such a market to be out of tune with the traffic of modern times; but it is a lively, colourful scene, well worth keeping. The cattle market used also to be held within the walls, at Hide Hill. This was removed to an exterior site at the close of the nineteenth century. Where the egg and butter sellers formerly congregated with their wares at the east end of the Town Hall, we now find the entrance to an unusual cafe and gift shop, in which clients sit at tables between immense stone pillars under a vaulted ceiling.

Before leaving this ancient and absorbing town of Berwick by the Scots Gate at the junction of the streets called Marygate and

Berwick from the estuary

Castlegate, we may put the traffic jams of today in perspective by glancing back at heavier burdens borne by citizens in Dr Fuller's time. He complains bitterly of the hardship caused by the practice of closing the town gates at nightfall, 'a custom no longer of any value as regards the safety of inhabitants, which had become a nuisance and in some cases a danger to life'. On one occasion his services were required at a difficult childbirth, and two girls sent as messengers were kept parleying for half an hour by rude and heartless sentinels. By the time the doctor reached his case, the new baby was dead and the unfortunate mother in a state of collapse. Physicians, surgeons, midwives and those sent to fetch them were supposed to be given passage, but the system was open to serious abuse.

Dr Fuller wrote:

If a person, upon his first coming up to the gate, quarrels with the guard, the greatest importunities afterwards for admission will more than likely be of no avail. Even medical people returning from the country, exhausted by fatigue and want of sleep, are sometimes detained for a long time at the gates. On some such occasions the sentry insists that the person is using a fictitious name, and he will not even open the wicket to inform himself whether it is so or not, either by looking at his passport or his person.

It sometimes happens, when they grant this indulgence in a rage, or in a state of intoxication, that they let go the great wooden bar of the gate, the consequence of which may be either the death of the rider or his horse. We know of several persons who, owing to that circumstance, have made narrow escapes at these gates.

Thoughts of these eighteenth-century trials, coupled with the sight of stocks beside the pavement just outside Scots Gate – a crude punishment only discontinued in 1857 – may help us endure the discomforts of the nineteen-eighties.

Having left Scots Gate behind, crossed the railway bridge and taken the right-hand fork, we have some three miles of the A1 to cover before the northern tip of Berwick Bounds is reached. Here, until recently, stood on the Scottish Border the remnants of two eighteenth-century cottages – Lamberton Toll and Marriage House, the latter being from 1798 to 1885 as much used by eloping couples from England (and by respectable local pairs in the normal course of events) as was the famous smithy at Gretna Green on the other side of Scotland. In a booklet dated 1933, issued by Northumberland and Berwickshire Newspapers Ltd. of Berwick-upon-Tweed, it is said that there may have been more marriages performed at Lamberton than at Gretna in the nineteenth century.

The 'Berwick Room' above the Public Library has on display a placard of 1850, in which a Mr W. Ness of the Blue Bell Inn offers to perform marriages at Lamberton

> in a manner which must give general satisfaction. . . . A correct Registry will be kept and carefully preserved, and the most honourable secrecy, when required, will be maintained. . . . By these means Mr N hopes to restore to its pristine purity this ancient heirloom of our Ancestors, and to render this primitive and romantic Institution as reputable as it is popular and as honourable as it is binding and legitimate.

Mr N also offers 'Private tuition in English Grammar, Book-keeping, Geometry, Algebra, Surveying, Etc', together with 'French Language and Rudiments of Greek and Latin'. Nor is this all, for he offers as well to write letters and prepare petitions for applicants 'to the various Government Offices and other Public Institutions'.

Many members of old Border families, remembering grandparents and great-grandparents who were married at Lamberton in the Marriage-house beside the Toll, had hoped to see the buildings restored and cared for – possibly for use as a folk museum, where pictures of old-time weddings, marriage certificates and other relics would have made a tourist attraction. Unhappily, Government Departments did not look with favour on the idea, and insisted upon sweeping away the ancient Toll and Marriage House. These have now been demolished, leaving no trace. Had Mr W. Ness been alive, he might have drafted a petition so moving that even stony-hearted officials would have been prevented from causing such witless destruction of local history.

3

Abbeys and their Towns

Kelso

Kelso stands on a limestone bank above the Tweed. In earlier times, before paved streets and built-up terraces obscured the chalky nature of this ridge, it appeared strikingly pale by contrast with the warmer coloured soil of most fields in the vicinity, and so gave to Kelso the name which means 'chalky height'. Down the ages this has been variously spelt Calkon, Kelcon and Kalyhow. Chalkheugh Terrace, a narrow turning near the bus station, still reminds us of the chalk cliff bordering Tweed to north-west of the town. At one end of this terrace foot-path is a little public garden with seats, giving the exploring pedestrian a restful viewpoint up above the weir where Teviot joins Tweed in a flurry. Beyond that is St James's Fair Green – a narrow neck of land between the rivers; the Teviot bridge – a handsome stone structure half hidden in trees; the site of old Roxburgh Castle and, on the north bank of Tweed, vast wooded parkland dominated by the Duke of Roxburghe's castle of Floors (see chapter 7).

All that remains of the once powerful medieval stronghold, Roxburgh Castle, green mounds where sheep may safely graze, lies but a short distance away between the two rivers. Except to the mind's eye they are not discernible from here. No doubt the imagination of Sir Walter Scott was at work when he dubbed this prospect, seen from Walton Hall, the oldest House in Roxburgh Street, 'the finest in Scotland'. Most travellers who have admired the country of Tay and Spey, the wild sea-lochs of the West Highlands and the homelier Trossachs may think that he was exaggerating. But a patient observer of the scene below Chalk-heugh at Kelso, with time to sit and stare, will come under a curious spell, particularly on those days of stillness and clarity in spring and autumn when the limpid water of Tweed appears to reflect, not sky alone, but a gateway to realms of the spirit beyond mortal ken, for which no words exist. I have felt nothing to match this elsewhere.

No doubt there was some small cluster of dwellings on this chalk ridge before David I established the abbey; but to that great medieval foundation the town now known locally as 'Kelsae' owes its importance. The place is still very much under the thumb of its grey ecclesiastical ruin, and in the surrounding country are many sites, now reduced to names marked in Gothic letters on the Ordnance Survey, which speak of monastic influence. Near Teviot bridge there was a convent, with the church of St Michael not far off; south of Springwood Park is the site of *Maison Dieu*, and opposite the racecourse that of St Leonards Hospital. All trace of these buildings has vanished.

The Tironensian monks (reformed Benedictines) came from Tiron in France, migrating first to Selkirk about 1119 and moving to Kelso in 1128. Although practically unknown in England, this Order had several Scottish houses, including the rich abbey of Arbroath. Kelso's abbey also obtained possession of much wealth, with manors, farms, mills and fisheries throughout southern Scotland. The abbots played a considerable part in Scottish affairs, appearing at the Court as ambassadors and special commissioners. In 1215 one of them attended the fourth Lateran Council in Rome. Kelso, which had long held the senior position among Scottish abbeys, was ultimately ousted from that eminence by St. Andrews.

In the year 1460 the infant James III was crowned in the Abbey Kirk, after his father, James II, had been killed when a cannon blew up at the siege of Roxburgh Castle, then held by the English. Fifty-three years later, the state of anarchy existing after the death of James IV at Flodden resulted in expulsion of the abbot and annexation of the abbey by Lord Home. Before long the English sacked and burned the place and unroofed the Kirk, a process more or less repeated in 1542 and 1545, so there was little left for Scottish Reformers of 1560 to smash. The last line of an epitaph in Melrose comes inevitably to mind: 'The earth says to the earth all shall be ours.'

For more than a hundred years the transept which was patched up in 1649 served Kelso as both church and prison, until in 1771 a collapse of the roof made it unusable. A new parish church was then erected elsewhere. The massive remains seen near Tweed bridge today are part of the twelfth-century west end of the Abbey Kirk.

Of the large range of conventual buildings, only a little parlour adjacent to the gable of the south transept can still be found – an oblong barrel-vaulted cell, much altered. The modern arcade beyond it, built in memory of the eighth Duke of Roxburghe, contains a thirteenth-century doorway that may have come from the Chapter House.

Someone has likened the ruins of Kelso Abbey to a gigantic tombstone. I could wish that all tombstones enhanced the environment as this does. The surviving tower has the strength of a fortification, and was indeed so used in 1545, after English artillery had demolished the abbey walls. The beleaguered inhabitants withdrew into the tower, and next day this last defence was forced by Spanish mercenaries. Its garrison was put to the sword, except for the few who had let themselves down from windows and escaped under cover of night.

According to Scott-Moncrieff, the ruins of Kelso Abbey Kirk caused controversy over a long period, owing to the fact that no record of its original plan could be found. Wars had destroyed most of the building, its occupants and archives. In comparatively recent years a description of the great Kirk came to light far away in the Vatican Library in Rome. This shows that the design took the form of a double-ended cross, giving the Kirk a dark central nave looking out to brilliantly-lit transepts at either end.

A mixture of Norman (or Romanesque) style architecture having round-headed windows and arcading, with transitional period pointed arches, and built of sandstone in which mica sparkles, the ruined Kelso Abbey Kirk does not stand aloof in monastic seclusion. It is almost part of the great central square, like many a cathedral in France. To my mind the whole place has a character so markedly French that I was once guilty of referring to Floors (or *Fleurs*) Castle as 'The chateau'. This lapse caused some local annoyance, but there was reason for it. After all, Kelso owes its importance to an abbey built by French monks.

Another powerful influence which later added to the renown of this, the most immediately attractive town on the banks of Tweed, is that of Sir Walter Scott. He spent a short but fruitful period of youth at his aunt's house in The Butts, near the present parish church, and attended Kelso Grammar School. There he was taught by Lancelot Whale, an enormous man of great learning, who improved young Wattie's knowledge of the classics. Poor Mr Whale. So weary was he of puns upon his size and his name, that all

The town square at Kelso

references to Jonah were taboo in his presence. He persuaded his son to spell the name Wale, which only landed the young man in further trouble, for the military mess to which he belonged nicknamed him 'Prince of Wales'.

Scott's later references to Kelso were laudatory if a little odd, for he described it as 'the most beautiful *village* in Scotland'. He could trace to his half year in this Border town what he called

the awaking of that delightful feeling of the beauties of natural objects which has never since deserted me. The neighbourhood of Kelso . . . is eminently calculated to awaken these ideas. It presents objects, not only grand in themselves, but venerable from their association. The meeting of the two superb rivers, the Tweed and the Teviot, both renowned in Song – The ruins of an ancient Abbey – The more distant vestiges of Roxburgh Castle – the modern mansion of Fleurs, which is so situated as to combine the ideas of ancient baronial grandeur with those of modern taste – are in themselves objects of the first class; yet are so mixed, united and melted among a thousand other beauties of a less prominent description, that they harmonise into one general picture.

While in Kelso, Scott made friends with the Ballantyne brothers, whose ill-starred venture as publishers involved him in great financial stress later on. He never blamed Kelso for his involvement in that calamity.

Jane Austen wrote, referring to her brother Henry's travels in Scotland in 1813: 'He met with scenes of higher beauty in Roxburghshire than I had supposed the south of Scotland possessed.' English travellers of that time knew very little of the Scottish Borders. Sir Walter Scott spread, through his *Border Minstrelsy* and his novels, vivid descriptions of the countryside and its people which were read throughout Britain and far beyond these islands. Yet today there are still multitudes who rush through the Borders Region as though the real Scotland is only to be found when Edinburgh has been reached. It may be that rising costs will now cause many to stop at Kelso and decide to go no further, a decision which they will have no cause to regret.

In the central square, paved with stone setts, the traveller may park his car and step out into a precinct with seats and gay flower-tubs which needs only a few striped umbrellas and tables to suggest a continental *place*. All around are elegant Georgian facades of the eighteenth and nineteenth centuries, ornamented with window boxes and hanging flower baskets. The Bull Ring in the centre has long been disused, and markets are no longer held in the streets leading off the Square, with such names as Coalmarket, Woodmarket and Horsemarket. Other activities have taken their place, and there is never any lack of lively bustle in the heart of Kelso.

Farther out there is the racecourse, where racing 'over the sticks' has been continuously promoted for nearly a century. Before 1883 there was flat racing here at the Berrymoss site, and the stone stand in use to-day was built in 1822 by the then Duke of Roxburghe for spectators of flat racing. At present there are five meetings a year at this well-laid-out and attractive course. It is the only racecourse known to me which has a golf course (nine-hole) within it. This was first made in 1913 and redesigned by James Braid in 1927. It is certainly an improvement on the seventeenth-century Kelso game, played in the churchyard. There is a contemporary account of a tragedy, the 'slaughter and death of Thomas Chatto, who within the Kirkyaird of Kelso was given ane deidlie straik with ane golf club under his left lug [ear] . . . thairof he shortlie thaireftir deceissit.'

Angling is perhaps the most popular outdoor sport in Kelso. With two fine rivers and many smaller mill streams, it is not surprising that most natives are born within reach of a rod and line. Those visitors who frequent the Ednam House Hotel, an attractive building of 1761 which overlooks the Tweed, will be familiar with its spacious entrance hall in which not only glass-cased exhibits but newly-caught salmon and trout may be seen, the latter often lying around unattended as if on offer as free samples. While fathers of families try a few casts, the mothers and children are usually to be seen enjoying the green banks of the Mayfield picnic centre, surely the most inviting and roomy place of its kind in Scotland. There is also a caravan park.

Whether viewed from Mayfield or from the opposite bank, or from up at Maxwellheugh, the Tweed bridge makes a splendid centrepiece to the Kelso scene. The five elliptical arches under a flat deck replaced an old hump-backed bridge in 1803. John Rennie designed it, and later used a similar form for his renowned Waterloo bridge in London. When that masterpiece was demolished in 1935, two of its lamp standards were brought to Kelso and erected at the south end of Rennie's Kelso bridge. In earlier days there was a toll here, and it became customary for pedestrians entering Kelso to scrape their pennies along the parapet while crossing the river. Grooves worn in the stone by this habitual exercise may still be seen. Although coins are popularly supposed to have been 'rolled' in the grooves, I believe their owners kept a tight grip on them, lest they fell off into the water. Held fast and used as blunt instruments, the Toll-pence would have made more impression on the stone.

The earlier bridge, built in 1754, was situated a short distance up river. It endured for only some fifty years, and was swept away by flood water a short while before Rennie's structure appeared. Prior to the Turnpike Act of 1751, there were very few roads worthy of the name linking Border towns. Thomas Telford, under the new Act, worked on a road from Wooler to Edinburgh and on the great highway over Carter Bar. Roadmaking gave an impetus to bridge building; before the middle of the eighteenth century the Tweed had only two from Peebles to Berwick. When Mary Queen of Scots came in 1566 from Jedburgh to Kelso, Hume Castle, Langton and Wedderburn and on to Houndwood House near Ayton, she and her large retinue must have ridden through many a ford.

Prince Charlie also came to Kelso, staying two nights before setting off for Carlisle on his abortive Rising of 1745. In the centre

Rennie's Tweed Bridge at Kelso

of Roxburgh Street (near the Co-operative Stores) the curious visitor may notice a horseshoe set into the road surface. This is said to be the one cast here by the Prince's horse. It is a matter for conjecture how many times the Stuart 'relic' has been replaced in nearly two and a half centuries. The interesting point is that Kelso takes sufficient care of its legends to see that the tradition is maintained.

Other traditions are honoured in Kelso's Civic Week in July, when the Kelso Laddie, bearing the beribboned Burgh Standard, leads a cavalcade of some 150 riders out to such places as Yetholm (where an eightsome reel is danced in the main street); Linton, which once had a dragon living in the 'Worm's Hole' in the field of Wormington, and still has an ancient stone tympanum above the south doorway of its Kirk, depicting a horseman thrusting his spear into the dragon's mouth; and home by Bowmont Forest, a ride which takes them almost seven hours – including refreshment stops. July also brings a great agricultural show to Kelso, and in September there are ram sales at the same Tweedside ground. Winter pastimes must not be omitted from a list of things to see and

47

do, since there is particularly good provision at the Border Ice Rink for ice skating, curling and skittles.

Kelso has two small industrial estates in attractive surroundings, where production of electronic equipment, tools and gauges, plastic goods, clothing and other articles is carried out. There is also an enterprising colony of artist-craftsmen, most of whom have centrally placed studios and workshops where the crafts of leatherwork, woodwork, pottery, gold and silversmithing, stained glass, welded steel and perspex mural decorations are all being pursued. The old smiddy in Hunter's Close has been re-opened.

A striking example of modern architecture – the Edenside Surgery – was designed by Peter Womersley, whose work may also be seen at Bernat Klein's High Sunderland studios near Selkirk. The unusual lay-out of Kelso's up-to-date medical centre is based on the form of four 'drums', and provides six consulting rooms, with waiting rooms and offices. Those who are in good health may enjoy this interesting conception from the outside. It earned a Civic Trust Award in 1967.

Jedburgh

The four great abbeys of Jedburgh, Kelso, Melrose and Dryburgh are so closely related to the Scottish Borderland that the Border history may justly be said to have begun with their foundation in the twelfth century. At that period there was no sharp division between Scotland and England; Cumberland, Northumberland and Durham had not then been finally acquired by the English, and communication between these counties and their northern neighbours was so freely maintained that inhabitants would have been puzzled by the word 'Border'. King David I (1124-1152, last of the three sons of Malcolm Canmore and Queen Margaret), who founded more monasteries than any other Scottish king, brought Augustinian Canons from Beauvais to Jedburgh in about 1138. A copy of his charter, dated 1147, to the monks for building here now hangs in Mary Queen of Scots House. According to Scott-Moncrieff, Jedburgh was raised in status from priory to abbey by 1152.

Only fourteen miles from Carter Bar, this abbey kirk must have been particularly vulnerable to English attack during the troubled

Jedburgh Abbey from the river

centuries that followed the death of Alexander III. When the numerous waves of assault from which it suffered are taken into account, it seems a marvel that so much is left standing. Roofless and weatherworn, the nave in Transitional and early Gothic styles of the twelfth and thirteenth centuries still adds grandeur to its fine hill site above the Jed Water, with a massive square tower rebuilt early in the sixteenth century. The great west gable is the only more or less intact Transitional front left in Scotland. Some remnants of monastic buildings have also survived.

The Burgh, which clusters round its stately ecclesiastical ruin, cherishes a number of old houses and an Inn, the Spread Eagle, which claims to be the oldest licensed house in Scotland. The medieval Canongate Brig, built in 1147, was for 400 years the only bridge in Jedburgh. As one of the few three-arched bridges of its period left in Scotland, it is being carefully maintained. In Castlegate there is the old lodging used by Prince Charles Edward Stuart – Bonnie Prince Charlie – in 1745, known to this day as 'Prince Charlie's House'.

Jedburgh's principal attraction, apart from its abbey, is the turreted sixteenth-century 'Mary Queen of Scots House'. Mrs Mary Hope, the custodian who showed us round, said that hitherto the building was known in the town as 'Queen Mary's House'. With the arrival of so many visitors – those from England in particular – it was discovered that many supposed the name to have been given in honour of the late Queen of George V. The title in consequence had to be made more specifically Scottish.

A painting of the sixteenth century shows the house roofed with thatch, instead of the present red tiles, but the stout structure is otherwise very little changed. Of six strongholds built around the town for protection in times of siege, only this one has survived. The gloomy barrel-vaulted basement has a cobblestone floor and walls of up to eight feet in thickness. This chamber had no internal communication with the three storeys above it before the seventeenth century, access to those being formerly by means of an outside stair on the north wall. Defenders of the building were lodged in the upper apartments.

This interesting house was presented to the Royal Burgh of Jedburgh by the late F. S. Oliver, and in the summer season is open to visitors at specified hours. It contains many articles of old domestic use, including a sixteenth-century roasting jack in the basement kitchen, and a 'saut buckie' (salt box) in a jamb of the banqueting hall fireplace, where salt was kept dry.

To most visitors the relics of the ill-fated Queen Mary, including her death-mask, have the greatest appeal. Here are the silver communion service given by Pope Augustine and used on the morning of her execution; her seal; a letter to the Laird of Cessford, and a French watch lost by the Queen on her ride from Hermitage Castle. This timepiece was found long afterwards – in 1817 – in the bog where she was thrown from her horse. After lying there for 250 years, it was disinterred by a mole, and appears to be little the worse.

In the sixteenth century a much-prized, almost unique feature of this house, one that rendered it fit for a queen, was the inside privy. This small closet within the wall is only partially floored. The colloquial name for it – 'the lang drap' – explains its simple design. Before the days of running water, such an opening, supplied with sphagnum moss in place of toilet paper, was considered to be the height of luxury, available only to ladies of high rank. At the time of the Queen's visit it was the only indoor privy in Jedburgh. She paid

£40 to Lady Ker of Ferniehurst as rent for the house.

The purpose of her visit in 1566 was not (as some believe) to be near the Earl of Bothwell, who lay sick in Hermitage Castle (see chapter 7), twelve miles south of Hawick. Her primary purpose was to hold a Justice Ayres or Circuit Court. The letter signed *Marie Regina*, which hangs on the wall today, had been written to the Laird of Cessford in September of that year, summoning him to come and discuss arrangements for her circuit visit: 'We intend, God willing, to repair in Teviot daill to see justice ministrat. . . .'

To horticulturists, the picturesque old pear trees in the small garden surrounding Mary Queen of Scots' House are of more than passing interest. Nobody can be certain of their precise ages, but the Jethart Pear has been famous since monastic times. In 1934, at the spot where stood a dying specimen traditionally called Mary Queen of Scots' tree, the late Queen Mary planted a replacement to carry on the venerable tradition of pear culture in Jedburgh.

This old Burgh also possesses what is known as 'the Castle'. It is in fact a Georgian prison, one of the best buildings of its kind, now preserved and furnished with relics as a unique museum-piece. It occupies the hill-top site of a medieval castle, which proved to be so great a magnet for invaders that a fifteenth-century Scottish Parliament ordered its demolition. It was rebuilt for use as a prison in 1820, in castellated style on ground then occupied by the town gallows. The Prisons Act of 1877 vested all gaols in the Prison Commissioners, and with the aid of improved transport, centralisation made many county and district prisons redundant. Jedburgh Castle was closed in 1886 and its inmates transferred to Edinburgh. The building was purchased by the Burgh in 1890. Those interested in penal institutions have opportunity here and at Berwick-upon-Tweed to see two authentic examples of old gaols.

In ancient times Ferniehurst Castle stood amid oak trees of the great Jed Forest. A famous survivor of that woodland, known as 'The Capon Tree', now stands alone in the meadow of Priorshaugh opposite Hundalee. The origin of the name 'capon' is not known; but as the site once held a monastery, it is supposed that the word is related to Capuchin, whose cowls or hoods were often referred to as 'capons'. Like the Jethart pears, this tree has no birth certificate and its age can only be guessed. It is commonly thought to be at least a thousand years old. Ferniehurst (now a Youth Hostel) and the Capon Tree are both on the A68 road, south of the town.

Dryburgh

The name of Dryburgh is said to have derived from the Celtic *Darach-bruach* – 'the mound in a grove of oak trees'. Fine trees still grow on this land. According to ancient tradition, a monastic establishment was founded here by St Modan in the sixth century, and later burned down by the Saxon Ida – 'the flame bearer'. Evidence for the legend is very slender. A calendar of Scottish saints lists against 4th February *Sanctus Modanus, Abbas Drijburgensis*; but the name of St Modan, one of Columba's followers, is more usually connected with Roseneath and the western lowlands. It may be that he had headquarters at Dryburgh, journeying far afield from it on missionary work. Invasion by the pagan king of Northumbria would probably have swept away traces of St Modan's influence, leaving Christianity in abeyance here until St Aidan, St Boisil, and St Cuthbert caused a resurgence from the monastery of Old Melrose.

The Abbey of St Mary, whose glorious remains stand in a wooded bend of the Tweed opposite to St Boswells, was founded in 1150 by the Order of Premonstratensians, or White Canons. They owed their inception to St Norbert in 1121, and followed the Rule of St Augustine (with some modification), their first seat being at Pre Montre in the French diocese of Laon. They came to the Scottish

Dryburgh Abbey from the east

Borders from Alnwick in Northumberland, arriving at Dryburgh on St Martin's Day, and as the first stage in the establishment of their abbey they consecrated a cemetery. The identity of the abbey's founder is often debated. King David I of Scotland granted certain territories to the abbey in his great charter, but the contemporary Chronicle of Melrose ascribes the foundation to Hugo De Morville, Constable of Scotland. De Morville and his wife endowed this creation with the churches and lands of Channelkirk and Saltoun, and the church of Bozeat in Northamptonshire.

The king presented the new abbey with the churches of Lanark, Pettinain and Cadisleya; Lessuden was given to it by some person whose name is not recorded. During the first century of its existence, the abbey received many and varied gifts. The work of administering scattered property must have encroached upon the time given by the canons to their religious vocation, although secular vicars were usually appointed to churches possessed by the abbey.

The isolated position of Dryburgh, separated – as it still is today – from main highways by the Tweed, may have accounted for the mainly uneventful nature of its early religious history. The Chronicle of Melrose does not trouble to detail the familiar and ordinary happenings, so the daily life and building progress at St Mary's Abbey are not described. The first abbot, Roger, held office for an unusually long period, during which three Bulls were obtained from Pope Alexander in Rome. One gave Dryburgh the privilege of holding divine service in such time as the country was under interdict. Roger was succeeded in 1177 by his prior, Gerard. The latter's successor, Adam, earned renown as a preacher and writer. He became a Carthusian and ended his days in the Charterhouse at Witham.

Up to the death of Alexander III of Scotland, Dryburgh took little part in affairs of state. The community led a peaceful, prosperous existence and was held in high esteem as a place of refuge from the cares of this world. Then began a long period of conflict, in which the Prior of Dryburgh was involved, as one of the commissioners nominated to assist the English king, Edward I, in making his choice between rival claimants to the Scottish throne. The monks swore fealty to 'Longshanks' in 1296. This did not save them for long.

When in 1322 Edward II was retreating from his abortive invasion of Scotland, his army pitched tents near the monastery, and so terrified the inmates that they celebrated departure of the troops by pealing the abbey bells. They rejoiced too soon, and so angered the English that soldiers paid a return visit and burned the place down. Another version says that soldiers failed to obtain provisions from the monastery and burnt it out of revenge. This wanton act of destruction was followed by gifts from the faithful, including Robert I, for rebuilding and repair. The continuing disturbed state of the Borders probably accounts for much incompleteness in the Dryburgh records. Andrew, who was abbot here in 1354, was present at Edward Baliol's resignation of the kingdom into the hands of Edward III of England at Roxburgh, in 1355. By their submission he and three other Border abbots saved their establishments, while others – including Haddington – were damaged.

Dryburgh was not long preserved. Richard II raided it in 1385, when the abbey is said to have been 'devastated by hostile fire'. King Robert III, like his predecessor, gave the stricken community what assistance he could, including the lands and revenues of a dissolved Cistercian convent at Berwick-upon-Tweed. In 1522 war again afflicted Dryburgh, and a letter of 1523 to the Cardinal Protector of Scotland at the Papal Court requests the appointment of a Superior to give attention to the repair of the abbey. In 1545 the notorious Earl of Hertford caused havoc, followed by some 700 English who 'rode into Scotland upon the waters of Tweide to a town called Dryburgh, with an abbey in the same . . . and they burnte the same town and abbey – and got very much spoylage'. The abbey and its town were never rebuilt.

The custom of allowing government of abbeys by commendators – that is, by persons appointed to levy the fruits of a benefice during vacancies – became a scandal during the reigns of James IV and James V. Abbeys and their benefices were granted to laymen, often the illegitimate offspring of royalty, or to influential churchmen, and such puppets had little to do with the abbeys except to take the proceeds of their offices. In 1541 Dryburgh was in possession of Thomas Erskine, second son of Lord Erskine, to whose family it belonged until the early seventeenth century, when the ecclesiastical title disappeared. The abbey changed hands more than once. In 1700 it passed to Thomas Haliburton of Newmains. In 1786 it was acquired by the eccentric Earl of Buchan (an Erskine, descended from one of the commendators). He founded the Society of Antiquaries of Scotland and did much restoration work at

Dryburgh Abbey, not always in the best taste. He had the enormous statue of Wallace erected up above the abbey overlooking the Tweed. From his heirs, Dryburgh was purchased by Lord Glenconner and given to the nation.

Having been used as a dwelling-house for more than a hundred years after the reformation, the domestic buildings survived longer than most similar structures adjoining Scottish monastic churches. Unfortunately local tradesmen in the eighteenth century, here as elsewhere, used the place as a source of building material. What is left of this abbey indicates that it must have been very beautiful. The site, a secluded promontory where the Tweed makes a horse-shoe bend, is a gentle stepped slope, on which the monkish planners designed their kirk at the highest level, with cloister garth immediately beneath, and the barrel-vaulted chapter house, principal day apartments, cellars and kitchen below that. The stone, which came from freestone quarries both north and south of the river, is of particularly pleasing hue, warm and mellow and yet with a clean, pure radiance about it as if lit from within.

The cloister is unusual. Instead of being surrounded by monastic buildings, it was enclosed on the west by a high wall. To the north, almost flush with that wall (part of the original structure) is the fifteenth-century west end of the Abbey Kirk, with a fine round-headed doorway, heavily moulded. Only the bases of pillars remain to show how the nave was aisled. Beyond are the more substantial remains of transepts and presbytery chapels, which belong basically to the first building period. After the Reformation, the north transept and its eastern chapels were taken over as burial places for the great Border families who at different times owned the Abbey. Sir Walter Scott is buried here, together with his wife and his biographer, Lockhart – a place chosen by Scott by virtue of his Haliburton ancestry. The Haigs, whose ancient tower of Bemersyde stands above the Tweed to north of the Abbey, also have right of burial within its walls. Field-Marshal Earl Haig, Britain's Commander-in-Chief during World War I, has a simple grave with a headstone similar to thousands placed above his men in cemeteries on the battlefields of Europe.

Never famed as a place of pilgrimage in its monastic days, Dryburgh has attracted visitors from all over the world since that day – 26th September 1832 – when Sir Walter Scott was laid to rest within its ruined walls. The scene was described by Lockhart in his *Life of Sir Walter Scott*:

His funeral was conducted in an unostentatious manner, but the attendance was very great. Few of his friends then in Scotland were absent – and many, both friends and strangers, came from a great distance. His domestics and foresters made it their petition that no hireling hand might assist in carrying his remains. They themselves bore the coffin to the hearse, and from the hearse to the grave. . . .

'The court-yard and all the precincts of Abbotsford were crowded with uncovered spectators as the procession was arranged; and as it advanced through Darnick and Melrose, and the adjacent villages, the whole population appeared in their doors in like manner – almost all in black. The train of carriages extended over more than a mile; the yeomanry followed in great numbers on horseback; and it was late in the day ere we reached Dryburgh. Some accident, it was observed, had caused the hearse to halt for several minutes on the summit of the hill at Bemersyde – exactly where a prospect of remarkable richness opens, and where Sir Walter had always been accustomed to rein up his horse. The day was dark and lowering and the wind was high.

This quiet kirk, now so still, is permeated by memories. One can almost hear the canons chanting, and in the remnants of the chapter house it is not hard to imagine that a chapter from the rule of their order is still being read each day to the assembled monks.

I once saw this seat of earlier piety in the month of December when no other visitors were about, and stood alone within what had been the great nave of the abbey kirk. (Being in State ownership, Dryburgh is open to the public at all seasons.) 'You can't miss the Field-Marshal's grave', the custodian said. 'The poppy wreaths are still there, laid on Remembrance Sunday.' Although I had gone with the express purpose of visiting the tombs of Scott and Haig, my inward ear soon became attuned to far older ceremonial than the funerals of 1832 and 1928. The sound of distant voices, apparently wind-borne from outside the church, suggested religious chanting. The sound alternately gained strength and died away, in a regular throbbing rhythm. It was uncanny. Except for the gate-keeper, no other human being was in sight. I left the ruins, preferring not to become too deeply involved with the occult.

Only when I reached the footpath alongside the Tweed was the mystery solved. Five swans in neat formation were flying up and down this stretch of the river, and their throbbing wing-music reverberating off the water, had a curious hollow timbre. This 'chanting' had no religious significance, after all. Yet someone afterwards told me that swans had been regarded as holy birds in the early days of Christianity, and were still quite frequently to be found flying to and fro over places anciently hallowed.

Melrose

The rose-pink ruins made famous by Sir Walter Scott and known to all who pass through Melrose today, are not those of the original building, nor are they on the site of the first abbey. That humbler Celtic (or Culdee) church was established as long ago as the seventh century, on a bank of the Tweed some 2½ miles downstream. At this place, Old Melrose or *Maelros*, St Cuthbert started his life in religion. Long after the Celtic colony left for Monkwearmouth, a chapel dedicated to him was maintained at Old Melrose as a place of pilgrimage. A corbel stone of the twelfth century, taken from the demolished chapel of St Cuthbert, is now preserved at the museum in the Commendator's house in the precincts of the present abbey.

In 1136 a colony of White Monks (Cistercians) from Rievaulx in Yorkshire, having found a patron in King David I of Scotland, came to Melrose and began building their monastic kirk at a place then known as Little Fordell. These Cistercians, who specialised in agriculture, particularly the breeding of sheep, horses and cattle, found this valley of rich alluvial soil ideally suited to their way of life. Their orchards made Gattonside noted for its fruit, which is still grown there. By royal charter they also acquired extensive lands and rights of fishing, pasture and timber as far away as Selkirk and Traquair. Their abbey church was completed by 1146 and dedicated to the Virgin Mary.

The new abbey of Melrose became a centre for the development of agriculture and the wool trade; of architecture, building and sculpture; of scholarship, education and the production of books. The Scottish Chronicle, begun by the Celtic monks of Old Melrose in the eighth century, was carried on by Cistercians until in the thirteenth century the long and disastrous series of wars with England disrupted their peaceful existence. English armies employed what we now call 'scorched earth' tactics, with the great Border abbeys as their primary targets. Situated on the old Roman road from England into Tweeddale and the Lothians, Melrose was especially vulnerable. It was sacked by Edward II in 1322 and burnt by Richard II in 1385, being in English hands for much of the interim period.

The ruins now extant are chiefly those of the late Decorated and early Perpendicular styles, inspired by the great minsters of York and Beverley, and date from the rebuilding of between 1400 and

1500. Most of the warm ochre and rusty-pink stone came from the quarries at Dryburgh. Timber for roofing was obtained from local forests; Kelso supplied lime; tiles were manufactured at a place near Darnick, still known in the eighteenth century as 'Tile House', while lead was brought up to Melrose from England. A mason named John Morow has been given a memorial stone in the wall of the kirk, 'John Morow . . . born in Parysse'. In the abbey museum there is a beautiful, lively little head sculptured by this master-mason of French birth.

King James IV visited Melrose in 1502 and 1504, and distributed drinksilver to the masons. A panel carved with his arms on a western buttress bears the date 1505. In a niche on the westernmost high buttress is a mutilated sculpture of the Virgin and Child. Local legend has it that the man who struck off the head of the infant Christ was so injured by the falling stone that he lost the use of his impious right arm ever after. In centuries when few of the people could read, religious buildings were sermons in stone and sometimes provided light entertainment as well. One of the humorous gargoyles at Melrose depicts a pig playing bagpipes. The abbey kirk was also enriched by stained glass and carved woodwork, none of which survived later onslaughts by the English. Sir Ralph Evers in 1544 set fire to the town and pillaged the abbey kirk, and in 1545 the notorious (and still hated) Earl of Hertford destroyed the monastery and further damaged the kirk.

The Scottish Reformation completed the ruin with expulsion of the remaining monks and plundering of the abbey. Even after that, a fanatical religious zealot went round with a hammer, toppling statuary from niches and battering it into shapeless stumps. For this vandalism he was given the by-name of 'Stumpy'. Not all reformers advocated such wild destruction. There was a post-Reformation Minister of the Kirk at Melrose who got himself into trouble for composing a litany with the line 'From all the knock-down race of Knoxes, Good Lord deliver us'.

So great was the influence of the Reformation in Scotland, with its general abhorrence of 'images', that one can find at the present day older folk who speak of any representations in the round, even plaster gnomes and rabbits sold at garden centres, as 'images'. These are regarded with traces of unease which bear no relation to artistic taste. Such residual fears do not, apparently, extend to the mercat (market) cross, which became a centre of community life in Melrose from 1662. Its slender shaft is capped by a unicorn, much

Melrose Abbey and the Eildon Hills

eroded by weather, with the royal arms of Scotland to remind people that this was once a Royal Burgh.

An ancient building in the High Street houses the local Freemasons, who claim that theirs is the oldest Lodge in Scotland. Each year in December, on St John's Eve, the masons march by torchlight round about the mercat cross, to the tune of 'Hey the Merry Masons'. After this ceremony there is a procession to the ruined abbey, which is picturesquely lit up by the flickering glow of many torches. At such times the visitor may recall that scene in *The Lay of the Last Minstrel*, when a monk leads Deloraine to the tomb of the wizard Michael Scott. The mosstrooper, having lifted the stone, takes from the fingers of the corpse his dreadful book of spells. Michael Scott spent much of his life outside Scotland, at the court in Palermo of the Emperor Frederick II. He was noted for scholarship as well as familiarity with evil spirits. Dante consigned him to hell. Others respect Scott for his early scientific researches and his translations of Aristotle. One of the tombs is pointed out as that of the wizard, who died in 1292. I doubt if the precise spot is known.

It is generally accepted that the heart of King Robert the Bruce was interred at Melrose, some say within the Abbey Kirk near the high altar. Scott-Moncrieff writes of a mummified human heart in a leaden casket which still lies buried beneath the floor of the chapter house, saying that this may be the relic of Bruce – who regained his country's freedom at Bannockburn in 1314. There is nothing in the casket indicative of its origin, and it is more likely to relate to an abbot. King Alexander II is also buried within the abbey. A later grave, which can be identified beyond any doubt, is that of Sir Walter Scott's forester and friend, the faithful Tom Purdie. The gravestone erected by Scott stands not far from the great south window of the abbey church.

The hurried tourist who thinks that Melrose consists of a ruined abbey and little else is mistaken. Within a short walk he will find at the Greenyards a rugby pitch where the variation of that game known as 'seven-a-side' was first played. Men of the Borders have rugby in their blood, and this pitch is crowded with enthusiastic supporters for the annual knock-out tournament held in April. Weddings of team members customarily give rise to an unusual game in the High Street of Melrose. The bride, using a diminutive model known as 'The Bride's Ba'', kicks off somewhere near the mercat cross, and there follows a scrummage among parked cars and bystanders.

Melrose, with its many hotels, is a convenient stopping-off point for Abbotsford, the home of Sir Walter Scott, which has become almost a Border shrine (see chapter 6). For those who take their overnight accommodation with them, there is a good municipal caravan site, centrally positioned. Melrose is well provided with public park and recreation facilities, and it is an ideal centre for walkers. The heather-clad Eildon hills are almost on the doorstep. Bowden village, with its twelfth-century church, Newstead, where masons who built the abbey are said to have lived – this village was the site of the original Lodge of Melrose Freemasons – and Darnick with its stout defence tower, are all within easy reach for the pedestrian.

Since 1425 Darnick Tower has been in the possession of the Heiton family. The present sixteenth-century version of the original, with a modernised interior, is still used as a dwelling house. Sir Walter Scott, who was foiled in his desire to purchase the place (the owners refusing to sell), acquired instead the farmhouse of Cartleyhole beside the Tweed, and transformed it into the imposing mansion which he named Abbotsford. The more modest Chiefswood, which he built in 1820 and gave to his daughter Sophia and her bridegroom J. G. Lockhart on their marriage, is situated in a lane running southwards from the Melrose to Darnick road. It is currently in the hands of Professor Trevor-Roper (now Lord Dacre of Glanton), whose wife, Lady Alexandra, sister to the second Earl Haig of Bemersyde, has made a charming garden, backed by a glen with trees planted by Sir Walter. The unique well, capped by a stone quatrefoil brought by Scott from the Melrose abbey ruins, is scheduled as an ancient monument. Scott used the well as a wine-cooler. Chiefswood garden is open occasionally.

An attractive little public garden, always conspicuously well groomed by its dedicated custodian, will be found alongside the abbey; and the National Trust for Scotland in 1975 opened an information centre, Priorwood, in the same vicinity. This has an old walled garden at the rear. Beyond it is a Youth Hostel. There is plenty of young life in Melrose; yet over it all broods the great ruined Abbey Kirk, reminding us of the words on one of its gravestones, dated 1761:

> The earth goeth on the earth glistring like gold
> The earth goes to the earth sooner than it wold
> The earth builds on the earth castles and towers
> The earth says to the earth all shall be ours.

4

Some Border Towns

Lauder

lsewhere in Britain, this little place would be described as a
large village of some seven hundred inhabitants. Here in the
Scottish Borders it was a burgh, formerly the only Royal
Burgh in Berwickshire, being thus honoured in the reign of William
the Lyon (1165-1214). Much fought over during long years of
Border warfare, Lauder suffered the loss or destruction of its
original charter in the turmoil; but in 1502 James IV granted a
charter of *novodamus* (renewal) confirming the town's status.
Curiously enough, this was not ratified by Parliament until 1633.

In the twelfth century Lauder was known as a 'kirk town'; in
1235 a chapter of clergy from East Lothian met here. Towards the
close of the thirteenth century Edward I, trying to cement
Scotland's reluctant allegiance, visited Lauder on two occasions.
Edward II, James IV and James V were all familiar with the little
burgh. The most memorable royal visit, that of James III in 1482,
was an occasion when king and court tarried at Lauder on the way to
succour Berwick, then under siege by the English. A group of
discontented Scottish nobles here seized a number of the king's
favourites and hanged them from a bridge (no longer in existence)
in what are now the grounds of Thirlestane Castle. Archibald
Douglas, Earl of Angus, took responsibility for this crime; he is
popularly known as 'Bell the Cat' – with reference to the fable of
some mice who, annoyed by a prowling feline, thought to hang a
bell round its neck. Walter Scott wrote of the grisly affair in
Marmion. With the king virtually a prisoner, the army returned to
Edinburgh, while Berwick was taken by the English. It has
remained part of England ever since.

Each time I visit this well-kept little burgh, with its high-shouldered town hall standing sentinel over the wide market place, and its newly-harled cruciform church across the street beside it, I have the feeling that it is all a stage set, one made, perhaps, for the Lyric Theatre at Hammersmith in the days of Nigel Playfair's production of 'The Beggar Opera' and 'Polly'. The sensation of unreality is heightened when, at a short distance along the A68 road to the east, the curious silhouette of Thirlestane Castle is seen above encircling trees. Although the roof of the central tower is ogee-shaped, and not an onion dome, the effect is that of a northern version of Brighton Pavilion; an oddly theatrical and unwarlike outline for a Scottish castle.

Even the hotel at which we stayed, comfortable though it was, had elements of fantasy about it. These ranged from a particularly belligerent painting of a bull's mask used as the inn sign, to a bar thickly spattered with murals and photographs of dachshunds, while elongated caricatures of the same canine breed, made in wrought iron, dangled from the ceiling. When asked if the management took a particular interest in these dogs, the young waitress replied laconically that the proprietor used to keep forty of them on adjacent premises, but now had 'only twenty-two left'. There are other good hotels in Lauder, but the rest are of more everyday character outside the 'theatre set'.

The present kirk, belonging to the Church of Scotland, was built in 1673, at a period when the Duke of Lauderdale, King's Commissioner for Scotland, planned the enlargement of the old Lauder Fort into what is now Thirlestane Castle. For nearly five hundred years before that, the original kirk built by Hugo de Morville had occupied a site near the Fort. We may safely assume that when the Duke extended his dwelling he did not care to have kirk and kirkyard on his doorstep. With the sanction of Scotland's Parliament, he employed Sir William Bruce to design and erect the present church on a central site in the town, and caused its predecessor to be demolished. The ancient burial ground was levelled and a lawn made above the bones of Lauder's former residents, with a sycamore tree planted to mark the position of the original kirk.

The seventeenth-century replacement is in the unusual form of an equal-armed cross, so that with lectern and communion table placed centrally as at present, one-fourth of the seating lies behind the officiating minister. In the centre, supported on four square pillars linked by round-headed arches, is an octagonal bell tower with a pointed roof. James Guthrie, the first martyr minister of the Covenant, served in the parish from 1638 to 1649. Another well-known Scottish divine, Dr John Wilson (1804-1875), was born at 19 The Row. He was a founder of the Free Church of Scotland and first Vice-Chancellor of Bombay University. Lauder Kirk is thought to resemble that of Balleroy in Normandy, whose chateau bears a likeness to Thirlestane Castle after its enlargement by Sir William Bruce.

The resplendent pomp of Restoration architecture, visible in Bruce's work at the Castle – particularly in the heavily intricate Dutch plaster-work ceilings – had exterior additions made to it in Victorian times, when the west front was somewhat mauled by David Bryce. The bell-shaped roof on the central tower, which seems to possess a seventeenth-century character, may well be part of Bryce's later alterations. It does not appear on a print of 1673.

The long and involved history of the Maitland family cannot be fully dealt with here. The Thirlestane Castle estate was dis-entailed at the turn of the century, and the late Dowager Countess, widow of the fifteenth Earl, left the Castle with its policies and farms to her grandson, Captain the Hon. Gerald Connelly-Carew, second son of Lady Sylvia (Maitland) and Lord Connelly-Carew. He has now changed his name to Maitland-Carew, and is living at the Castle with his wife, whom he married in 1972.

John Maitland, the second Earl (later first Duke) of Lauderdale virtually ruled Scotland as Charles the Second's Secretary of State. In general his reputation is not pleasant; but a local tale, that of 'Midside Maggie', shows that his inflexible nature had a kindlier side to it. Thomas Hardie held the middle of three farms on Tollis Hill as tenant of the Earl when, in 1643, he married Margaret Lylestone from Westruther. Times were hard, for a series of severe winters played havoc with their sheep on the exposed hills 1,200 feet above the sea. When rent fell due, they had no money to pay it with. Maggie made her way to the Castle and managed to see the Earl. She asked for time, and so appealed to him that he was moved to show some mercy. He agreed to remit the rent for one year, if she could prove her case about the snow lying until late into the season by bringing him a snowball in June. Snow does lie long in crannies of the Lammermuirs, and Maggie made sure that it would do so by packing it tightly away from the sun. The Earl kept his word, and accepted her June snowball in lieu of rent.

Maggie, too, was honourable and generous. The Earl, who was

captured at Worcester and kept prisoner in London until after Cromwell's death, made his escape to Holland in 1660 with the aid of some gold coins which Maggie smuggled to him in a bannock. Outside the gaol she stood singing the Border song 'Leader Haughs and Yarrow', which the prisoner recognised. Warders must have been less suspicious in those days, for at the Earl's request Maggie was allowed into his apartment. After his return to Thirlestane, he gave her a silver chain girdle, now on display at the Museum of Antiquities in Edinburgh. There are still descendants of the Hardies living in Lauder.

The foundations of the Tolbooth, which has been burned and rebuilt a number of times, probably date from the fourteenth century. Lauder was then a walled town, and the magistrates collected tolls and customs duties on goods at the Tolbooth. The upper storey of this building also served until 1975 as Council Chamber and at one time as Court House, with three prison cells below. A bell in the clock tower was used to summon councillors to meetings. The prison went out of use in 1843. Until slates were applied about 1770, the roof was of thatch. In front of the flight of steps leading up to the Council Chamber, an old mercat cross, thought to be of thirteenth-century origin, formerly stood, together with a 'tron' for weighing heavy goods. The wide market place was then in regular use for the sale of animals, farm produce and other merchandise. At that time there was no road to the north of the Tolbooth; the narrow one between it and the kirk took all traffic through the town.

At night, and when the gates were kept shut all day because of plague or other epidemic, travellers passed outside the walls of Lauder by means of lanes known as 'Upper Back-side' and Lower Back-side'. In recent years people living on these streets have found such names unacceptable as addresses, and so those ways to the south are now re-named Factor's Park and Crofts Road, while that beside the estate is called Castle Wynd. From just inside the old West Port a road named Route de Roi ('Rotten Row') led in earlier times to Lauder Fort, which, when it was not in English hands, served as a hunting lodge for Scottish Kings. All this history may be forgotten, now that the road is simply known as 'The Row'. Between the two entrances from High Street the "Sumer Tree" (Maypole) used to stand.

The fronts of most Lauder houses are sited right on the street, and have large plots of ground at the back. This arrangement originated in days when burgesses occupied substantial town premises, with cottage property for labourers, and cow-byres and stabling for horses behind them; often hen-runs too. These prosperous citizens, who were usually engaged in business in Lauder, had as a sideline an interest in farming. They cultivated the arable land known as the 'Burgess Acres' and maintained small steadings within the walls, for as burgesses they were obliged to live inside the town. For centuries Lauder employed a communal herd – often some poor lad of limited intelligence – whose job it was to blow a horn twice daily, as a signal to cows grazing up above on the Common Lands amid the hills. The beasts then made their way down in a stately procession, each turning off when her own byre was reached. After being milked, the cows ambled uphill back to their pasture. This age-old custom ceased after World War I, when motor cars began to monopolise the roads. Cottages, even cow-byres, are now converted to make attractive homes; the Lauder cows are things of the past, and common land is given up to sheep.

In his booklet, *Lauder, Its Kirk and People*, the Rev. Richard James gives an interesting account of the role of burgesses in the town.

The Royal Charter in effect freed the Burgh from any feudal superior, confirmed to it the ownership and free use of lands, gave authority to elect its own bailies and other officers . . . to have a cross and weekly market and public fair, to levy tolls, to hold burgh courts, to engage in trade and commerce, and to have bakers, brewers, fleshers and sellers of flesh as well as of fish, in respect of all of which a yearly duty was to be paid to the Royal Exchequer and customs duty levied on goods leaving the town. In addition the King's justice could be administered and his courts held there, and probably the Burgesses and Freemen of the Town were liable to be called to the King's standard in case of emergency.

The system was in fact for the great benefit of the place, since it set the townspeople free from any form of service to a feudal superior and enabled the Burgesses to employ servants to till the land and attend to cattle and sheep while they themselves engaged in industry or commerce. It must have encouraged an influx of people into the town. At first they probably lived in rather primitive wooden houses clustered around Lauder Tower. To become a burgess, a man must own (by inheritance or purchase) one of the town's 'Burgess Acres', which may be anything from 1¾ to 3½ acres in extent, and he must reside in the Burgh. He must then be admitted by approval of the Town Council and take the Burgess oath, whereupon he receives his Burgess ticket and the right to graze his sheep and cattle on the 1,700 acres of common land.

This system is still operating in Lauder, which appears to be the last remaining Royal Burgh to perpetuate it. Most of the 'Acres' have passed by inheritance to women, who cannot be burgesses, or to men no longer resident in the Burgh, and so there has been a steady decline in the number. In the late 19th century there were 37; in 1973 only three.

Under the new Regional Government scheme due to operate in 1975, it seems that Lauder will not only lose its Town Council (like other burghs), but will also see the end of the ancient burgess system and lose community possession of the Common lands. The community, which has stood fast through so many extremities of fortune, can and will look forward with hope. Through its Common Riding, which in early days safeguarded the boundaries and blessed the lands in a religious festival, it will retain its pride in the past, its unity of purpose and spirit and its determination to build a happy, peaceful and prosperous community for the future.

Another relic of the past, the Lauder Light Railway, had a very short life and is now closed. From 1899 until the 1930s Lauder folk were able to travel by this small railway to Fountainhall and thence by the Waverley route between Edinburgh, Carlisle and London. Passenger services ended in 1932 and all goods traffic ceased in 1957. The disused track would make an admirable accident-free pathway for walkers and naturalists, if local farmers were able to remove cross-fences. Lauder is already rich in moorland walks

Thirlestane Castle

suitable for those able to manage the rougher tracks and steep gradients. For the antiquary there are many hill-forts and traces of Roman encampments. Anglers may obtain excellent sport in the Leader and its tributaries. There are also wayside flowers. In two short rambles I found a tall aconitum with cream flowers, identified as Wolfsbane; an elegant giant bellflower with white flowers; and several hedgerow bushes of a white spiraea, presumably a garden escape.

This beguiling little town has an attractive caravan park in wooded surroundings alongside Thirlestane Castle, with a picnic area near by. The castle has been saved for the nation by a massive scheme of structural repair and restoration under the direction of Crichton Lang of Ian Lindsay and Partners, financially supported by the Historic Buildings Council of Scotland. The splendid Restoration interior may be seen by the public on certain days in summer. An unexpected bonus of more modern date is the interesting collection of photographs taken by the fourteenth Earl at the turn of the century. In a wing to the right of the main entrance, an important exhibit of early agricultural implements and domestic 'bygones' is being mounted at the time of writing. This new Borders Museum of Country Life will be opened in 1983.

As we came out from the tearoom into the courtyard, we saw a charming little unrehearsed tableau in the shape of Emma, small daughter of the house, mounted upon an elderly Shetland pony. The great building, typifying the pomp and power of the 1st (and only) Duke of Lauderdale, who was an intimate friend of Charles II; the rows of family portraits by Lawrence, Lely, Hopner, Reynolds and others; the Louis XVI furniture, candelabras, clocks and gilt mirrors, were instantly transformed into a family background for Captain Maitland-Carew, his wife and three young children whose home it is now.

Hawick

This bustling town of some sixteen and a half thousand inhabitants has proudly proclaimed itself to be the twenty-seventh largest Burgh in Scotland. The name is said to come from the Anglo-Saxon *Haga*, a place of safety, and *Wic*, a dwelling. Its hallmark today is cheerful efficiency coupled with friendliness to the stranger. Between the modern shopfronts on the east side of the High Street are some ancient alleyways or 'pends', leading back to the depth of two or three buildings and in some cases no wider than my walking-stick. That old-established newspaper, *The Hawick News*, for 100 years kept its offices up one of these narrow entries at 24 High Street, and the Editor told me how awkward it can be at times when heavy furniture or crates have to be moved out to the street or taken into the offices. For much of its life this paper, the only one actually produced in Roxburghshire, had its printing works situated alongside the office at the end of the alley. This has now been shifted to more modernly accessible premises outside the town centre. Down many an old pend the exploring visitor may discover enormously stout buildings, with circular turrets attached to them, housing spiral stone stairs.

At the south-west end of the High Street stands the Tower Hotel, a forty-bedroom hostelry associated with the Douglases of Drumlanrig. A plaque to the right of the main entrance reads:

> Incorporated in these walls is the Black Tower of Drumlanrig, Hawick residence of the Douglas family, and later of the Scotts of Buccleuch. This tower, built in the 16th century on an L-shaped plan, almost certainly replaced a still earlier tower, which in its turn had been preceded by the late 12th century tower of the Lovels on the Mote.

This mote, motte or moat is a flat-topped hillock situated in a small park to the south-west, reached through Howegate and The Loan. It is about fifty feet high, with a flight of thirty-six rather crooked steps up it; a climb well rewarded when the bird's-eye view of Hawick is observed from the summit.

Returning to The Tower, which became an inn in 1773, we find that one of the original compartments is still visible, and its cool depths are in use as a bar. To the hotel in September 1803 Sir Walter Scott brought William Wordsworth and his sister Dorothy; a plaque to the left of the entrance records that the trio stayed here for a night. The interior is a pleasant blend of ancient and modern, the modernisation not too blatant and the ancient atmosphere kept in check by an efficient and active staff. Next door is a large garage whence a taxi may be summoned at any moment – a luxury becoming less common every day. This is an excellent tourist centre for visitors who do not arrive by car. Bus services connect Hawick with Langholm, Jedburgh, Kelso, Selkirk and Galashiels, making it a simple matter for anyone to obtain a picture of some of the best

Border country. Many tourists, with or without their own transport, would find Hawick an admirable place in which to spend a leisurely week of exploration.

Behind The Tower, on its own little hill – the original 'Wick' – stands the church of St Mary. Historical records show that a place of worship stood here at least as early as 1183, and the original settlement of Hawick grew up around the shrine, on a triangle of land between the River Teviot and its tributary the Slitrig. The first dedication to St Mary, made by Adam Bishop of Caithness in 1214, must have involved a stout building, for it served the parish for nearly 600 years. When, in 1763 that church had to be demolished, the Buccleuch vaults beneath it were sealed off before the present building was put up. Until 1884 St Mary's served as the parish church, and in 1860 it was turned into a separate parish, taken out of the official one for ecclesiastical purposes. Although it had to be largely rebuilt after a serious fire in 1880, the Georgian character has been retained.

Inside the handsome wrought-iron gates of the churchyard is the tomb of Bailie John Hardie (1722-1800), who brought the first knitting machines, known as stocking-frames, to Hawick. At the house where Hardie lived, 37 High Street, above the present chemist's shop, is a tablet recording that he procured four of these novel frames in Glasgow in 1771 and brought them back to his home town, where he became the founder of the main industry – that of hosiery manufacture. The beginnings of this mechanical device provide a striking example of invention mothered by necessity. In the Hawick Museum (of which more later), is a picture of the Reverend William Lee, curate of Calverton, Nottingham, seated near his wife and child and observing intently the movements of her fingers as she knitted. William Lee, who was expelled from St John's College, Cambridge, in 1589 because he chose to marry contrary to the College statute, accepted the ill-paid Calverton curacy in order to earn a living of sorts. His wife was obliged to add to their income by knitting garments for customers, and her husband with desperate ingenuity invented his 'stocking-frame' to speed up production.

He profited little by the brilliant invention; but it certainly led in after years to fortunes being created in the huge knitwear industry which developed from that necessitous beginning.

A little farther east, on the same side of High Street as the newspaper office, is another spacious and hospitable old hotel, The

Crown, where willing service makes the guest wish to come again. From the first-floor lounge a wall plaque above Mosgrove's shop may be seen. It carries the curious legend:

ALL WAS OTHERS
ALL WILL BE OTHERS

Meaning, I suppose, that all material things are destined to perish. Although Hawick is well provided with hotels – there are several more which I have not had opportunity to sample – I thought at first that it lacked accessible cafés, handy for the High Street shopper at ground-floor level. Then I found one not far from the 1514 memorial, known familiarly as 'The Horse'. The little restaurant is also near the terraced gardens of Trinity Church, where gay flower beds and plenty of seats are much patronised in summer by townsfolk and visitors. One evening, after the corner café had closed, I walked on down Bourtree Place and came upon an Italian restaurant with the unusual name of *Quo Vadis*. Having spent a good deal of time in Italy, and acquired a liking for that nation's food, I went in, to discover that the venture had only just opened its doors. The interior is very well designed and furnished, and the proprietor seems wholly dedicated to the job, so I drank to his future success and wished the new café a long and useful life.

The Horse is a bronze equestrian statue, life-size, placed at the junction of the A7 (Selkirk) and A698 (Jedburgh and Kelso) roads. It was erected by public subscription in 1914 to mark the quater-centenary of a major event in local history. After the Battle of Flodden, a band of marauders from Hexham advanced up Teviotdale to attack Hawick. Most of her fighting men were gone, and only a muster of old men and youths was available to defend the town; but they came upon the enemy beside a deep pool at Hornshole and, falling on them suddenly by night, were able to rout them and capture their standard. This, in replica, is carried by the Hawick Cornet at the Common Riding ceremony each June.

On the opposite side of the High Street are some more pends, and one or two narrow roads leading down to the banks of the Teviot. Here we come upon one of the most famous of the numerous knitwear factories. Some people say that the history of that industry is largely the history of Pringle of Hawick. If you are in the mood to see how expensive cashmere twin-sets and men's cardigans are made, you are at liberty to enter the main door of Rodono Mill, and (at stated times) a guide will show you round. I had been standing near this entrance, thinking how clean the air remained in this industrial town, when Pringle's stack belched out a column of black smoke. As I stood looking up at this unseemly exhibit, a man near me said that he was the official concerned with smoke abatement and had come round to reprimand the employee responsible for stoking. I left him to get on with the good work, pleased that the Burgh kept such a sharp eye on pollution.

The swift-flowing Teviot, whose water is sparkling and clear, was regrettably marred by tin cans, bottles and plastic litter on its verges and caught on reefs in midstream. This, I thought, might surely be cleared by a Civic Society or Youth Group as a piece of voluntary service to the community. I learned that in fact such work had been done, but within a few days the river brought down a further supply of refuse from up-stream. It is an unending battle fought by public-spirited townspeople against the selfish, don't-care section of humanity, for whose irresponsible behaviour no effective method of prevention has yet been devised.

Hawick has a very remarkable asset which is not sufficiently publicised. The Burgh, at its Victorian baronial-style Town Hall in the High Street, would do well to exhibit a pictorial map, large enough to attract attention, showing the principal places of interest, with particular reference to the location of the fine Wilton Park and Museum. How many towns of this size can boast of having 107 acres of flower garden and grassy slopes, of shrubbery and wooded glen, enhanced by a burn and waterfall, almost on the doorstep of many residents? This domain was originally the home of the Langland family, descendants of the Norman Longueville, friend and ally of William Wallace. He reputedly visited here in 1297, and a stone marks the spot where Wallace is said to have hitched his horse to a thorn tree.

In 1451 the Langlands were created Barons of Wilton. They remained on the estate until 1783, when the last laird, an Edinburgh doctor, disposed of what was left of the estate to Thomas Elliot. Seven years later it was sold to Lord Napier, who re-named the house Wilton Lodge, instead of Langlands. In 1805 James Anderson, lately returned from service with the East India Company, acquired the estate, leaving it in due course to his daughter Mary. She married the Borderer David Pringle, born at Yair and educated in Selkirk. In 1859 the Pringles added an extra storey and bow windows to their house, which stands today essentially as it was in their lifetime. In 1889 it was purchased for

£14,000 from the Pringle trustees by Hawick Town Council, with the intention of maintaining a section of the land for recreation and using the rest for housing schemes and industry. Luckily for the town, that kind of development took place elsewhere and the whole of Wilton Park is reserved as an open space for the benefit of the public.

The house, now used as a Borders Museum, has been extended to include a spacious gallery for art and other exhibitions. Of the small number of paintings in the permanent collection, mostly portraits of local worthies, a group by Adam ('Yedie') Brown, an early nineteenth-century shoemaker of Hawick, may be classed as folk-art of very high quality. Eight of these are full-length Hogarthian caricatures of well-known local characters going about their business or pleasure. They are painted with an enchanting mixture of decorative charm and pithy comment, one or two being composed on fluid lines reminiscent of Japanese wood-cuts. The ninth example of Brown's art is a commissioned portrait, a head and shoulders in conventional style, done after he had left his shoemaker's last to earn a living as a painter. It is competent but dull, not equal to the inspired 'Sunday' paintings of its neighbours. At one time the museum possessed fifteen of Brown's pictures, and it is sad that during years of change and removal six should have been mislaid. If galleries in London or Edinburgh ever stage a comprehensive show of folk-art, Yedie Brown merits an honoured place.

In an adjoining room there is a collection of old knitting and sewing machines, spinning wheels, winding wheels and cop-holders, including a 14-gauge stocking-frame of 1798. Presumably this resembles the machines used by Bailie John Hardie, founder of Hawick's knitwear industry. There is also a Bentley-Cotton machine, similar to those now in use, except that it turns out only four garments simultaneously. Modern equipment produces eight (a few giants twelve) garments at a time. In glass-topped cases there is a good selection of work produced on these and other machines, including stockings in 'Dandy' or 'Sanquar' designs. These bold traditional patterns seem to be closely akin to those being revived by hand-knitters at Sanquhar in Dumfriesshire.

Among many other exhibits, a beautiful gas street lamp, made of copper, with a delicately cut edging to the canopy of the rectangular lamp, and a little fluted umbrella top to the circular chimney, is a reminder of more gracious days when street furniture was an asset and not an ugly intrusion. There is also an excellent scale model, made by Tom Horne in Hawick, of a famous little railway engine, built in 1835 by George Stephenson and originally used to haul passengers from Manchester to Liverpool. Over three decades ago we saw the actual steam engine running between Freshford in Somerset and Westbury, Wiltshire, at a time when it took the star part in that well-loved film of rural life, 'The Titfield Thunderbolt'.

There are examples of local journalism, including *Hawick Observer* (1842), *Hawick Newsletter* (1846), *Border Times* (1882) and *Hoggs Journal* (1886), none of which lasted very long. Near these are letters in the hands of Sir Walter Scott and James Hogg; poems by Hugh MacDiarmuid, a native of Langholm; by Will Ogilvie; and the manuscript of music written by Francis George Scott to MacDiarmuid's poem 'Crowdieknowe'. The Curator of this museum (until 1976), Mr R. E. Scott, is a son of the composer and one of the most quietly knowledgeable people, where the Borders are concerned, to be found in the area. He is the author of an informative booklet, *Companion to Hawick*, obtainable at the museum.

He collected a great many exhibits himself, particularly in the field of rural and domestic 'bygones'. There is a room full of these treasures, beautifully arranged and cared for. Here I found a 'dally pin', used by field workers who bound up sheaves at harvest time and were known as 'bandsters'. That labelled implement explained to me the titles given to a group of standing stones above Hownam in an eastern valley of Cheviot. Tradition has it that a party of reapers with sickles went out sinfully to work on a Sabbath day, and as a punishment were turned into stone. Their metamorphosed figures have been called 'The Shearers and Bandsters' ever since. So completely have old country crafts disappeared that I was unable to find anyone locally to supply the precise meaning of 'bandster'.

Mr Scott also staged a fine collection of nineteenth-century shopkeepers' billheads, full of delicate printers' ornaments and flourishes. A neat trade card measuring about four inches by three is a small period piece with immense evocative power. It is headed SEASON 1889, and reads:

> Miss Thomson begs to announce that she will show after 28th March her recent purchases in various markets, embracing all the Novelties for the Coming Season. She respectfully solicits an inspection of her MILLINERY, BONNETS & HATS in the leading Parisian fashions.

Miss Thomson has carefully selected a Large Stock of Straw Bonnets and Hats in Plain and Fancy Straws, newest colours, New Flowers and Foliage. Ostrich Plumes and Mounts. Choice stock of Rich Brocades & Fancy Ribbons, New Laces, New Embroidered Millinery Lisse, etc.

Miss Thomson had her hat shop at 29 High Street, and in the current guide-book I saw an advertisement for Miss A. Burnet, Millinery Specialist, 81 High Street, Hawick. Thinking to compare today's stock with that of 1889, I paid a visit to Miss Burnet's shop – only to find the windows gaunt and empty, the door locked, the shop deserted. Sad to say, there is now no 'Millinery Specialist' left in Hawick. It is a great loss to the shopping centre, for an array of fancy hats in gay colours, each on its little pedestal, has for most of my life played an important part in every town. There was always entertainment to be had from trying to imagine what faces and figures they were destined to adorn, even for such a woman as I, who seldom bought these wares.

A different kind of museum relic in the 'folk' class is the wooden model of a fulling or waulk mill, made as a political gimmick in late Victorian times. After Gladstone's government had passed a Bill to integrate the voting systems of counties and burghs, to give the people fairer political representation, the House of Lords (under Lord Salisbury) rejected it. Protest demonstrations followed all over the country. In September 1884 people from all the Border towns gathered in Hawick, and this model waulk mill was borne aloft at the head of a procession. On the front it has in large red letters 'PUBLIC OPINION', and both sides carry the slogans: 'FRANCHISE HOUSE OF LORDS SALISBURY & CO. OBSTRUCTION & RETROGRESSION. HOUSE OF COMMONS GLADSTONE & CO. REFORM & PROGRESS.' One hopes that 'Gladstone & Co' were pleased by this unusual form of tribute.

I have dwelt at some length on Wilton Lodge and with reason. Not only is it a very well arranged and interesting collection, in a delightful setting, but it has been awarded the status of principal museum for the whole of the new Borders Region.

Hawick takes pride in being the birthplace of the famous soprano Isobel Baillie, who was born in the town on 9th March 1895. In March 1975, during a radio programme in celebration of her eightieth birthday, the great singer's voice still sounded as pure as spring water, always right in the middle of the note and free from 'wobble'.

In a charmingly modest letter to me she recalled her childhood

Isobel Baillie, 1975

in the Borders, and holidays spent in the cottage of her grandfather, a joiner who worked on the Bowhill estate of the Duke of Buccleuch. Long afterwards she came back to it, having earned international fame, to sing at the wedding of the Earl of Dalkeith and Jane McNeill, now the Duke and Duchess of Buccleuch.

There may be a link between the exceptional quality of Isobel Baillie's voice and the purity of the atmosphere around her birthplace. Anyone who has walked out into the Border hills early on a fine May morning will know what I mean. The whole environment seems newly created. Every prospect pleases and even man is transfigured. The sheep have a kind of silver radiance on their fleeces, and when their shepherd comes up from a hidden ravine he appears against the flush of sunrise like some unearthly presence – perhaps the Good Shepherd himself. This heavenly light, this freshness and clarity, come to mind each time I hear Isobel Baillie sing. Much of her work has been connected with oratorio performances, and it is peculiarly fitting that she should sing of sheep and the Shepherd.

Selkirk

If ever I wished to exemplify the idea that bigger is not necessarily better, I would point to the old Burgh of Selkirk. This 'bonnie toon, The Favoured Forest Queen', as the song describes it, has barely six thousand inhabitants – about one-third the population of Hawick – yet it crowns the hills with such assured dignity that to number the inhabitants almost savours of discourtesy. I have stayed in different parts of the town, have attended the Common Riding ceremonies and walked in all the processions; have wandered about, talking to people and standing to watch them at work and play; yet the secret of how this small place quietly stamps a powerful impression of its own importance on the visitor's mind has eluded me. Perhaps it is all due to immense local pride and to an exceptionally strong community spirit. *Yince a Souter, Aye a Souter* is the legend on the golden banner of the Selkirk Colonial Society, and the bond between folk who are able, however far back, to trace a thread of Selkirk ancestry is unbreakable. The word 'souter' is Scots for 'shoemaker'. In bygone days, before the power looms and the tweed arrived here, Selkirk was so famous for its shoes that the burgesses became known as 'Souters of Selkirk'. (It has now spread to all of Selkirk birth.)

In those early times the hides were obtained from Ettrick Forest and tanned in the town; one tannery of long standing is still at work. Particularly famous were the 'single-soled shoon', a type of brogue with a thin sole to which thicker leather could be applied at the option of the wearer. At least one pair has survived in the town; it was brought out at an exhibition in 1975. There is a local tradition that about half the shoes required by Edinburgh to equip the Highlanders in the '45 rebellion were made at Selkirk. The craft is honoured each time a newly-created burgess is given the freedom of the Burgh, at a ceremony when the birse – a bunch of the boars' bristles used by shoemakers – is dipped in wine and 'licked' by the candidate for the honour. The word 'burgess' has altered its meaning through the centuries, for it originally denoted an inhabitant of a burgh (more strictly one who possessed full municipal rights); but later the meaning was restricted to freemen, those who had received 'the Burgess ticket'. Now the old Scottish Burghs and all their traditional ceremonies have been swept away for new groupings (made on the assumption that bigger *is* better) under the umbrella title of 'regionalisation'.

The old Royal Burgh of Selkirk, which, it is claimed, was created by David I, lies at the north-eastern tip of Ettrick and derives its name from 'Shiel-kirk', the church near the summer shiels of the foresters. For some unknown reason the monastery which David I founded, with a colony of Tironensian monks, remained at Selkirk for only twelve years, and was then removed to the new abbey at Kelso. At that time there was a royal castle (now no more than a mound, on the Haining estate), and twin townships, Selkirk Abbatis and Selkirk Regis. In addition to David I, William the Lyon and Alexander II and III and possibly Robert the Bruce, also dwelt at Selkirk. Castle and Monastery have long since gone, together with the ancient mercat cross and tolbooth; so has the old Forest Inn where Burns wrote his 'Epistle to William Creech' in May 1787. A tablet marks the site in West Port, and another records that the great Montrose stayed in a house nearby before his defeat at Philiphaugh.

Compared with some Border towns, Selkirk seems to have escaped many of the worst ravages of troops from south of the line. After the Battle of Flodden, however, it was burnt to the ground. In recognition of the great part played by the Souters at Flodden, the young James V allotted 1,000 acres of his royal forest to the burgh as common land, with permission to fell enough timber to rebuild the town. Of the valiant band that went out to march behind the standard of James IV in 1513, led by the Town Clerk, William Brydon, it is said that only one – John Fletcher – came home to Selkirk. Wounded, exhausted, carrying an English pennon, he waved the captured flag round his head and 'cast' it on the cobbles of the Market Place, thus indicating to the assembled crowd that all was lost. The Common Riding ceremonial – which is certain to continue long after the Royal Burgh has been deprived of its trappings – is held each year in June to ride the bounds of the common lands, and to commemorate the dead of Flodden and all subsequent wars. When at the close the flags are 'cast' on a dais before the old Court House, the unique circling and dipping, carried out by all the Standard Bearers with great skill, recalls the silent mime with which Fletcher broke his tragic news four and a half centuries ago. The tattered remnant of the English pennon is now framed and hanging in the Selkirk Public Library.

Flags play a large part in the life of Selkirk. The Burgh ensign is popularly supposed to symbolise the discovery on Ladywood Edge, after Flodden, of a dead woman, wife to one of those killed in

A standard-bearer at the Common Riding, Selkirk

battle, with a live infant still suckling at her breast. (A picture of the scene by Tom Scott, RSA, a well-known local artist, hangs in Sir Walter Scott's courtroom in the Town Hall.) It is more likely that the Selkirk Burgh flag and the armorial bearings depict the Virgin and Child, especially as the arms show halos round the heads of both figures. Other flags carried at the Common Riding are those of the Merchant Company, the Weavers' Company, the Colonial Society, the Incorporation of Hammermen, and the British Legion. On the 'Nicht afore the Morn' each of the flags is 'bussed' by a lady with knots of coloured ribbon, a rite based on the giving of favours to their chosen knights by the ladies of long ago.

From flags it is a natural step to the statue of Fletcher (by Clapperton) outside the Victoria Hall, which shows him bearing the English pennon. In front of the Town Hall is an imposing statue of Sir Walter Scott, affectionately known to Souters as 'The Shirra', who officiated as Sheriff of Selkirk from 1799 until his death in 1832.

His effigy, the first memorial to be erected to him, is set up on a high plinth above the traffic and the flower-beds, and occupies the site of the old tolbooth. Another famous man of the former county of Selkirkshire, born in 1770 just outside the Burgh at Foulshiels – the African explorer Mungo Park – is commemorated by a statue at the eastern end of the High Street. He married Alice Anderson, daughter of a local doctor to whom Mungo was apprenticed at the age of fifteen. The Anderson home, an attractive Georgian building, still stands nearby, shaded by a fine horse-chestnut tree which the explorer planted after returning from his first expedition.

On the other side of the street, set back from the road in its garden, is the house called 'Viewfield' where the author Andrew Lang was born. A plaque at the entrance records this fact. Sir Walter Scott was a frequent visitor to the Lang home, and to the County Hotel a few yards farther west, where he attended meetings of the ancient Forest Club. Here his daughter Sophia, who married Scott's biographer, John Gibson Lockhart, once sang (at her father's special request) the traditional 'Souter' song, 'Up wi' the Souters o' Selkirk'. Every visitor to the Common Riding today will hear this sung, shouted, whistled and played until he knows words and tune by heart:

> Up wi' the Souters o' Selkirk
> And down wi' the Earl o' Home!
> And up wi' a' the braw lads
> That sew the single-soled shoon!

Sir Walter's courtroom in the Town Hall is sometimes shown to the public, with Scott's Bench and worn chair, his robing room, and the great window through which he often admired the encircling hills when he grew weary of litigation. For most of his term, his Sheriff clerk was Andrew Lang senior, grandfather of the poet and essayist. Until 1974 the silver Burgess cup, which Sir Walter himself designed, was on view, together with the birse, during visiting hours. Unfortunately the dreadful occurrence at Hawick Common Riding in June of that year, when the gold chain of Hawick's Provost was stolen, caused the Provost and Bailies of Selkirk to think twice about exhibiting their silver cup. Unless some burglar-proof case or other safety measure can be devised, it seems that a pleasure hitherto available must be withdrawn.

Still to be seen are portraits of James Hogg, of Mungo Park's father-in-law, and a bust of Scott; also letters written by Burns,

'Crying the Burley'

Lang and Park; a plan of Abbotsford made by Scott; copies of charters relating to Selkirk's twelfth-century abbey, and a charter of James V, dated 1535, in which ancient privileges were renewed. From the steeple of the Town Hall curfew is still rung at eight-o'clock as it used to be in medieval times, when Selkirk was a walled town. The halberds carried by Burgh officers on ceremonial occasions have turned into museum pieces, and there is no longer a Burgh officer to 'Cry the Burley' (from 'Burlay' – a court of neighbours in a district to settle local disputes) on the 'nicht afore the morn', dressed in his white-faced livery and silver-braided topper. There have been no Provosts since May 1975, so chains of office are no longer worn in the old Scottish Burghs. On the one hand, large sums are spent on the Tourist Board and advertising of all kinds, while on the other the pageantry and old, unique customs which the tourist wants to see are being curtailed at an alarming rate.

In 1976 John Guthrie, the last working 'souter' (shoemaker) in Selkirk, retired. His tools have been presented to the town. During over fifty years at his last, John has been visited and photographed by people from Canada, the United States, Australia, New Zealand

and elsewhere. His little shop in Westport, where his father and grandfather made shoes before him, had been left unchanged since the beginning of the century.

Grandfather Robert Guthrie was renowned as a fiddle-player, and in his time the evenings were spent in music and song. He was still playing his violin at the age of ninety-four. Many a night had his family and neighbours joined in the traditional song:

> There sits a souter in Selkirk
> Wha sings as he draws his thread –
> There's gallant souters in Selkirk
> As lang as there's water in Tweed.

Unfortunately the thread has been broken by modern mass-produced footwear. When John started part-time work for his father as a schoolboy of twelve a good pair of hand-made shoes cost only fifty shillings. The Guthrie shop employed four or five assistants, and there were some twenty other shoemakers' shops in the town.

One by one these closed down, and the United Crafts Corporation to which they all belonged came to an end. John Guthrie in 1934 cast the Shoemakers' flag at the Common Riding ceremony for the last time.

An interesting relic always open to visitors is the old roofless 'Kirk o' the Forest', which stands on its grassy knoll above the Kirk Wynd. Here in 1298 William Wallace was proclaimed Guardian of Scotland. Within these walls, in an enclosure known as the Murray Aisle, lie the remains of the maternal ancestors of Franklin D. Roosevelt, thirty-second President of the U.S.A. Among many older stones in the surrounding graveyard is one which has stayed clearly legible for over three centuries. The words are cut in bold, plain lettering, arranged to fit the stone to the very edge without wasting space. There is a curious charm in its naive simplicity:

> HEIR LYIS MASTER
> JOHN ANGUS
> BAILLIE OF SEL
> KIRK WHO DE
> CEASED THE 26
> OF SEPTEMBER
> 1662 HIS AIGE
> WAS 48 YEARS
> VIVIT POST FU
> NERA VIRTUS

G   *John Guthrie, the last shoemaker in Selkirk*

Reference has already been made to the Forest Club, to which Sir Walter Scott belonged. Of old, Scottish people who spoke of 'The Forest' invariably meant Ettrick Forest, with Selkirk as its 'queen'. This wild territory, which has played so important a part in Scots history, comprised some 350 square miles of Selkirkshire – most of that county, in fact – together with a good deal of Peeblesshire and a section of Dumfriesshire. Always isolated and remote, even in this motoring age, 'The Forest' has only the three small towns of Selkirk, Moffat and Peebles on its perimeter with about 13,000 inhabitants between them. It was once a part of the old Caledonian Forest which covered most of Scotland. Oak, hazel, Scots pine and the bonny birken tree supplied food and shelter for deer, wild cattle, swine – and the most valuable cover for men. Edward I never succeeded in cracking this hard core of the Borders, where both Wallace and Bruce in their time found safe harbourage.

Although tree-cover was not of great density or continuous, the fact that Ettrick had no roads and few landmarks, but held many places where invaders might be ambushed, and little scope for deployment of mounted troops, greatly favoured the exploits of natives who were familiar with the terrain. In 1528 James V staged a grand hunt there, taking about 350 harts and managing (as if by accident rather than by design) to round up some troublesome free-booting Borderers as an additional sport. After that he introduced sheep to Ettrick – as many as 10,000 of them, it is said. When sheep took over the ground, trees gradually dwindled and died out. Woodland cannot regenerate itself if seedlings are steadily grazed down.

A number of tree-planting Border lairds added good timber to their estates in the late eighteenth and nineteenth centuries, Sir Walter Scott being one of the most diligent. He wrote several papers on afforestation, and to him we owe the modern custom of calling the native Scots pine by its rightful name. Before that, Scots were accustomed to calling *Pinus sylvestris* 'fir'. In our own time considerable planting has been carried out by the Forestry Commission, notably at Yair, Elibank, Traquair, Cardrona and Glentress near Peebles, all in the old Ettrick region, and totalling 13,000 acres. About four miles to the south-west of Selkirk lies Bowhill, a seat of the Duke of Buccleuch, whose 1,400-acre estate rises from 420 feet at the meeting of the Yarrow and Ettrick Waters to over 1,000 feet at Pernassie. A fine collection of trees flourishes here, including Norway and Sitka spruce, Douglas fir, Lawson cypress, sycamore, oak, ash and birch. Many come up freely from seed to ensure natural regeneration, and there is also a forest nursery and a sawmill. A stretch of 150 acres of birch scrub at Howebottom is believed to have survived from the ancient Ettrick Forest, without any recorded replanting.

5

More Border Towns

Coldstream

Because a well-known regiment bears its name, most people have heard of Coldstream. Too often that minimum knowledge is linked with the erroneous belief that the place lies on the English side of the Tweed. In a pleasant little public garden, Henderson Park – which overlooks the river from the Scottish side – is a large block of stone inscribed 'Presented to the Burgh of Coldstream by the Coldstream Regiment of Foot Guards on the day on which they were proud to receive the Freedom of the Burgh, 10 August 1968'. It was from here that General Monck and his men crossed the River Tweed to start their long march to London, which culminated in the Restoration of Charles II. Although they helped to restore an English monarch, they came from Scotland.

Smeaton's fine bridge, which now links Coldstream with Cornhill, Wooler and Newcastle, was not built until over a hundred years later, between 1763 and 1766. It has seven arches, is 305 feet long and 25 feet wide. Robert Burns first set foot on English soil after walking across this bridge in May 1787 – an event recorded on a tablet erected by the Coldstream Burns Club in 1926. For centuries before it had the benefit of a bridge, Coldstream was in the hot line of communication with England, having the first reliable ford upstream of Berwick. Not that the Tweed has been invariably placid. In the wall of the riverside walk below Henderson Park, a path which is itself high above the normal river, there are two plaques at waist-level, recording high-water marks during great floods on 2nd February 1831 and 13th August 1948.

Sections of the riverside path, known here as Nuns Walk and a little farther upstream as Penitents Walk, are the sole surviving reminders of Coldstream's medieval convent, a Cistercian Priory founded in the twelfth century by Cospatrick, Earl of March, an ancestor of the Douglas-Home family of The Hirsel. The coat of arms of the now defunct Coldstream Burgh, a salmon between a wheel, sun, crescent and five planets, is taken from the seal of a vanished priory, which Hertford destroyed in 1545.

The little Georgian toll-house at the Scottish end of the bridge was formerly used as a marriage-house. At one time it seems to have been as popular as the more famous Gretna Green smiddy and Lamberton Toll at the northern extremity of Berwick Bounds. Until 1856 marriages could be effected without prior notice and were perfectly legal. After that date, three weeks' residential qualification was required. Runaway marriages have attracted so much attention from the romantically-minded that it is often forgotten how much the toll-cum-marriage houses were used by ordinary local couples. Many people living in the Borders today will tell you of grandparents and great-uncles who were married in these places, which were cheaper and less formal, and – to the shy – less alarming than a ceremony in the kirk. As to cost, old Will Dickson at Coldstream used to ask five shillings, adding to this modest request his hope of sharing a dram with the happy pair at a later date.

A few months before re-organisation of local government in May 1975 swept away Scotland's old Burgh Councils, Provost Lloyd of Coldstream told me that all the Border Provosts, who used to meet regularly in amicable conclave, had between them persuaded the planners not to throw this area in with Edinburgh and the Lothians, as originally suggested, but to create a separate Borders Region with its own Regional Council. He added that Coldstream, the only Scottish Border town to be situated right *on* the Border, maintains the friendliest relations with England. 'This is partly due to the difference in licensing laws. In Coldstream, bars open at five, and thirsty folk from England cross over the bridge to our hotels. Down there, they close half an hour later, so the tide of drinkers then turns and flows in a southerly direction.'

This picturesque stretch of Tweed, fourteen miles west of Berwick and nine miles east of Kelso, with a ford where the Leet runs into it, has seen many an army, both English and Scots, passing through to lay waste the opposite countryside. Visitors might therefore imagine that the statue raised high above the town on a great column near Coldstream bridge commemorates some military triumph. The truth is more prosaic. That lonely figure represents Charles Marjoribanks, elected first Member of Parliament for Berwickshire after the Reform Bill of 1832. The monument was set up by jubilant Liberals during the lifetime of the subject and so does not record the dates of his birth and death. He was a son of Sir John Marjoribanks of Lees, an estate at the west end of the town at the confluence of Leet and Tweed.

The story of The Hirsel and its distinguished owner, former Prime Minister Lord Home, has been kept for a later chapter. There is little else in Coldstream to be mentioned, except for a house in the Market Place, built on the site of seventeenth-century headquarters of the Coldstream Guards. The original building was replaced in 1865. Here will be found the local museum, with military and other relics. These treasures have recently been joined by the Provost's robes and chain of office, no longer in regular use but given an airing each year at the festival 'Presenting Coldstream', at which the ride-out and memorial service at Flodden Field is the highlight.

The old heart of this pleasant little town, consisting largely of one long, winding street, is fast being hemmed in by modern building estates; yet the character of the original still contrives to exist, overcoming the stream of long vehicles going through all day long and the massed modern housing on the perimeter. That essential to tourism, the caravan park, has been well placed at a lower level alongside the Tweed, conveniently close to the centre without being obtrusive.

Although the river is not normally seen by shoppers in the High Street, there are sudden, delightful glimpses of it from rear windows of buildings on the south side, and a very short stroll to Henderson Park brings a wide panorama into view. The name of this splendid salmon river is familiar to people all over Britain and far beyond our shores, chiefly because the sturdy woollen cloth known as 'tweed' is thought to have taken its name from the Tweed-side Border country.

While it is true that people here have woven and exported such cloth in great quantities since the late eighteenth century, the name is believed to have been born of a misunderstanding. To begin with, the Scottish weavers called their product 'twill', a word pronounced in their Border speech as 'tweel', and some English buyer, unable to grasp this, is said to have substituted the letter 'd' for 'l'; and so the cloth shared the name of the great river ever afterwards.

In spite of an interesting history, Coldstream is to some extent an upstart town, supplanting the ancient village of Leinhall (now Lennel), which is named in deeds of the twelfth century. The original church of this place is but a ruined remnant, although its burial ground still serves the neighbouring town. Lennel village, now reduced to a hamlet, no longer has a shop, kirk or inn; the old house across the corner which used to serve as a hostelry has become a private dwelling.

Sir Ilay Campbell's former home (now occupied by Mr G. Bowie) is a Georgian house whose fine frontage may be admired from the road through Lennel. It is beautifully sited above the Tweed. The garden consists of a series of long terraces parallel with the river and bordered by beds of old-fashioned flowers, such as madonna lilies, delphiniums, astrantias, single hollyhocks and white bellflowers. All the herbaceous plants and the many roses are expertly tended, the turf is close and even, the yew hedges always trim. At the lowest level are two large rectangular pools full of exuberant pink and white water-lilies.

There are many fine trees, including a larch which the last occupant believed to be contemporary with the house. An impressive range of walling, statuary, wrought ironwork – with a charming little well-head near the sundial – completes this fine Scottish-Italian garden. Beyond it the fertile Merse stretches to distant Cheviot hills. The garden is open to the public occasionally.

A cottage on the Lennel estate for many years housed three sisters – Mary, Jean and Ellen Margaret Hutchinson, all unmarried, who lived most amicably together. Jean had an unusual career and became one of the best-known local characters.

Shortly before the outbreak of World War I she began her life work on the land as a ploughwoman. She was fourteen years old, and her wages were five shillings a week, of which her mother returned sixpence as pocket-money. Jean had to be in the stables by five o'clock in the morning to feed the horses an hour before yoking time. Her day ended at six in the evening.

Jean worked like a man and spent her weekly sixpence manfully on Woodbine cigarettes. When she grew older she took to wearing a man's working suit and cloth cap, long before the days of ladies' slacks and unisex garments. Horses were her passion, and in 1921 she won a championship at the Glendale Ploughing Matches against twenty male competitors. In the 1930s she had her own farm at Cornhill, on the English side of the Border. By the 1950s she reluctantly learned to drive a tractor, when horses were being phased out of farm work.

Over the years Jean made a habit of collecting horse-brasses, which she cared for lovingly and sometimes lent for exhibition in Coldstream. In old age she invented the ideal hobby, dressing porcelain models of working horses with authentic reproduction harness, perfect in every detail.

No visit to Coldstream and Lennel is complete without a short excursion into Northumberland to see the battlefield of Flodden near the village of Branxton. It is well signposted. Each summer, during the 'Presenting Coldstream' festival, the young 'Coldstreamer' and his cavalcade ride their horses out to Flodden, where a service is held and a wreath laid at the memorial stone.

Every year some well-known Border personage is invited to give an oration after the ceremony, a duty which seldom falls to a woman. In 1973 Miss Grace Elliot of Birgham, who had recently been awarded the M.B.E. for her historical researches, gave the address. In it she described how in 1910 the Berwickshire Naturalists' Club, which erected the Flodden monument, invited suggestions for an inscription. The simple and moving words carved there:

TO THE BRAVE OF BOTH NATIONS

were submitted by Miss Elliot's father.

I am indebted to Major P. R. Adair, a contributor to the Civic Week programme dated 1968, for information about the Coldstream Regiment of Footguards. It is the 'oldest Corps by continuous existence and sole representative by lineal descent of the first Regular Army, which was raised and organised by Oliver Cromwell under the title of "New Model" '. In June 1650 Cromwell wished to offer a Command to General Monck, but as that officer fought on the Royalist side in the Civil War, the regiment selected for him did not favour the new Commander. The problem was solved by taking half a battalion from each of two regiments and combining ten companies on the Border as 'Monck's Regiment of Foot'.

After Cromwell's death, Monck (then General Commanding the Army in Scotland) in the winter of 1658 moved his headquarters to Coldstream, where the most bitter cold and privation were experienced. The cheerful endurance of hardships gained for the

Jean Hutchinson of Lennel in her 74th year

Regiment the title of 'Coldstreamers'. On 1st January 1660 General Monck led them out of Coldstream on a march to London, which took thirty-four days. They were quartered in St James's and employed in repressing riot and disturbance. At the end of May Charles II was restored to the throne, and General Monck, now Captain General of the Land Forces, was created Duke of Albemarle. On his triumphal entry into the capital, King Charles inspected the Coldstreamers and expressed satisfaction at their appearance and discipline.

By an Act of Parliament, Cromwell's New Model Army was disbanded, with a proviso that Monck's own Regiment of Horse and Foot were to be retained to the last. In January 1661 Monck's Regiment of Horse was about to be disbanded when insurrection necessitated using troops to restore order. It was then decided to keep the Regiment for the security of the monarch. In February Monck's men were mustered on Tower Hill. Having been required to lay down their arms and accept formal disbandment, the Regiment of Foot was immediately ordered to take up arms as the Lord General's Regiment of Foot Guards. From that time the already distinguished Regiment became a personal Guard to the Sovereign.

In 1664 another change occurred, when 500 extra men were raised by royal warrant to augment the Foot Guards for sea service. Twelve years earlier, in 1652, General (then Colonel) Monck had been one of three 'admirals' who led the British Fleet against the Dutch Navy. He is recorded as having issued an order to his ships in the heat of action, using the unorthodox words 'Wheel to the right – charge!' Coldstreamers were thus prepared to act as parents to the corps which ultimately developed into the Royal Marines. On the death of George Monck, Duke of Albemarle, in 1670, the Lord General's Regiment was conferred upon the Earl of Craven, and from that date became known as The Coldstream Guards.

Eyemouth, Coldingham and St Abbs

Eyemouth stands at the mouth of the River Eye, some eight miles from the English boundary stone to the north of Berwick-upon-Tweed on the A1 road. Its long history as a seaport can be traced back to William the Lyon, when the great Priory of Coldingham carried on a substantial maritime trade from Eyemouth. In 1214 a harbourmaster named Kinghorn was accused of overcharging a ship for anchorage dues. Alexander III encouraged fishing and introduced fish-curing processes, so that trade in these local products with the continent grew and flourished.

During the sixteenth-century wars between Scotland and England, galleys landed French soldiers here for service with the Scottish armies. As a result, the English established themselves in a fort on the northern promontory overlooking the bay. Like so many other fortresses in these parts, this one became a bone of contention. It was occupied at various times by English, French and Scots; demolished, rebuilt, and again destroyed.

The old house of Gunsgreen, in a conspicuous position on the opposite arm of the bay overlooking the inner harbour, had better fortune. It is popularly supposed to have been built on the proceeds of smuggling, and local tales of secret chambers and hidden passages abound. Some say that a concealed spring controlled a panel in the great fireplace of the kitchen. The stone slab rolled aside to disclose a flight of stairs into cellars which were connected by tunnel with the shore.

Another tale relates a happening of over a hundred years ago. A horse plough fell into a pit which suddenly opened beneath it in a field, supposedly part of the Gunsgreen subterranean network used in the profitable contraband trade. The present house, of early eighteenth-century construction, stands on or near the earlier one owned by Logan of Restalrig. Sir Robert Logan took part in the Gowrie Conspiracy, and two of the incriminating letters were written at Gunsgreen in 1600 by his Notary.

Eyemouth Bay is protected by a ridge of rocks called The Hurkers. Years ago there was a projected scheme to unite them to the land to form a complete breakwater, but this idea was abandoned on account of the high cost. In 1747 William Crow of Netherbyres planned the Old Pier at Eyemouth and had it carried out by private subscription. His tombstone, scarcely decipherable, is in the precincts of Coldingham Priory. In 1768 further improvements to the harbour were made under the direction of Smeaton.

In May 1787 Robert Burns set out from Edinburgh on a tour of the Borders, which took him to Coldstream, Jedburgh, Kelso, Berwick-upon-Tweed and Eyemouth. Here he was taken for a sail after dinner, and admitted as a Royal Arch Mason of St Abbs Lodge. Others at the same admission ceremony paid a fee of one guinea. The record shows that Burns, 'on account of his remarkable poetic genius', was by unanimous vote admitted free. He saw a flourishing port and a busy fishing industry, before disaster struck Eyemouth.

In October 1881, on a day known ever since as 'Black Friday', a sudden freak storm took terrible toll of the fishing fleet. Some vessels tried to make port and were dashed to pieces on the cliffs or the Hurker Rocks. Others attempted to ride out the storm at sea, but few managed to survive. Twenty-three boats belonging to the port were destroyed and 129 men drowned. Many Eyemouth families lost all their menfolk in one blow, and other fishing communities along the coast – Burnmouth, St Abbs and Cove – also had severe losses. It was a very long time before the local fishing industry recovered from this disaster. A commemorative service was held in October 1981.

Today there are big changes afoot in the town, which is expanding, with some factories and new housing estates. Alleyways and wynds of the old fishing port are making way for industrial traffic and tourists. But it is still possible to watch boats unloading catches right in the heart of the place, where the cleaning and packing of fish goes on, and boxes are sold by auction. To make the perfect background to all this, there is usually a new fishing vessel to be seen, high up on the stocks of the Eyemouth Boatbuilding Company. Nowhere else can so many aspects of the sea-fishing industry be taken in at a glance. This advantage should be enjoyed before an ambitious new scheme for more modern facilities takes the fish landing and market away to a less congested site.

I am indebted to Commander James Evans for the following account of boat building.

It is probable that the building of small boats in Eyemouth started at an early date. There are records of fisheries dating back several hundred years. The recollection of older members of the community, derived from grandparents, is that small sailing vessels were built on the beach where the gantry now stands. In 1827 the land on the Ayton side of the river was sold by the Robertson family of Gunsgreen to the Weatherhead family for a boatyard and brewery. The Weatherheads had come to Eyemouth from Alnwick by way of Berwick-upon-Tweed.

It would appear that the first fishing vessel was built about 1843 on the site of the present yard. Many others have followed. Most of the boats lost in the Eyemouth disaster of 1881 would have originated in the

Building Valhalla *at Eyemouth*

yard. It had a very good reputation as builder of Scottish fishing vessels, and in 1909 the *Amanda Jane*, built in 1903 as a sailing vessel, was converted to the first internal combustion engine with a petrol/paraffin engine, the first Scottish fishing boat to have this. In 1911 the first diesel-powered boat, the *Bolinder*, was built here. The Bolinder Company, now Volvo Penta UK Ltd, still has the Eyemouth Boatbuilding Company as a Volvo agent.

Weatherheads closed down in 1954 and the boatyard was later acquired by Thomas Evans, who had been a Director of the earlier firm. His son James is now Managing Director of the Eyemouth Boatbuilding Company Ltd. Between the 1950s and the early 1960s the yard concentrated on pleasure craft, but since that time it has reverted to the construction of fishing vessels.

In 1978 a major reconstruction was carried out, with slipways realigned and the river bed lowered by one-and-a-half metres. A ring circuit of compressed air was fitted to allow the use of air tools, sandblasting, paint spraying and other modern techniques. The yard was also equipped to manufacture in aluminium alloy as well as in steel and wood, and a new crane was introduced. At the height of the fishing vessel boom in the late 1970s, seventy-six men were employed, building four new vessels a year as well as carrying out complete maintenance and repair work for the local fleet. In the depression of the early 1980s this was reduced, only thirty-four men being employed at this time.

A fishing boat at the time of the disaster in 1881 would have cost about £400. When ownership of the boatyard changed in 1957, the standard Eyemouth vessel was about fifty-five feet in length and cost around £11,000. In 1981 the standard vessel was somewhat larger, sixty feet, and cost around £350,000. Not all the rise in cost is caused by inflation. Vessels have become very much more complicated and include more gear. Before 1950 there were no electronics in these boats. Now the wheelhouse is full of electronics and with the microchip and control circuits now available, this change will become even greater in the next twenty years.

Prices now go out of date before they can be published, but there is an object in quoting them. Housewives are helped to understand that the catching of fish has become an expensive business, with very high fuel costs, all of which must be reflected in the price per pound of this valuable food. Eyemouth pays tribute to its fishermen every summer, when a local girl is chosen and crowned as the 'Herring Queen'. Together with her maids of honour she is voted into her throne by fellow pupils at Eyemouth High School. Her maids, dressed in capes of silvered herring-net, walk behind their queen in positions marking the points of the compass. Very appropriately, they arrive at the harbour in a fishing boat.

A famous native of Eyemouth, Captain John Willis, began his career as a cabin boy in a local boat. Later he went to London and became a prosperous shipowner. It was a period of intense competition in the trade, each trying to acquire the fastest ship in order to win the 'blue riband' of the sea. In 1869 Captain Willis was successful with the *Cutty Sark*, which has been carefully preserved and is now on view at Greenwich.

Another distinguished resident, Captain Samuel Brown, RN, who bought Netherbyres in the early part of the nineteenth century, invented a new type of chain cable, which was adopted by the navy. He utilised it to construct a suspension bridge across the Eye to his own grounds, an underslung design which he called a tension bridge. Next he took out a patent for a suspension bridge, and went on to build these in several places.

In Scotland he constructed the Union Bridge over the River Tweed at Horncliffe, which has recently undergone repair; then came the old Spey Bridge at Fochabers and the chain bridge at Montrose. In England he made himself famous by constructing the Chain Pier at Brighton, an achievement for which he received a knighthood from Queen Victoria in 1838.

The present mansion of Netherbyres, built by Captain Samuel

Brown *circa* 1830 and later enlarged, stands on the site of an older house, above the Eye Water within a fork made by the A1107 coast road and the B6355 road from Ayton. Formerly enclosed by a wide belt of trees, it has in recent years suffered from some destruction of valuable shelter because improved road access to Eyemouth sliced off part of the policies. Netherbyres now belongs to the Furness family.

Its chief glory is an oval walled garden, probably designed by William, an eighteenth-century member of the Crow family who owned the earlier house of Netherbyres. The outside walling is built of stone, faced inside with brick, thought to be Dutch. Bricks were often brought back from Holland in ships trading out of Eyemouth with wool and linen goods. This charming enclosure measures 200 yards in length and 100 yards in width, and is very well laid out and maintained. Oval gardens are rare, but there is another, only partially oval, at Carolside near Earlston, also built in the eighteenth century. Netherbyres also possesses an attractive herb garden, with a white clapboard garden house made by Furness shipyard workers during a period of unemployment. Both Carolside and Netherbyres are open from time to time, and will be found listed in the Scotland's Gardens Scheme booklet.

Coldingham Priory, about three miles north of Eyemouth, has been the site of a Christian foundation since the seventh century and possibly even earlier. In the twelfth century it developed into an important priory, dependent on Durham. Dedication of its church of St Mary was attended by King Edgar in 1100. After being sacked by King John early in the thirteenth century, it was rebuilt on a larger scale. In 1509 Coldingham was attached to Dunfermline instead of Durham.

Cromwell destroyed the south-west walls of the choir of the monastic church, which was rebuilt after the Restoration. It was renovated in 1850 and again a hundred years later, and the choir is currently in use as a parish church. The surviving north and east walls, with unusual combined clerestory and triforium, together form one of the best pieces of ecclesiastical architecture left in Scotland. Under the auspices of the Berwickshire Naturalists' Club, a large programme of excavation has been carried out recently at the remains of the great Priory.

The small village was at one time a centre of handloom weaving, Coldingham gingham and shirting being much in demand locally. At the east end, there is a modern caravan park and camping site,

The nature reserve at St Abb's Head

Scoutscroft, within easy reach of Coldingham Bay. That sandy shore is a favourite place for bathers and family picnics, while the little fishing port of St Abbs attracts many skin divers.

The fine promontory known as St Abbs Head and part of the Northfields Farm, 192 acres in all, were purchased in October 1981 by the National Trust for Scotland, to be maintained as a Nature Reserve with a resident Ranger in charge. This area, part of a Site of Special Scientific Interest, Grade 1, is described by the Nature Conservancy Council as a 'fine series of sea-cliffs with considerable botanical interest, and the most important locally for cliff-breeding sea birds in South East Scotland'. Kittiwakes, guillemots, razorbills, shags, fulmars and herring gulls breed here, and skuas, terns and shearwaters are frequent visitors. The headland is also a staging-post for migrants. Details of admission to the Reserve will be found in the appendix, together with the latest attraction in Eyemouth, a museum of local artefacts.

The headland takes its name from St Ebba, daughter of a king of Northumbria who in the seventh century founded a religious establishment here. This was sacked in the ninth century, probably by Vikings. There is a lighthouse, built in 1862 at a height of 225 feet above the sea.

Duns and Gordon with Earlston

> I stood upon Eyemouth Fort
> And guess ye what I saw?
> Fairnieside and Flemington,
> Newhouses and Cocklaw;
> The faery folk o' Fosterland,
> The witches o' Edincraw,
> The rye-riggs o' Reston –
> But Duns dings a'!

Outside its own district, Duns has two main claims to be remembered. As birthplace and name-town of the medieval scholar, John Duns Scotus, it became known from the Borders to Oxford (where he was Professor of Theology at Merton College); from Paris (where he defended his doctrine of the Immaculate Conception) to Cologne, where he died in 1308. The scholarly debates in which he took part gave rise to another link with Duns. When John Duns Scotus and Thomas Aquinas founded the Scotist and Thomist schools of thought, the Thomists derisively referred to every Scotist as a 'Dunse'. From that epithet our word 'dunce' has come down into everyday speech.

The tomb of Duns Scotus in Cologne bears an inscription in Latin which means:

> Scotland bore me;
> England adopted me;
> France taught me;
> Cologne holds me.

In 1966 the Franciscan Order (to which he belonged) erected in Duns Park a striking bronze of Duns Scotus by Frank Tritchler, to commemorate the 700th anniversary of his birth. There is also a stone near the Pavilion Lodge at Duns Castle, marking the site of the house where the scholar was born. Everywhere the Catholic Church celebrated his 700th anniversary.

A divine of very different outlook, the Calvinist Thomas Boston, was born in Duns in 1676, at a house in Newtown. After being licensed as a minister by the Presbytery of Duns and Chirnside, he was called to Simprim, the smallest parish in Berwickshire. He was transferred to Ettrick in 1707. Later in life he wrote memoirs and much else, his best-known work being the *Fourfold State of Man*.

Duns – sometimes seen on old milestones as 'Dunse' – played a great part in upholding the Covenant. In 1639 an assembly of 30,000 armed men was encamped on Duns Law under General Leslie, while Charles I, trying to force Episcopacy upon the people of Scotland, waited with his army to cross the Tweed at Paxton. In the end the English monarch thought better of it, and battle was not joined. Each summer during the Duns Festival an open-air service is held on the Law near the Covenanters Stone, which commands a very wide view of the surrounding country. As the ministers of various local churches assemble with their congregations, the Duns Reiver, bearing the town's banner and attended by his followers, fifty or more young people on horseback, comes riding up the brae to take part in the ceremony.

Below the Law to the east lies the Duns Castle estate, a large area of which is now a Nature Reserve managed jointly by the owners and the Scottish Wild Life Trust. No cars are admitted, but there is a parking place within the Oxendean entrance, on the road B6365 at the northern boundary of the Reserve. There is a good-sized lake, known as Hen Poo', where swans, coot, moorhen, heron and various kinds of duck may be seen. In the woodland red squirrel, roe deer, badger, stoat and otter have been observed. Among the nesting birds are pied flycatcher, redstart, green and spotted woodpecker, and woodcock. Duns is fortunate in having such a sanctuary within a stone's throw of its streets.

The little town itself, once so pleasantly attractive in an unpretentious way, has suffered rather badly from the influx of motor traffic, for which its narrow winding streets were not designed. From its heart the imposing late-Georgian Town Hall of

1816, which dominated the scene, was removed in 1966, ostensibly for reasons of safety, although many residents believe the deed was done to make way for parked cars. Then a new road came to divide up the town, with many more changes to come. Most of the modern houses already built are purely functional, adequate as dwellings but without the character and charm of earlier homes, which could probably have been renovated. Whatever may be missing in the sphere of architecture, its absence is compensated for by the kindly inhabitants of this place, formerly the county town of Berwickshire.

Leaving by the A6105 road in a south-westerly direction, the motorist will skirt the edge of the Lammermoors, passing through Greenlaw to Gordon. Although it is no more than a village, this place has a curious air of consequence, so that one is tempted to call it a town. In situation very near the Merse, it is unmistakably not part of that rich arable country but a moorland settlement, with sharper air, heather slopes near by, and curlew crying overhead.

Its main built-up street, busy with traffic, has no great merit; but Gordon is like a plain woman who sets out to make the best of herself. It invariably looks tidy and well-washed, with sparkling windows and fresh paint. Above all, it has flowers. There are tubs, pots, troughs, window boxes, hanging baskets and, on the wide pavements, permanent concrete-edged 'raised beds' full of flowers. At the entrance to the village, regiments of rose bushes have been massed along the grass verges in a wordless welcome to the stranger. It is no surprise to hear that Gordon wins prizes for the best-kept village.

Most appropriately, members of the great clan of Anglo-Norman origin which settled at Gordon in the twelfth century and removed to Aberdeenshire two centuries later, have always been known as the 'Gay Gordons'. One of the family's titles, Huntly, corresponds with the name of hamlet, now vanished, which once formed a part of Gordon parish. Their castle has gone too. The existing remnant of a pele tower of later date on the western outskirts was a Pringle stronghold. Although the Gordons left it so long ago, Gordon is certainly gay.

From Gordon the road descends to Earlston, which really is a town, although of small proportions. Most people in Scotland know the place as Ercildoune, the home of Thomas the Rhymer. Battered remains of his tower still stand, close to the Leader Water. Until May 1975, Berwickshire claimed the place; but after that date it was annexed by Ettrick and Lauderdale.

One mile north of Earlston, on the A68 to Lauder, are the gates of Carolside. Far below the road, the dignified house of Adam date may be seen in its broad green valley where the Leader runs glistening. In her garden Lady Mary Gilmour gathered the best collection of Old Roses in southern Scotland. Those who indulge in this hobby will be glad to see that varieties are labelled. Other roses get off the ground and reach great heights. A huge willow acts as host to Paul's Himalayan musk rose, whose garlands of delicate pink rosettes may be seen waving amid the topmost boughs. On a breezy day, when the willow leaves ripple like cascades of silver rain, the effect is marvellous.

There is a fine elliptical walled garden here, less obviously an oval than the one at Netherbyres. Fruit and climbers trained on curving walls live in comfort, being reached by the maximum amount of light and warmth. Although Carolside is large and impressive, it somehow manages to give an effect of simplicity, almost reproducing the character of a cottage garden.

Two ancient thorn bushes on a knowe, or knoll, near the house have a homely, Darby-and-Joan appearance. Lady Mary told me of their strange history. In 1790 Lady Sarah Lennox (Bunbury) eloped with Lord William Adam Gordon and took refuge at Carolside, where the young lovers planted a pair of thorns to commemorate their stay. The idyll was short-lived, for the Duke of Richmond soon forced his sister to come away with him, to a house he had built for her at Goodwood. Only the thorn bushes were free to live out their lives together side by side into extreme old age.

The garden of Carolside, now owned by Mr and Mrs Hugh Poole-Warren, is open occasionally and will be found in the booklet *Scotland's Gardens*, obtainable from Scotland's Garden Scheme, 26 Castle Terrace, Edinburgh.

Peebles

This ancient town is said to derive its name from the 'pebylls' – tents – of wandering *Gadeni* tribes. The inhabitants of today are, in modern English, properly known as Peebleans and not (as heard from the lips of a slightly confused visitor), 'Plebeians'. Those who still use the old local speech dub such incomers 'stoorifits': that is, people newly arrived with the dust or 'stoor' of travel still on their boots; while true-born natives are known as 'gutterbluids'.

Dorothy Wordsworth in 1803 thought Peebles 'very pretty from the Neidpath road – an old town, built of grey stone'. That greyness is particularly noticeable if one travels, not from the west as she did, but by the Innerleithen road. The terra-cotta ploughland of the Berwickshire and Roxburgh Districts and the rosy stone quarried in those areas to produce buildings of rich, warm hues, are replaced as one journeys westward by yellowish grey at Galashiels and paler grey stone in Peebles. Arable soil is a comparatively rare sight here, for grassland and sheep predominate between afforested hills.

Peebles is built on a peninsula at the confluence of Eddleston Water and the river Tweed, and the place most short-stay visitors know best is really the 'new' town, a separate collection of buildings from that of the 'old' town, which is situated on rising ground to the north of Eddleston Water. In the fifteenth century it was known as 'Peblis', and the poem attributed to James I, *Peblis to the Play*, derives from that monarch's frequent visits in search of diversion.

This old Royal Burgh, one of many to lose its burgh status and privileges under the regionalisation of local government scheme inflicted upon Scotland in May 1975, has a resident population of some 6,000 people – a number considerably increased in the summer season by hotel guests, caravanners and campers. A mere twenty-three miles by road from Edinburgh, it is a popular residential area for commuters with daily occupation in the capital city. All rail links having been severed by the Beeching axe after World War II, there are no straphangers here. In the Borders, the business fraternity is obliged to travel by car.

The original town developed round the early churches of St Andrew and Holy Cross, both now in ruins. Before the Cross Kirk was built, someone dug up a magnificent cross on the site, believed to have been hidden below ground in the time of Maximilian's persecution. It was unearthed in 1261 and a slab of stone found beside the cross bore the inscription: 'Place of Nicholas the Bishop'. Miracles were claimed for this hallowed place, and Alexander III ordered the construction of a church, to which monastic quarters were added to house seventy Red or Trinity Friars. In medieval times this place became famous as a centre for pilgrimages. Some three centuries later church and monastery were proscribed by the Protestant Lords of the Secret Council, and by the eighteenth century they had been totally abandoned. Local builders had for some time been helping themselves to the stone. Thanks to the efforts of a twentieth-century Peebles physician, Dr Gunn, this wanton destruction was halted, the ruins restored so far as possible, and eventually taken over by the Office of Works, long before it turned into the Department of the Environment. The late eighteenth-century parish church of Peebles was replaced in 1887 by the present structure, which stands at the west end of High Street in the 'new' town.

Where there are rivers, people need bridges – although a certain Dr Russell in his *Reminiscences of Yarrow* wrote that in the past, when there were only two bridges across the local rivers (at Deuchar in Yarrow and Ettrick Bridge), people crossed either on horseback or by means of stilts, and very few accidents occurred even when the rivers ran deep and the fords were rough. Peebles, if footbridges are counted, now has more than twice the number mentioned by Pennicuik in his rhyme of 1715:

> Peebles, the metropolis of the Shire,
> Six times three praises from one require;
> Three streets, three ports, three bridges it adorn,
> And three old steeples by three churches borne.
> Three mills to serve the town in time of need,
> On Peebles Water and the River Tweed.
> Their arms are proper, and point forth their meaning,
> Three salmon fishes, nimbly counter-swimming.

Chambers, in the *History of Peeblesshire* says that there were really four ports, not three, and mentions that the mill on Eddleston (or Peebles) Water was a waulk-mill for cloth, while the others were used for grinding malt and meal. The arms of Peebles, with three salmon, the fish at top and bottom facing one way and the middle one heading in reverse direction, represent the increase (by spawning) given to those who swim against the flood. The motto *contra nando incrementum* is commonly translated as 'success will come by resisting obstacles' – a good, tough precept for a little town which has had many to overcome. These arms are found on the Burgh seal of 1682.

Weaving here, as elsewhere in the Borders, was for centuries the principal industry, and there are still mills in the town. In early days, before people had timepieces, communal methods were used to summon workers and sound curfew. Not only were steeple bells rung, but the town drummer beat his drum robustly in the streets to ensure that nobody slept late, and at one time the sound of bagpipes increased this early morning clamour. By five o'clock the townsfolk would be at breakfast. Work began at six. The weavers were at their looms until eight o'clock, when the bells rang for curfew, and drummer and piper again serenaded the town. I have not discovered how much cloth each webster was expected to produce in his long day's work. An old ledger (*circa* 1500) records exports of cloth known as 'Peebles White', which was sent all the way to Antwerp for dyeing red. The journeyings of people and goods, in times when roads were vile and transport uncomfortable and tedious, never fail to astonish the pampered jet-propelled travellers of today.

By nine o'clock all was quiet in Peebles, with bands of citizens taking it in turn to patrol the streets until daybreak. I wonder if these early 'Home Guards' had to turn up at the usual hour for work, after their nights on duty keeping close watch at the ports. These medieval gateways were not linked up by an encircling wall until 1570, and it is clear that the town had not increased appreciably in size by that date. In fact, Peebles remained almost static until the last quarter of the eighteenth century.

Among the famous names associated with Peebles are those of William and Robert Chambers, brothers who were born (1800 and 1802) in a small house in Biggiesknowe at the east end of the old town. They founded the publishing house of Chambers in Edinburgh, and I remember the late Alasdair Alpin MacGregor, author of so many books about Scotland, telling me that Chambers' Dictionary had been a much-used and cherished possession throughout his long life as a writer. The brothers are commemorated by the handsome Chambers Institute in Peebles High Street, which William converted to combine a hall, reading-room, library and museum under the one roof. Andrew Carnegie later gave £10,000 to develop this as a centre of community life.

On this site once stood a house belonging to the Cross church, which by charter of James VI (1624) came into the hands of Baron Hay of Yester. Towards the end of the seventeenth century it passed to the Duke of Queensberry. The Fourth Duke – 'Old Q' of whom Wordsworth wrote so scathingly – was born here in 1725. In the spacious quadrangle of the Chambers Institute stands the Peebles War Memorial, a hexagonal shrine of white stone. As a climax of the annual Beltane Festival in May, the young Beltane Queen places flowers here in memory of those who died that she, and succeeding generations, might live in peace. In the seventy-fifth

Anniversary booklet (1974) of this festival, a former Beltane Queen wrote:

> Although I was only twelve, the ceremony of laying a bouquet at the war memorial moved me deeply. I really heard the 'Last Post' for the first time, and felt a surge of sympathy for the woman who was laying a posy quietly at the side.

Among other benefactions, the Chambers family also set up a tombstone in Manor churchyard to the memory of David Ritchie, the prototype of Sir Walter Scott's 'Black Dwarf'. There is a rowan tree overhanging Ritchie's grave, put there to repel witches and evil spirits. One of the most rewarding short expeditions from Peebles is that to the Manor Valley, taking a left-turn southwards off the A72 about a mile beyond Neidpath Castle. Not far from the churchyard, at the mansion of Hallyards, Walter Scott and his friend Adam Ferguson were staying in 1797, and walking thence one day across the haugh ('Mucklestane Moor'), they visited 'Bowed Davie', as Ritchie was known locally. So deep was the impression made on Scott, that nineteen years later he was able to use still vivid memories of the dwarf as a basis for his novel.

Continuing along the same road for about a mile, explorers will find the cottage of the Black Dwarf on the left-hand side. The whole valley is rewarding. Higher up, St Gordian's Cross marks the site of a pre-Reformation chapel, and beyond that is a cairn erected to the memory of John Veitch, Peebles-born Professor of Logic, Rhetoric and Metaphysics in St Andrews and later at Glasgow University. Professor Veitch wrote two volumes of verse, mostly in praise of Tweeddale and the Border hills.

Another writer, admired by readers all over the world, John Buchan (later Lord Tweedsmuir), made frequent visits to Peebles. In 1935, as 'Warden of Neidpath', he delivered a speech at the March Riding, after welcoming the Cornet to Neidpath Castle in his official capacity of standard-bearer of the Burgh. His sister, Miss Anna Buchan, JP, gave the Neidpath address in 1937. As 'O. Douglas' she was the author of many popular novels and had her home at Bank House. Her brother Walter served as Town Clerk for many years, and compiled a history of Peeblesshire. The fine old house where Anna wrote her books is threatened with demolition by so-called progress. It stands at the north-west corner of the High Street and is said to impede the traffic.

To quote again from the 1974 issue of the March Riding and Beltane Queen Festival booklet,

Peebles has a long history. The Roman Legions passed this way on the march to a camp at Lyne; its medieval church was a place of pilgrimage; several of the Kings of Scotland galloped down its streets to the royal castle after a day's hunting; from that castle (now gone) bands of daring men set out on forays over the Border; James the First, scholar king, knew and sang of its Summer Fair; the ill-starred Mary Queen of Scots passed a night at Neidpath Castle; during the Napoleonic Wars local militiamen kept watch and ward, as did their descendants, the Home Guard, in the anxious years of World War II.

Many elderly men may be seen about the streets of Peebles today who must have known those war years of the 1940s. The bracing air seems to encourage longevity, and great alertness of mind and body is noticeable in Peebleans of advanced age. The celebrated violinist Horace Fellowes must be given pride of place among them, seeing that he was alive and active for a hundred years from his birth on 26th May 1875, and in 1975 still brought out his violin to delight audiences with his playing. He was born in Wolverhampton and taken to Glasgow as a child. After a distinguished career as violinist in several orchestras and quartets, Horace Fellowes became Leader of the Scottish Orchestra. He also became a member of the staff at the Royal Academy of Music. His autobiography, *Music in my Heart*, was issued in 1958. He was the oldest member of the Glasgow Arts Club. Everyone in Peebles seemed to know this energetic senior citizen. It was no surprise to residents when the minister of the Old Parish Church suggested that the thirteen bells, which are keyboard-operated, should be used to play 'Happy Birthday to You' to celebrate the violinist's hundredth birthday. Horace Fellowes died before his 101st anniversary early in 1976.

In addition to its hotels and guest-houses, Peebles provides an excellent caravan and camping park (the publicly-owned Rosetta Park), with modern facilities, including a play area for small children and a picnic site. It has room for 100 caravans and thirty tents, and is in a delightful wooded setting. A second caravan park, in private ownership, will be found on the A703 road to Edinburgh.

Angling for trout and salmon is good and not too expensive – this advantage led Horace Fellowes to make his home in Peebles. There is some free sport for children under sixteen, and half-price fishing for pensioners. The eighteen-hole municipal golf course is easily accessible, pleasant to play over, and open seven days a week at moderate fees.

107

6

Open Houses and Grounds

Abbotsford

Where would you expect to see a piece of oatcake taken from the pocket of a dead Highlander on Culloden Field; David Garrick's mulberry-wood box, made from the timber of Shakespeare's tree; a lock of Nelson's hair, sent to the Prince Regent by Lady Hamilton; Napoleon's cloak clasp in the form of two golden bees, said to have been found in his carriage after the Battle of Waterloo? It sounds like one of those quiz questions. Until recently, my own reply would have been: 'Either in a jackdaw's nest or in some museum.' The correct answer, of course, is at the head of this page. These things are part of the huge collection amassed by Sir Walter Scott at his cherished home, where they are still carefully preserved just as the Wizard of the North left them on his death in 1832.

Although it sounds like a museum, this great house – a romantic concept inscribed by the author in pinkish stone on the banks of the River Tweed – has retained its own warm and lively atmosphere: a rumbustious character which the glass-cased collection, formidably equipped with burglar alarms, cannot overlay. We are told that the rooms on exhibition have not been lived in for many years, yet the whole place is still unmistakably a home. The vigorous blood of the Scott family courses through it, and thousands of tourists who buy admission tickets every year are caught up in the intimate friendliness which makes them feel like guests. Were it practicable to invite them all as her personal guests, Mrs Patricia Maxwell-Scott would wish to do so. She admits to a fundamental desire to share Abbotsford with all admirers of her great-great-great grandfather. Leaving aside private invitations, I have, in common with scores of fellow-travellers, been allowed (on payment) into many other great houses, from Blair Castle in Perthshire to the Wiltshire mansion of Longleat; the Sackville's Tudor splendour at Knole in Kent (birthplace of that great gardener Vita Sackville-West); Berkeley Castle on the Severn and Corsham Court, all occupied to some extent by descendants of the original owners; but nowhere else have I felt myself to be more than a politely tolerated intruder.

No doubt the radiant enthusiasm of its chatelaine plays a considerable part in creating the atmosphere of intimacy and homeliness at the shrine of this pre-Victorian author; yet I jalouse that some secret at a deeper level must be nourishing the roots of his family tree. There is nothing like it at Jane Austen's Chawton, or at Shaw's Corner; at the residences of Dickens, Kipling and Henry James, or even at Chartwell, so recently beloved by Sir Winston Churchill. Churchill – whom I had seen in the flesh; the man who wrote pithy comments, in the red ink reserved for his pen, upon our Admiralty dockets when he was First Lord in the early months of World War II; the nation's overlord in its darkest days, whose voice became a trumpet call on the radio, his V-sign and cigar elevated into symbols of heraldic significance for the people. Who would have thought that the presiding genius of a long-dead Scots writer could maintain an aura of greater brilliance than that left behind at the home of our contemporary giant?

On my first visit to Abbotsford, in 1973, I was not wholly aware of its unique vitality until after I had left the gates and walked towards Melrose by a narrow country road overlooking the Tweed. This literary pilgrimage had been undertaken from a sense of duty rather than in expectation of pleasure, and the illumination it brought had a kind of delayed-action fuse built into it. A spell of peaceful contemplation at home before an evening fire was necessary to bring out the flavour of the day's experience, like the later effects of a fine claret. Only then did it become clear to me that visitors to Abbotsford are still being right hospitably entertained at the good table of Sir Walter and his family –although the stimulus is of mind and spirit, not flesh.

Abbotsford. That name echoed in my mind all through the winter of 1973-4. We planned, when Easter came, to be among its first visitors of the season. Instead, there were unexpected guests of our own to be entertained during a brief, rare spell of June warmth in April. After the holiday, winter threw a final tantrum and kept up squalls until the month was nearly out. A room had been booked in

109

Abbotsford

Melrose for the last week-end in April. It was a dismal one, with streets awash and passers-by hidden under umbrellas. A wet week-end in a strange little town can seem inordinately long. It was not shortened for us by a couple of young dogs in an adjacent room of the hotel, which kept up a shrill yelping until the small hours. When the chambermaid brought early morning tea, we asked her if the little pests were miniature dachschunds, having met hysteria in that breed before. Stooping down and waving her hands about near her ankles, she said wryly: 'Two of those wee *scooterie-about* dogs.' Walter Scott would have been pleased to find such expressive speech still alive in his Border country.

Monday put on a shining morning face – such a day as that described by the bereaved Laird when, in early May 1826, he hastened from Edinburgh to Abbotsford on receiving news of his wife's death. In his diary he wrote:

> Another day, and a bright one to the external world, again opens on us, the air soft, the flowers smiling and the leaves glittering. They cannot refresh her to whom mild weather was a natural enjoyment.

His sorrow was profound. Today there is no suggestion of grief here at Sir Walter's Abbotsford, whose well-washed frontage is glowing rosily in the clear sunlight, its guardian trees all freshly clothed, its grassy banks sparkling with daffodils which seem to have opened their buds within the last half-hour. Blackbird and thrush are fluting from every corner of the wooded policies, and various small birds, perched on pinnacles and turrets, are ringing miniature glass bells and working away on tiny anvils with little silver hammers. The place seems to be wrapped in a kind of sanctified peace. It suggests one of those idealised story-book backgrounds to an early religious painting. Perhaps the monks of Melrose – Boisil the Prior, who welcomed Cuthbert into the priesthood and later gave his own name to St Boswells – and maybe Saint Cuthbert himself – still brood upon this land (which in their day belonged to the Abbey), and watch over their Tweed crossing-place: a ford whence Sir Walter took the title for the house he built.

It has had many owners, for the earlier heritors were short-lived. Scott's son, Walter, died in his forties, leaving no heir. (None of Scott's children lived to be old. Anne, worn out with nursing her father, did not long survive him. Sophia, the wife of Lockhart, died at thirty-seven, while her brother Charles only lived to be thirty-five.) Young Walter Lockhart succeeded Walter Scott, the author's son; but he too had not long to live. Charlotte Lockhart then inherited Abbotsford, with her husband James Hope, and the couple assumed the name of Hope-Scott. These devout Anglicans, influenced by the Oxford Movement, entered the Roman Church along with their friend the future Cardinal Manning. At this period the wealthy Hope-Scotts enlarged the house and added the private chapel.

The only surviving child of this couple, Mary Monica, 'Mamo', married a Constable-Maxwell and the pair assumed the name of Maxwell-Scott. Their eldest son, Walter, succeeded to Abbotsford, and in 1932, the centenary of Scott's death, the baronetcy was revived in his favour. Writing in the Abbotsford guide-book, Sir Walter Maxwell-Scott said that at the time of her marriage in 1874, his mother was not merely the only living great-granddaughter of the author, but Scott's sole surviving *descendant*. By 1952 that position had greatly changed, and there were nineteen living descendants. The last Sir Walter died in 1954 and was buried near his famous great-great grandfather in Dryburgh Abbey. His two daughters, Patricia and Jean Maxwell-Scott, now share the

Hope-Scott wing and care with selfless devotion for the literary shrine which Sir Walter Scott built. Scott would have quietly accepted his great-great-great granddaughters' Catholic adherence, for in the last year of his life he said 'It is a comfort to me to think that I have tried to unsettle no man's faith, to corrupt no man's principle.'

As we walk in at the unpretentious white gate by which tourists are admitted to the domain, and pass down a sloping path beside a high wall into a little dark tunnel entry, we might be going to buy eggs at a small chicken farm or plants from a nursery. Only when some stone steps have been descended and a corner turned, is the surprise packet opened and the large rambling house with its crow-stepped gables and clustered chimney-stacks suddenly in full view. Sir Walter's romantic dream in stone has been called a 'folly', an 'architectural nightmare', and many other rude names. It could more justly be described as a special kind of jumble, made harmonious by the owner's imagination, which fits into the Tweedside landscape as though ordained for the position since the Borders began. The ornately splendid Scott monument in Edinburgh may be the largest construction in stone ever set up in honour of a writer, but Abbotsford, for all its fantasy, creates an overall impression of solid, forthright honesty better suited to commemorate the incorruptible Sir Walter.

We enter through a side door. Within is a room arranged as a shop for the sale of admission tickets, postcards, guide-books, souvenirs, biographies of Scott and a selection of his Waverley novels. (In Edinburgh's famous bookshops it is now difficult to find many of these, except for paperbacks of television versions.) The assistant is welcoming. From an inner sanctum the custodian, John MacAlister, emerges, gives us a brief summing-up glance, and then withdraws. Somewhere a vacuum cleaner hums. We have already learned that everyone lends a hand at Abbotsford. Sometimes the ladies of the house serve coffee in the restaurant near the gate. At other times they are geared to dust, mop, 'tackle the whole thing', as they put it.

Having been shown the way, we are left to ascend the stone stair, and at the top immediately find ourselves inside Scott's study, with the author's writing-desk and leather armchair in the centre. It looks used, so very much on the *qui vive* that he could be walking in at any minute. We catch ourselves listening for an uneven footfall, remembering his lameness, and are ready to apologise for our intrusion. Even the books appear poised, expecting his hand to reach for them. The shelves are arranged on two levels, with access by a small stair to the narrow gallery above. In one corner of the study an open door gives entry to an octagonal turret room ('Speak-a-bit') which houses one thing only, a bronze cast of Sir Walter's head taken on his death-bed. Death seems an irrelevance, seeing that all around us the essence of Scott so palpably survives.

These first intimate chambers open into a larger room, the library proper, whose volumes, together with those in the study, number about 9,000. While my companion appraises Chantrey's marble bust, made in 1820 – the year in which George IV bestowed a baronetcy on the author – I am drawn to a glass-topped showcase in the bay window. The scene outside, the smooth lawns with the Tweed running clear and full between the banks, cannot for long keep my eyes from the collection of relics displayed in the showcase. Napoleon's cloak-clasp and his ornate pale green blotting-book and pen case are strange bedfellows for the mother-of-pearl crucifix reputedly carried by Mary Queen of Scots at her execution, and the gold and enamel snuffbox of Prince James Edward, the Old Chevalier. Sir Walter's great-grandfather, 'Beardie', who vowed never to shave until a Stuart returned to the throne, would have liked to see his drinking cup kept near these royal treasures.

The box of Irish bog oak, decorated with carved harp and shamrock, is of humbler origin – a present to Sir Walter from Miss Maria Edgeworth, who stayed here at Abbotsford. 'Everything about you [said Maria to her host] is exactly what one ought to have had wit enough to dream!' Her box companions the amber-handled knife and fork with which in childhood little 'Wattie' used to eat his dinner, and the moleskin purse he had in later life. The fur is worn off in several places, leaving bald patches. The author's fingers manipulated its silver frame when good fortune filled the purse – he earned £10,000 a year while his writings were best-sellers – and during those later lean times in second-rate lodgings, when he slaved continually to write off the huge debt incurred by his publisher, Constable. Over that worn, expressive purse a tear must fall. The eye shifts to a toad-stone amulet, sole memento of the author's mother. It was often borrowed by parents of new-born babies, to be hung round soft little necks as a charm against the evils of witchcraft and sorcery. Near it are examples of that nineteenth-century fetish, the lock of hair: Nelson's, Bonnie Prince Charlie's

Sir Walter Scott by James Saxon

and Sir Walter's own, taken by his coachman Peter Mathieson after the author's death.

We move on to the drawing room. Each of these apartments opens out of the other. The absence of corridors gives a concentrated form to the whole, helping to maintain its character as home rather than museum. Hugh Scott, Sir Walter's cousin, presented the decorative hand-painted Chinese wallpaper upon the walls, gay with oriental flowers and birds against an emerald green background. Having passed through from the library, visitors who stop, face about, and look downwards near the left-hand side of the door frame, will see two Chinese gentlemen (lifelike though not lifesize) in conversation among the entwined flowering trees. One of them might be the identical twin of George Bernard Shaw. Sir Walter must have contemplated this bearded sage on many occasions, ignorant of the fact that he owned a portrait which forecast with accuracy the appearance of an Irishman destined to find a permanent place in our literature, rivalling his own.

Over the fireplace Scott, in the famous portrait by Raeburn, averts his eyes from G.B.S., while the greyhound 'Percy' gazes up earnestly into his master's face. A stringless harp of French make stands at one side of the room. 'Aha', says my companion, 'Sophia used to entertain her father's guests on this.' A ponderous roll-top desk and matching chairs, finely carved in Portuguese ebony, seem out of key with this elegant room. They were given to Sir Walter by George IV, and royal gifts may not be disposed of or hidden in a basement store.

We hasten through the armoury to the dining-room. This most restful part of the exhibited area, its white walls half-panelled in pale oak, has a sturdy centre table and sideboard made from oak grown in the policies at Drumlanrig Castle. The maker, George Bullock, worked in London, so the timber had to be taken from the Duke of Buccleuch's seat in Dumfriesshire to the English capital, and when the furniture had been fashioned to Scott's liking it travelled north to the Scottish Borders – a considerable undertaking for the horse transport of the period. In this room hang portraits: Sir Walter's great-grandfather (the stalwart and genial 'Beardie'); Lady Scott, the French-born Charlotte Charpentier; the younger of Scott's daughters (Anne) and his great-great grandson Major-General Sir Walter Maxwell-Scott, in khaki and red tabs.

A showcase in the bay window holds, among other weapons, a sword given by Charles I to the Marquess of Montrose, originally the property of James VI of Scotland, I of England. Outside, the river runs swiftly between green banks, making the sound that Sir Walter loved above all others – the ripple of Tweed stroking its pebbles. He died in this room on a perfect day in early autumn, so warm that all windows were wide open. He was only sixty-one. In his own words, 'We must take what Fate sends.' It had sent him outstanding imaginative power, which was based on love – love of his country, its people and scenery, and love of creative activity with the pen. His indefatigable use of these great gifts brought him world-wide admiration and love. Surely the secret of Abbotsford's astonishing vitality must lie in that simple word. In *The Lay of the Last Minstrel* Scott summed it up: 'For Love will still be Lord of all.'

Bowhill

This estate, part of the ancient Forest of Ettrick, was granted to the Douglas family by Robert the Bruce in 1322. They kept it for almost 130 years, after which it reverted to the Crown, becoming a favourite hunting-ground of successive Scottish Kings. The Tower of Newark, two miles to the north, was used as their hunting-box. Legend handed down for centuries relates how a member of the Scott family, whose men had been active Rangers since medieval times, came upon a cornered buck which had turned on the King's hounds in a deep 'cleuch' or ravine, and seizing the antlers threw the animal over his shoulder. This exploit caused the King to dub him 'Buck-cleugh', from which the present ducal owner derives his name. In 1590 one Walter Scott was knighted by King James VI, and in 1606 he became the First Lord Scott of Buccleuch. His son was created Earl of Buccleuch. In the mid-sixteenth century much of Ettrick Forest was portioned out among members of the Scott family. The earlier Douglas connection was happily revived in 1720 by a marriage between the Scotts and Douglases. Meantime the first Earl's granddaughter Anna had married the natural son of King Charles II, James, Duke of Monmouth, who obtained the titles of Duke of Buccleuch and Earl of Dalkeith. In 1767 the third Duke united Scotts and Montagus of Boughton by marrying Lady Elizabeth Montagu, heiress of the Duke of Montagu.

The original Bowhill House of 1703 has been replaced by a building begun early in the nineteenth century, which has sustained many later additions. By the time three Scots architects of distinction – William Atkinson, William Burn and David Bryce – had finished with it, the house and stables formed one continuous block, 437 feet long. Sir Walter Scott, who in his *Lay of the Last Minstrel* called it 'Sweet Bowhill', watched over much of the extension work. He is now remembered by an exhibit in the study at Bowhill.

The house provides a splendid series of exhibition rooms for the display of pictures, tapestry, furniture, silver, china and glass, collected by many generations of the Scott, Douglas and Montagu families, together with gifts made by Charles II to his son. The lovely seventeenth-century Chinese wallpapers sent home by Lord Macartney, first British Plenipotentiary in China, used on these walls in about 1760, and the eighteenth-century silk wall-hangings, are in fine condition except for fading of silk hangings from crimson

Bowhill

to pale pink in places, which is not unattractive. Probably dyed with plant or other natural material, these old fabrics know how to grow old gracefully.

Following the death of the eighth Duke of Buccleuch in 1973, his successor decided to throw open the house and grounds to the public. On a visit before the house was opened, I had thought of Bowhill as a palace of the Sleeping Beauty, closed up with drawn blinds and not a living person to be seen. I had no prior knowledge of the transformation that was to take place in twelve months' time. Now the windows and doors are open, grounds provided with busy car-parks, the stables have become an attractive centre for refreshment and shopping. Visitors throng the lawns; banked rhododendrons do not bloom unseen; the lake is no more a mirror of unpeopled walks under the spell of some enchanter.

In spite of the new activity, my first impression of this house as the home of a sleeping beauty had been so powerful that I entered with a sense of expectancy, as though she might still linger within the walls. As a rational being I knew that this was pure fancy, without hope of realisation – or so it seemed. Yet there are times when in this too solid world fact and fancy mingle, and this happened to be one such day for me. I ranged through the entrance and gallery halls; stood in the Dalkeith dressing-room, with its

117

four-poster bed where General Monck slept (or maybe stayed awake, planning the Restoration) during the Commonwealth of Oliver Cromwell, whose miniature, warts and all, hangs here; admired the Monmouth room with its magnificent saddle and trappings, used when Monmouth was Master of the Horse to his father, Charles II; and so, engrossed in English history, moved on to the 'Italian' room, with its masterpieces of landscape painting. After these sunlit apartments and the Mediterranean pictures it was a shock to find the adjacent dining-room in subdued artificial light, the heart of my Sleeping Beauty's domain with all its windows shuttered.

Instead of the half-expected bed, there was a handsome table with much fine glass and silver, laid ready for the evening company to assemble. No princess here, after all. And then I saw her. She is very young. Not more than four summers have greeted her. She wears a wide-brimmed hat covered in black tulle, a black silk pelisse over her white dress, and she carries a pink silk muff. Her eyes are open wide, but they have that wondering, half-focussed look which is always noticeable in small children when they are aroused from sleep. The Sleeping Beauty, just awakened, hangs on the dining-room wall. Her portrait by Sir Joshua Reynolds is called 'Winter'.

The story goes that Reynolds had been commissioned to paint little Charles, Earl of Dalkeith (later the fourth Duke of Buccleuch), and while he was at work the tiny sister, Caroline Scott, entered the room, exactly as shown. The artist was so enchanted that he insisted on painting her portrait as well as that of her brother. Charles, wearing pink satin, is depicted fondling a young owl, symbolical of learning, with a spaniel (indicating sport) beside him. He is known as 'The Pink Boy'. His delicate air and faintly roguish smile linger long in the mind, although the infant sister takes precedence. I cannot recall any other great house or gallery where interest is centred so powerfully on young children. It is worth while visiting Bowhill for these pictures alone, even if there is little time for anything else.

But there is a great deal more, from the famous Canaletto of Whitehall to the huge collection of porcelain, much of it Meissen; the handsome boulle furniture; chairs and settees covered in Aubusson tapestry; an enormous silver wine cistern (4 feet 6 inches wide, weight 9 stone) which stands on a plinth carved from a block of coal; gems of needlework; relics of Queen Victoria, and a fine unfinished portrait of the Duke of Wellington by Sir Thomas Lawrence. The Duke's character seems to be so completely realised that any further 'finish' would be superfluous.

Another notable exhibit, worthy of detail in a book about Scotland, is a long-case clock in the 'Italian' room. This was made by a superb craftsman named John Smith who lived in the little fishing village of Pittenweem in Fife. In an advertisement of 1775 he informed patrons that he had been bred to the trade and had never been out of the country. His great clock, seven feet high, has a mahogany case with fluted columns at each side, partly gilt, with brass Corinthian capitals and bases. This case contains an eight-day musical clock with a chime of sixteen bells, which play at the quarters. A tune is played at the hour.

There is within the clock a large musical barrel containing eight popular Scottish tunes, which are played through every twenty-four hours at three-hourly intervals. A dial shows the days of the week, and when the Sabbath comes it casts up 'remember Sunday'. The music stops religiously at midnight on Saturday, not to be resumed until midnight on Sunday. This is an intricate piece of mechanism by any standards, and amazing work for a rural craftsman in an obscure village.

At the left-hand side of the case there is a charming peepshow, representing the front of a town house with an open door in centre, guarded by sentries of the Edinburgh City Guard. Inside stands the Macer of the Lords of Council and Session, wearing his robes and holding the mace in his right hand. As soon as the clock begins to play a tune, he takes off his hat with his left hand and walks past the open door, followed by fifteen Lords, all robed. When the procession has passed, the Macer comes back to the door and puts his hat on again. The Lords are said to be faithful likenesses of the Edinburgh dignitaries of John Smith's time.

The owner of all these treasures, the ninth Duke of Buccleuch, has been confined to a wheel-chair since a hunting accident some years ago, a handicap which has not been allowed to interfere with a great range of activity. His Grace in former years was well-known to a large public, when, as the Earl of Dalkeith, he served as the Conservative Member of Parliament for Edinburgh North, from 1960 to 1973. In the main hall there is an early portrait of him by Edward Brock, next to a more modern triptych of his wife, who was Jane McNeill of Colonsay. This delightful composition by John Merton won an Academy 'A' award in 1957.

Their son and heir, Richard, Earl of Dalkeith, in October 1981 married Lady Elizabeth Kerr, youngest daughter of the Marquis of Lothian.

Manderston

Most people would find it as difficult to picture Manderston without its sumptuous gardens and wooded parkland as to visualise them without the great mansion for centrepiece. The whole suggests some grand theatrical scene, larger and more colourful than real life, a fit stamping-ground for heroes and goddesses of operatic stature. Yet the truth is that, during the lifetime of the former owner, when the grounds were occasionally open to the public and crowds thronged the garden walks, a modest grey-haired man in a dark suit could be seen slipping among groups of visitors as unobtrusively as some private detective. The contrast between Major Hugh Bailie and his opulent setting provided a kind of anti-climax which never failed to surprise the uninitiated, when I chose to point him out.

At other times Major Bailie would take me round, free of crowds, to show the progress of what he called his 'little Inverewe', a plantation begun in the 1950s, wherein some natural species; Rhododendrons, Azaleas, Primulas, Erythroniums, the stately Himalayan 'Blue Poppies' and much else reminded me of my old home on Loch Ewe in Wester Ross. This delightful woodland garden had taken many years of patient work and is now one of the chief glories of the place, and a fit memorial to him. Major Bailie died in 1978.

Although the property was always well maintained and inhabited by the family, the knowledge that Douglas Bailie, the only son and heir, had been killed in World War II left an unspoken query hovering over the house. Who would inhabit it when Major and Mrs Bailie were gone? A happy solution appeared in 1978. Their grandson, Adrian Palmer, and his young wife shouldered the responsibility and in 1979 opened both house and grounds to the public in summertime.

First of all there was much refurbishing to be done and difficult decisions to be taken. Some adjuncts were perforce dispensed with.

The splendid range of hothouses required too much labour to be practicable in the 1970s. But most of the property has been maintained intact, just as it was in the days of James Miller, Adrian Palmer's great-uncle, who in 1903 began his remodelling of the original eighteenth-century house.

In 1895, before beginning on his appointed task, the architect John Kinross had to pass an unusual test. He was commissioned to design and carry out erection of the handsome range of stabling, which may still be seen in its original glory – except for the horses. Such as are kept will be out at grass during the summer months of the visiting season. Marble nameplates, Mystery, Monarch and many more act as their memorials above empty stalls. With arched roofing of teak, polished brass posts, gleaming halter-rings and door furniture, these equine apartments (which cost £20,000 to build) far surpass most human dwellings of that period – or any other.

Apparently James Miller, who inherited a title in addition to a fortune, embarked on lavish improvements to his estate in order to impress the father of his chosen bride-to-be, the Hon. Eveline Curzon. She was the fourth daughter of Lord Scarsdale of Kedleston Hall in Derbyshire, and sister to a famous Viceroy of India. Presumably Sir James succeeded in his aim, for the marriage duly took place. Nine years after the wedding, at Eveline's wish, Manderston House was largely rebuilt, to include many features copied from her birthplace.

In order to make room for entertaining on a lavish scale, the roof was taken off, a floor added, and the house was doubled in size by the addition of a wing. An outstanding feature of all this work is the supreme quality of materials and craftsmanship. The fine stucco work, rich mahogany and other beautiful woods, variety of marbles – even in stabling and dairy – and a whole range of artefacts, down to the ornate silver-plated balustrade of the stairs, are sights which we in a cement-and-plastics age may view with astonished delight. The interior richness of the remodelled house has the more impact by reason of the plain mould in which Kinross cast his new frontage, in a style designed to blend with the original house.

The entrance, through a pillared portico, takes one into a square, domed hall floored with marble and decorated in Adam-style Greek ornament. The main staircase is modelled on that of the Petit Trianon at Versailles. Opening out of the hall is a morning-room, with circular ceiling, and some french windows set into a curved wall adjoining the south terrace – a facade of the Georgian house, dating from about 1740. The ballroom has a rich plasterwork ceiling with painted inset panels, a classical marble mantelpiece and handsome chandeliers. The walls are hung with brocade in primrose and white, Sir James's racing colours, the curtains being of silk interwoven with gold and silver thread. This is a setting in which young Edwardian beauties, chaperoned by stately mammas, can, in the mind's eye, still be seen waltzing to 'Blue Danube' or 'Merry Widow' with gay but outwardly decorous gentlemen.

Like his monarch, King Edward VII, Sir James Miller had a passion for horse-racing, and his career on the turf was one of remarkable success. Portraits of his two Derby winners, Sainfoin (1890) and the latter's son, Rock Sand (1903) hang in the house. Rock Sand, bred by his owner, also won the Two Thousand Guineas and the St Leger – a triple crown achieved by only one other horse, the Aga Khan's Barham. Sir James was a subaltern in the 14th Hussars when Sainfoin won the Derby in 1890. There is a firm belief among local residents that his commanding officer refused him leave to see the race run at Epsom, but the late Major Bailie declared this to be a fabrication. James Miller did not live very long. He died at the age of forty-two, only three months after his palatial reconstruction of Manderston had been completed.

In 1974 a Duns tradesman told us that he had experienced the shock of his life when, upon entering the back door of the house to service some kitchen equipment, he found the butler at work cleaning a large collection of gold plate. 'Something out of a fairy-tale!' he said, 'but I found out that it was real gold.' The plate, six George III goblets and two ewers, two nineteenth-century candelabra and various condiment sets, was purchased with Derby stake money. There were also several gold cups won for other races.

The huge kitchen and range of domestic offices in the basement are well worth a visit. There is an island cooking range with six separate ovens to provide various temperatures, the whole powered by solid fuel, and in addition an open fire for spit roasting. The adjoining scullery contains every conceivable appliance of its period for the preparation of vegetables and the washing of dishes and pans. Opening out of the tradesmen's corridor are larders designed to receive meats, poultry, fish, game and cooked foods. Outside the housekeeper's room is a collection of fifty-six bells,

The Formal Garden at Manderston

each having a different tone. In 1905 the staff consisted of six housemaids, three scullery maids and a cook. It would not be surprising to hear of even more servants indoors in this imposing house.

Not far from the great stables there is a replica of an old Border watchtower in miniature, which houses a dairy walled and floored with marbles collected in seven different countries. Above it is a tea-room copied from one of the small oak rooms in the Palace of Holyrood in Edinburgh. The ladies of Manderston had a pleasant custom of visiting this room above the dairy, where a collection of fine china is kept, and partaking of afternoon tea from one of the elegant sets. The architect, John Kinross, seems to have had a flair for palaces. He restored the ancient Palace of Falkland in Fife.

The pleasure grounds surrounding this strange, grand house of Manderston are equally lavish in conception. What is unusual in this utilitarian age is that these are still well maintained, full of colour in summer. The south terraces, overlooking a lake at lower

123

level, are laid out with formal precision. The original box-edged parterres have gone, but clipped evergreens, fountains, statuary and antique Italian stone urns are still there to make an imposing foreground to the picture, which extends to banks of rhododendrons framing the water, and in the distance the great blue humps of the Cheviot Hills.

From the mansion front you may walk across a wide spread of mown turf, with thousands of spring daffodils beneath the trees, to be followed in May by drifts of wild hyacinth. Beyond these lawns is a stately formal garden, an orderly array of bedding plants intersected by walls, pergolas, wrought-iron balustrades and a splendid yew hedge. This is a truly authentic Edwardian scene, wanting only to be peopled by gloved ladies in large hats and long dresses, squired by gentlemen in equally formal attire. The careless dress of today, comfortable though it may be, is out of place in this setting.

Having left this period piece behind, the visitor is given a fresh surprise. A shady woodland walk leads to a field gate. Within we find, not the expected cow pasture, but a fine cricket field. Of course those distant blue hills of Cheviot seen from the terrace are in England; but here we stand on Scottish soil, in the old County of Berwickshire. Scotland, as most people know, is not a traditional home of cricket. Golf, seven-a-side rugger, curling, bowling (including the indoor 'carpet' version) and more aggressive modern games fill the sports pages of newspapers. Possession of its own cricket field and pavilion puts this Scottish mansion into a rare, possibly unique, class. On a placid June day, when winds off the North Sea are taking a rest, and cries of 'Well played!' sound through the shelter-belt of great lime trees, it is hard to believe that one is not far south of the Border – perhaps in Taunton or Worcester.

Mr Adrian Palmer, who master-minded a great deal of work inside the house before putting it on show to the public, has also provided a pleasant tea-room in what was once the stable bothy, not far from the entrance where tickets are sold. There are modern toilet facilities in the same block. Beside the car-park we found a good selection of well-grown plants on sale.

A word of warning to older and less agile visitors. If Manderston is to be fully appreciated, a lot of walking is required, both indoors and outside. Climbing the stairs to bedroom level may be left to the more active members of one's own party, although it is a pity for those interested in needlework to miss the collection of samplers displayed in the north dressing-room.

The field used for parking being some way from the house, there is provision for disabled drivers to take their cars right up to the portico. It is advisable to inquire which part of the forecourt may be used for parking.

Mellerstain

The fame of Mellerstain has spread far beyond Scotland. I remember being given a glowing account of it by a Welsh friend, our neighbour in the West of England, long before I set foot in Berwickshire. The lady's praise was not exaggerated. In a way I would consider that she underestimated the interest of this house and garden, which must be taken as a whole, for she did not indicate that the summertime hours of opening, between 1.30 and 5.30 pm, are little enough to enjoy everything to the full. Although it has not the brooding antiquity of Traquair, it has held an important place in the Borders for some five centuries, since in 1451 Patrick Haliburton received from King James II 'the lands of Mellerstain'. They changed hands twice in the following 200 years, before being made over by Royal Charter of 1642 to George Baillie of Jerviswood, son of a merchant burgess of Edinburgh. At that time the house was known as Whytesyde and stood near the site of the present mansion. The sole remnant of that early dwelling is a ruined vault, believed by some to harbour a ghost, and known locally as The Bogle House.

A contemporary account of Whytesyde describes it as 'an old melancholick hous that had great buildings about it'. George Baillie, the first of his name to appear in the story of Mellerstain, did not live long to enjoy his new possession. He died in 1646, during the Civil War, to be succeeded by his eldest son, Robert. This man, an inflexible character, soon fell foul of the authorities; he was fined and imprisoned for rescuing his brother-in-law from what he considered wrongful arrest. While he was shut up in the Edinburgh Tolbooth, Sir Patrick Home of Polwarth (later Earl of Marchmont) sent his eldest daughter, Grisell, then only twelve years of age, to deliver a secret message to Baillie. This dangerous mission the child successfully accomplished. Some years later, in 1684, Robert Baillie, a staunch Covenanter, was arrested for high treason and condemned to death. His last words are still remembered; 'This night I shall be a pillar in the House of God to go furth no more.'

His estate and that of his ally Sir Patrick Home were both forfeited, and the latter fled with his family to Holland. Robert Baillie's son George, penniless after his father's execution, also went to Holland, where he obtained a junior's officer's commission in the Prince of Orange's Horse Guards. He had already met Grisell Home at the time of her daring errand to the Tolbooth, and their friendship developed in exile. In 1689 the Prince of Orange set out for London, taking Home and Baillie with him; after the Prince had been crowned William III of England, he restored the Home and Baillie estates to their former owners. George Baillie, no longer impoverished, asked for Grisell's hand, and 1691 they were married. After her father's elevation to the peerage in 1697 she became Lady Grisell Baillie, a name famous in the Borders. Her husband prospered. He became a Member of Parliament, and served as one of the architects of the Act of Union in 1707, afterwards sitting in the first Parliament of Great Britain.

This devoted couple then began to plan the extension of their house, and in 1725 foundations for the present east and west wings were laid, with William Adam as architect. For some reason his charming centrepiece in Dutch Palladian style was never built, and for a long time the Adam wings were separated by a gap where the old house used to be. George and Grisell Baillie had a younger daughter, Rachel, who married Lord Binning, the Earl of Haddington's heir. Rachel's younger son, George, in 1759 inherited Mellerstain and assumed the name of Baillie. His grandfather (and namesake) had died in 1738 and Lady Grisell, aged 81, in 1746.

So it happened that the building of Mellerstain once more proceeded in the hands of a George Baillie, one who had travelled abroad and acquired the classical taste which was all the rage. By the second half of the eighteenth century Robert Adam, son of William, had become the most fashionable architect in Britain, and Baillie secured his services for the extension of the house which Adam senior had begun some fifty years earlier. Although the exterior is not typical of Robert's influence, the interior is unquestionably his. The library ceiling of 1770, which suggests a piece of Wedgwood stoneware, is considered to be in the highest class of Robert Adam's design. In the dining-room is another of his fine ceilings, dated 1773 and decorated with eagles and sphinxes. That of the drawing room (1778) is one of the last to be completed. A design for the great gallery which occupies the raised centre block of the facade was never carried out. The architect's drawing, in various shades of green, is still extant.

In 1858 George Baillie's grandson, George Baillie-Hamilton, became the eighth Earl of Haddington, and from that date the Earldom of Haddington was united to Mellerstain. It is now the home of Lord Binning, the present Earl's heir. Later owners have all maintained the building as it was completed by George Baillie in the eighteenth century; only the gardens have been altered considerably. The present occupant's grandfather (then Lord Binning) in 1909 engaged Sir Reginald Blomfield to add the terraces on the south side of the house, and that architect also enlarged the lake, to which the land gently descends in slopes of mown grass enclosed by hedges. More recently, the terrace gardens have been planted with an interesting arrangement of roses, many of them the old gallicas, centifolias, Bourbons and Hybrid Musks.

The central block of Mellerstain is sometimes criticised for its over-heavy facade; but as a record of changing tastes the style is interesting. By 1770 the Romantic Movement had turned the attention of landowners to ruined medieval castles and towers, and builders were beginning to imitate aspects of ponderous Gothic architecture. Whether George Baillie insisted on having a castellated frontage is not clear, but this is hardly typical of Robert Adam, nor is it strictly in keeping with the wings his father designed. It suggests Adam trying to look back over his shoulder at earlier Border edifices, while keeping a tight rein on his horse and not permitting it to gallop into the past, as did so many later Scottish architects.

The great building of champagne-coloured stone, low in proportion to its total length, with the attendant wings of 1725 (each modest block suggesting to me a large English rectory where I spent part of my childhood), is set so deep in estate woods that it can scarcely be glimpsed until the forecourt is reached: then the whole north front looms up suddenly. The level sweep of parkland visible from the main entrance, the groups of broad-leaved trees and the grazing cattle, make a setting unsurpassed in its dignified seclusion and peace. Before going into the house I like to pass through the

Mellerstain in spring

garden entrance in the east wall, in order to experience contrast and swift surprise when an open prospect comes into view, of green lawns descending to the lake from rose-planted terraces, with blue humps of distant Cheviot hills beyond. From this southern aspect the house is seen to be poised 600 feet up on a hillside; a site which the earliest builders of that 'old melancholick hous' must surely have chosen for the splendid vista, even though untamed hills and woods were less popular then than they are now.

It is a place to linger in, and on my first visit I stayed too long outside to have sufficient time left to study the interior. The whole conception is the work of many minds and hands over more than two centuries, and so skilful a combination of art and natural beauty cannot be appreciated fully by a hurried visitor. Although staffing problems and the owner's need for privacy may have to confine daily opening to the afternoon, I wish there could be one extension each week for those who like to stand and stare; even if only the gardens could be seen in the forenoon. Given some provision for a snack midday meal in the existing tearoom, a strict ban on the undesirable picnic might be enforced.

The most interesting and lovable character Mellerstain has housed, Lady Grisell Baillie, is charmingly depicted in a portrait dated 1725 by Maria Varelst. The picture, which hangs in the front hall, is Scotland's equivalent of the 'Mona Lisa'. Its subtle smile is so compelling that, after looking at it for some moments, the idea of this lady being about to speak grows absurdly strong.

A recent addition to activities at Mellerstain is the bowmaking enterprise formerly situated in Kelso. The most sophisticated modern bows, fitted with pistol-grip handle sections and adjustable sights and stabilisers, are made from a variety of woods (often laminates), the limbs being faced with fibreglass. The only material I did not see was the traditional yew. Imported Canadian maple, Indian rosewood, beech, black walnut, padauk, bubinga and degamé (lemonwood) have supplanted the indigenous material.

Yew is tricky stuff. Bows being fashioned from it sometimes break during the process. They are expensive; but experienced archers regard the yew bow as giving 'the sweetest shoot of all'. When I visited Border Bows, then in Kelso, there was one craftsman left who knew how to make the longbow out of yew wood.

Traquair

Although most Scots have heard about the Bear Gates of Traquair, comparatively few seem able to pinpoint their locality and fewer still have ever seen them. The ancient house of Traquair – the oldest inhabited house in Scotland – stands a short distance from Innerleithen on the south bank of the Tweed. The famous gates, guarded by heraldic bears carved in stone, creatures whose savage toothed appearance is belied by a tame upright stance suggestive of the circus, have, it is said, been closed ever since the year 1745. The gates are known locally as 'The Steekit Yetts', and may be found at the end of a tree-lined avenue some quarter of a mile to westward of the house. The most popular legend relates how the fifth Earl of Traquair, after bidding farewell to his guest Prince Charles Edward Stuart, vowed that the gates would not be used again until the Stuarts were restored to the throne.

Another story has it that the seventh Earl shut up these gates in 1796 after the death of his wife, when he ordered that they were to stay closed until another countess should grace the house of Traquair. This never happened, for the title lapsed in 1861 on the death of the eighth Earl, a bachelor. In *Portrait of the Scott Country* Marion Lochhead has recorded an account of yet another incident, given to her by the late Sir Walter Maxwell-Scott, great-great grandson of the author of the Waverley novels. Like the Maxwell Stuarts of Traquair, to whom they are connected by marriage, the Maxwell-Scotts of Abbotsford are Catholics. In the days before the Catholic Emancipation Act of 1829, no Catholic might own a carriage and horses – although many in fact did so, trusting that neighbours would turn a blind eye. The Jacobite Lord Traquair was unlucky, for someone informed against him and the carriage had to be relinquished. As a gesture of contempt for the unjust law, he then closed the Bear Gates and the avenue, which have not been used since. The present owner has said that much information lies hidden in family archives, which have not yet been fully researched; so meanwhile we are left to speculate on the validity of these stories as best suits us.

Some account-books dating from the early eighteenth century show that the gates, built between 1737 and 1738, cost £12.15s for the pillars and £10.4s for the carved bears, with four gallons of ale to the men who erected them. Up to 200 years ago, brewing for home consumption had been carried out on the premises over a long period, so these men were probably refreshed with good Traquair ale. Mr Peter Maxwell Stuart, the present Laird, has revived the tradition, and is the only laird in Scotland licensed to brew and sell his own beer. Visitors may buy it for consumption in the tea-room or to take away, and the old brewhouse with equipment is on view. Here the Traquair speciality is made by Mr Maxwell Stuart in person, and an excellent brew it is. (The bottling is done by a small Brewery at Dunbar, but the contents are genuinely Traquair-brewed.) More domestic utensils of bygone days are exhibited in a stone-vaulted cellar reached by a passage from the entrance hall. Another chamber, candlelit, houses a tableau of spooky appearance to amuse young visitors. These vaults were long ago used for the safe housing of cattle in troublous times.

This remarkable old house began, like many a Border mansion, as a little rough tower. As early as 1107 it was occupied intermittently as a Royal hunting lodge. Wild cat, wolf, bear and

Traquair House

wild boar were then roaming the surrounding forests – animals now to be seen at Traquair only in mural decorations and early embroideries in the Museum Room upstairs. After the death of Alexander III in 1286, a long period of strife began to disrupt the old peaceful existence of this countryside, and the small tower was soon incorporated in a stronger defence peel or Border keep. By the time the Earl of Buchan bestowed it on his son James Stuart in 1491 it had developed into the 'Turris et fortalicis de Trakware' – a free-standing tower of three storeys and attics, with walls of stone from five to seven feet thick. James Stuart was killed with his king (James IV) at Flodden Field in 1513. His 'turris' is now built into the northern part of the main structure, its identity almost lost. It is otherwise at Earl Haig's Bemersyde, where an original tower – which is very like that of Smailholm – may still be seen, or at Lord Home's Hirsel House at Coldstream. Traquair was gradually enlarged, until by the middle of the seventeenth century the great central block looked the same as it does today. What are still referred to as 'the little modern wings' were added between 1660 and 1680, since when no exterior alterations have been made.

The main entrance, reached through a quaint little octagonal porch at the southern section of the main house, has a massive door – that on which the fugitive Montrose hammered in vain after his defeat at Philiphaugh in 1645. The first Earl of Traquair kept the place barred against the man who thought him a friend; this act no doubt saved Traquair's skin (and his house) from the vengence of General Leslie, who was hot in pursuit of Montrose. A grand knocker is of later date. It bears the entwined initials of the fourth Earl, Charles Stuart and his wife Mary Maxwell, and was made in 1705. We were told that Sir Walter Scott coveted this fine example of blacksmith's work, but had to go away without it. The iron screen and gates to the courtyard, and other ironwork, including some house locks, were fitted at the same time as the knocker.

Although it was for so long of considerable importance in Scottish history, Traquair now bears the stamp of tranquil domestic routine; Mervyn Horder's picture, taken on a summer evening as parkland trees wrapped it in shadows cast by a low sun, gives a good impression of this peaceful place. The small windows are like the eyes of a centenarian, which often seem to shrink with fatigue after long use, and withdraw into their shells. It is easy to re-create in imagination the Victorian life of Lady Louisa Stuart, an unmarried daughter of the seventh Earl, who inherited the house after the death of her bachelor brother in 1861. In earlier years she had known Robert Burns and was a great friend and regular correspondent of Sir Walter Scott, who paid many visits to Traquair.

Within a few days of her hundredth birthday in 1875, this vigorous old lady (of whom a characteristic portrait, reading a book, may be seen in the stillroom) made an expedition to Edinburgh to buy herself a new bonnet in time for Christmas. Unfortunately she caught a chill and died of pneumonia soon after. A staunch Catholic, she left endowments to provide churches in Peebles and Innerleithen. It would be misleading to suggest that this great house lacks mementos of royalty and battles, or works of fine and applied art ranking with the best in the land. It is indeed packed from ground floor to roof with such valuables, but manages to swallow up and digest them all, maintaining its own placid, homely character without interruption from throngs of sightseers who come to admire it during the summer months.

In the hall passage there is a significant arrangement of seventeenth and eighteenth-century weapons, hung on the wall beneath a frieze of servants' bells. Each bell has a label: 'Lord

Traquair's Room', 'Priest's Room', 'King's Room', 'Chintz Room', and so on. Perhaps the most desirable single exhibit – to those with an interest in music – is a lovely harpsichord made in 1651 by Ruckers of Antwerp, still in its original state, and kept tuned. There are some fine Jacobite drinking glasses, one with the forthright inscription:

> God bless the Prince of Wales,
> The true-born Prince of Wales,
> Sent us by Thee.
> Send him soon over
> And kick out hannover
> And then we'll recover
> Our old Libertie.

Other items of great historical interest include a rosary and crucifix of Mary Queen of Scots; a cradle used for her son James VI (and I); a magnificent state bed with yellow hangings, brought from Terregles House near Dumfries (a Maxwell possession) and used by Queen Mary on her visits there. The quilt was worked by the Queen and her ladies – 'The Four Maries'. The King's Room, used by Mary when she came to Traquair with Darnley on a hunting trip in 1566, has an adjacent powder closet fitted out with wig stand and block, wig powder and bellows.

Next to the closet a low door opens to the narrow stair, which originally formed the main access from ground floor level. We are now in the oldest part of the house, dating back to the twelfth century. The staircase connects with a second one from the King's Room to the floors above, emerging from behind a panel in the Priest's Room, where Mass was celebrated until the early part of the nineteenth century. It served as an escape route, very successfully, for there is no record of a priest being caught at Traquair, although articles used here were taken away during searches of the house. The secret stair has in recent years been opened up, and gives great delight at children's parties. Below the Priest's Room is the Library, with a fine collection of classics in seventeenth-century bindings.

In one of the 'little modern wings', situated to the left as you face the front of the house, is the family chapel, which was established here following the end of religious persecution in Scotland, probably very soon after the Catholic Emancipation Act of 1829, when the Stuarts were no longer obliged to worship in secret. It contains many treasures, including a set of oak panels made in

Holland, which some think show signs of having been carved by a Scottish hand. Below the chapel is the brewhouse, and alongside it are the gift-shop and a display centre, the latter attractively constructed in the old malt loft, where grain used to be prepared for brewing. Across the courtyard, the south wing contains the dining-room still used by the family. It is hung with hand-blocked French wallpaper, over a hundred years old, and a number of family portraits are on view. The lower drawing room, similarly papered, opens out of the dining-room.

Behind the house, the terraces are enlivened by a pair of pavilions with ogee-shaped roofs. A path known as 'Lady Louisa's Walk' runs alongside the brisk little river Quair, starting from the rear of the south wing and passing the croquet lawn. Here stands an unusual summerhouse made from heather – a gem of craftsmanship dating from 1834. Perhaps it commemorates the original house at Traquair, which is said to have been 'a heather hut of about 950 AD, deep in the Forest of Ettrick'. A pond called the Well Pool lies in the old bed of the Tweed, which at first flowed close to the old tower and threatened its foundations. For this reason the first Earl had the river diverted. It would be valuable to have details of how the work was done; it must have been an arduous task in 1640, before mechanical diggers were known. So far no account has been discovered. Mr Maxwell Stuart told us that in misty weather the thickest trails cling to and delineate the original course of the Tweed.

Until the river's course was changed, royalty had been pleased to divert itself on occasion by fishing for salmon from windows in the tower. Alexander I, who in 1107 stayed at Traquair and granted a charter therefrom, was the first to be named in a long record of royal occupants, and the house remained a royal domain up to the thirteenth century. The name is derived from *Tra* or *Tre*, meaning a house or small group of dwellings, and *Quair*, (a tributary of Tweed), which indicates a stream of winding habit. The Museum Room and Library contain a good collection of Traquair charters, some of which are always on show. Among them is one signed by William the Lyon in 1175. It authorises Bishop Jocelyn to found a Bishop's Burgh on the banks of Molendinar Burn, a site chosen some five centuries earlier by Saint Kentigern (or Mungo) for his chapel. The new Burgh, with its right to hold a market on Thursdays, has after 800 years grown into the teeming modern city of Glasgow.

Dawyck

This estate belonged initially to the Veitches, a name well known in the Lowlands of Scotland. The family is believed to be of Norman origin, its name derived from la Vache. In 1296 one William la Vache signed the infamous Ragman Roll. Veitches were in possession of Dawyck from about 1450 to 1691, when it was purchased by Sir James Naesmyth. Writing in 1715, Pennicuik mentioned Dawyck as being 'in the hands of Sir James Naesmyth of Posso, an eminent lawyer', who rebuilt the house and increased the ornamental plantations.

Pennicuik relates an amusing story which has been handed down by generations of Border people.

> Here [at Dawyck] in an old orchard did the herons build nests upon some large pear trees, and whereupon in harvest time are to be seen much fruit growing and trouts and eels crawling down the body of these trees. These fish the herons take out of the River Tweed to their nests; and this is the remarkable riddle that they talk so much of: to have flesh, fish and fruit at the same time upon one tree.'

Herons are usually adept at despatching their prey before carrying it aloft; but, accurate or not, the riddle is now part of established tradition. The heronry was famous, beyond doubt. King James IV obtained birds from it in 1497.

Although there has been a house at Dawyck since the fifteenth century, the original was destroyed by fire in 1797. The present house was built in 1830, by William Burn. In his vast work, *Aboretum et Fruticetum Britannicum* (1838), John Loudon mentions with approval the transformation made by Naesmyth, his plantings having changed the property from 'a lonely mansion in the bosom of a gloomy mountain into the extreme reverse. The vast improvements made by the present owner have proved not only an ornament to Tweeddale, but a worthy example for emulation.'

Since 1450 the estate has been owned by only three families – Veitch, Naesmyth and Balfour. The last two, being particularly interested in silviculture, have given constant attention to the care and improvement of the Dawyck trees and shrubs over a period of 295 years. Such continuity is enjoyed by very few woodlands and shrubberies.

In 1897 the grandmother of Colonel A. N. Balfour, the present owner, purchased this 5,000-acre estate, and from then on until his death in 1945 her son, the late F. R. S. Balfour – described by W. J. Bean as 'an enthusiastic arboriculturist and forester' – continued to plant rare species, particularly of conifers. Between 1900 and 1912 he travelled extensively in North America and there collected many specimens himself. The present owner continues to care with keen and informed interest for his father's aboretum and garden. The Balfours have also experimented with game birds. Capercailzie imported from Finland bred here and were later found at Stobo, Drumelzier and Glentress. Ptarmigan were introduced as well. In the seventeenth century both these birds were common in the Megget district of Peeblesshire. The Dawyck estate carries herds of roe and Japanese deer.

It has long been justly famous for the variety of its trees, and it is impossible to define the wealth of interest available to keen silviculturists here, without lapsing into a catalogue of botanical names and measurements. Colonel Balfour lent me a list which gives, *inter alia*, twenty-six varieties of *Pinus* (Pine), twenty-one varieties of *Abies* (Fir), seventeen of *Picea* (Spruce), and seventeen of *Acer* (Maple). Sir James Naesmyth was a pupil of the great Swedish botanist Linnaeus, who is said to have visited Dawyck and planted the first larch. This first European larch (north-east of the house) dates from 1725 and is thought to be the oldest in Scotland. According to Loudon, those at Dunkeld in Perthshire were introduced in 1738. The fastigiate Dawyck Beech originated here. The original tree may be seen through the yew arch some 200 yards south-east of the house. There is also a fastigiate oak. Fine examples of Douglas Fir in the glen, planted in 1835, have reached noble proportions. The *Picea breweriana* lifted in the wild by Colonel F. R. S. Balfour in Oregon in 1908 was destroyed by a gale in 1973, but there are other examples of this unusual spruce readily identified by their deep green fringe-like foliage.

Dawyck House stands over 600 ft above sea-level, surrounded by woods up to the 1,500 ft line. With an average rainfall of thirty-five inches, severe gales and very hard frosts, this is a tough environment. The soil, being lime-free, suits plants which thrive in acid conditions, and the Balfour family has introduced many rhododendrons, both natural species and hybrid forms. The protection afforded by the wealth of tree-cover enables these and other shrubs to endure the gales. The worst ever known (134 mph) occurred in January 1968, when very severe damage was suffered by the estate, some 50,000 trees being lost. Fortunately most of the rare specimens managed to survive, including the venerable *Abies pectinata* in the Silver Walk. This specimen dates from 1680.

The estate is reached from Peebles by the B712 road which forks left off A72 just before Lyne church is reached. The way runs close to Tweed – now a narrow stream in its upper reaches – as far as the drive entrance. Although it is sited not far from the road, the house has a delightful air of seclusion, almost a monastic feel about it, and the long, low facade of mellow greyish stone merges into the background, chameleon fashion, as if designed to be invisible. Architecturally speaking, this is not one of the most celebrated Border houses, but one that most of us – if given the chance – would choose to call 'home'.

Having spent part of my youth in the Italian province of Liguria amid terraced hillside gardens with steps, balustrades and vases of refined design and workmanship, I was immediately reminded of these by the beautiful stonework in gardens surrounding the house of Dawyck. It was therefore no surprise to hear that this had all been carried out in 1830 by Italian craftsmen brought over to Midlothian and engaged by the Naesmyths. The same men afterwards moved down into Kent and made the terraces at Chartwell, Sir Winston Churchill's home.

The Dawyck gardens and aboretum are never dull, but the best seasons in which to visit them are spring and autumn. In spring the bulbs seem to light up *every* nook and cranny, which is very nearly true, for the late Colonel F. R. S. Balfour obtained from Tresco in the Isles of Scilly a ton of bulbs each year over a period of twenty years. Before these flowers fade, the rhododendrons begin to show new colour from opening buds. Few of the very large-leaved varieties will thrive here, but *Rhododendron rex* has handsome foliage, and *R. campanulatum* with felty grey, russet-lined leaves is an attractive shrub whether in bloom or not. *R. souliei* does better here than on the west coast, and avoids frost by flowering late. In autumn the woods are a tapestry of yellow, gold and russet set off by dark green and blue-grey of the conifers. There is a beech walk on the south and a splendid avenue of limes, half a mile long, north-east of the house. This planting was shown on a map drawn in the early eighteenth century. In one of John Buchan's first novels, 'John Burnett of Barns', the hero rides up this lime avenue to visit Margery Veitch at Dawyck.

Smaller trees which develop special glory in autumn are *Prunus sargentii* (a flowering cherry with a talent for colouring and retaining its foliage like a blazing torch some weeks before winter extinguishes it); *Cercidiphyllum japonicum*, the Japanese 'Katsura' tree; *Cornus nuttallii*, an elegant Dogwood; and the rare *Disanthus cercidifolia*, which Mr Robert Blair, the head gardener, managed to establish with difficulty. It is now nearly thirty years old and was the first shrub to win an Award of Merit from the Royal Horticultural Society for foliage alone.

Dawyck also possesses a typical Scottish walled garden, situated a little way east from the house, where – for a thrilling contrast to woodlands and stone terraces – the visitor is plunged during summer months into a riot of roses, honeysuckles, clematis and all the good traditional herbaceous plants, set round an old stone well and protected by hedges of clipped yew in addition to walling. Some 4,000 visitors come to see Dawyck each year. A favourite spot with most of them is the glen, a cleft in the rocks with a burn tumbling down from Scrape Hill. Rushing water, clear and cool; resinous scents; bird song and the beautifully designed plantings, make this an enchanted place in which to linger.

Shrubs and trees of contrasting form and texture include *Tsuga heterophylla* (planted in 1860); the great Douglas Firs (planted in 1835); and a fine *Prunus sargentii* from the Arnold Arboretum in the United States, planted in 1908. Most of the shrubs and trees are labelled. The ancient parish church of Dawyck, restored in 1837, will be found up behind the house, half buried in woods, a place of peace. It is now a private chapel.

Although so picturesque, the woodlands of this estate are run as a commercial forestry enterprise by Colonel Balfour. He states that, with the exception of beech and sycamore, hardwoods do not grow quickly enough to make them an economic crop to plant, and therefore most of the woodland is composed of conifers introduced from America. He plants, not for himself but for his grandchildren. One hopes that political manoeuvres by government decree will not interrupt the long tradition of silviculture here, although recent fiscal legislation has made the planting of woodlands far less attractive.

Since October 1978 the Dawyck Arboretum has become an outstation of the Royal Botanic Garden in Edinburgh.

The Hirsel

This large, rambling yet unpretentious house looks most attractive when seen from the south-west, as one approaches up the main driveway. At the southern end of the west front stands a square tower, the oldest building on the site. It adjoins a three-storey house of the late seventeenth to early eighteenth century, consisting of a central block and two projecting wings. A long and slightly higher block running northwards from the older part dates mainly from the early nineteenth century. The warm pinkish-grey freestone of all these buildings harmonises well with wooded policies and gentle slopes of mown grass. It suggests 'Austere beauty slowly grown' – indeed, the whole place has an almost monastic air of timeless simplicity.

The main entrance is on the east front, where a long terrace overlooks a steep drop to the River Leet. The name 'Hirsel' derives from a term used to denote the area which would be put in the charge of one shepherd, and it can be seen that Hirsel House stands at the point where four drives meet, each about a mile long. The ancient church of 'Herishille' and some one hundred acres of land here formed part of the foundation charter (1166) of the Cistercian Priory of Coldstream. A charter of the barony of Hirsel was served on the second Earl of Home in 1621, and there is evidence that the third Earl lived here twenty years later.

The Home family took its name from lands in Berwickshire first mentioned in a charter of 1138. Hume Castle was the family stronghold until its walls were 'dinged doun' by Cromwell's forces in 1651. No doubt that event caused the Homes to adapt Hirsel House for use as their family seat. The fifth Earl died here in 1706, and there have been Homes in residence ever since. In these days, when golden handshakes are worth many thousands of pounds, the decline in values is strikingly illustrated by the mere £70 given to the early Home by James II for 'wines, victuals, spears and lances for the defence of his house of Hume'. That was in 1453, when the Earls of Northumberland and Douglas were threatening Hume Castle. The next in line was created Lord Home. (The family name is pronounced 'Hume'; the old Berwickshire castle is spelt as pronounced.)

Marriage of the young and lovely niece of the fifth Earl to the elderly Lord Polwarth (afterwards Earl of Marchmont) as his second wife created a stir in the Borders, but seems to have had a happy outcome. The tenth Earl married a daughter of the Duke of Buccleuch and built part of the nineteenth-century house. A group of the Buccleuch family of this generation (perhaps by Mercier) hangs in the present drawing room in the Regency wing, which has a very attractive curving staircase of elegant proportions. The great stone stair leading up from the hall and main (north) entrance has above it, on the ceiling of the stair-well, an interior weather-vane. Such devices are rarely found north of the Border.

With the marriage of the eleventh Earl to the sister of the last Lord Douglas, two of the greatest Border families were united, and in 1859, on the death of her mother, Lady Home inherited the vast Douglas estates. From that time onwards the fortunes of the Homes were assured. The eleventh Earl was created Baron Douglas of Douglas, and his son added the Douglas to the family name, becoming Douglas-Home. The thirteenth Earl, whose portrait by James Gunn hangs above the smoking-room fireplace, was the most courteous and modest of men. He played a large part in the founding of The League of Nations, and died in 1951. His son, later known as Sir Alec, had as a boy little knowledge of his likely inheritance. By the time he was ten it amounted to 134,000 acres and a gross annual rental of £93,000 with coal royalties on top of that, according to Kenneth Young's biography.

This distinguished family has, over a period of five hundred years, given a great deal of valuable service to the nation; but the present head of the Homes is the first of his line to have been Prime Minister. Unfortunately he did not hold that office very long. His parliamentary career began in 1931, when as Lord Dunglass he was elected MP for Lanark. When in October 1963 he was asked to form a government, the fourteenth Earl of Home relinquished his peerage and then found himself in the unprecedented position of being Premier of Great Britain without having a seat in either the Lords or the Commons. The latter defect was soon remedied, for at the Kinross and West Perthshire by-election early in November, George Younger stood down in favour of Douglas-Home, who was elected with a majority of 9,328. Sir Alec still retained his one title, as Knight of the Thistle. That, and his offices of Premier and, later, Foreign Secretary, have all been won by own exertions and not bestowed upon him by heredity. The Home earldom has been put into cold storage for the rest of Sir Alec's life. Afterwards it may be revived by David Douglas-Home if he so wishes. In 1974 Sir Alec accepted a Life Peerage, becoming Lord Home of The Hirsel.

The Woodland Garden at the Hirsel

Some gardens cannot be described without their homes – in this case, without Homes and the house they inhabit. It is impossible to imagine The Hirsel bereft of its family. An amazingly vigorous current animates them all, and they dart about the place as though provided with roller-skates instead of feet. By contrast with their owners, the planted-up sectors of the grounds have a slightly hesitant air. It seems that all those handsome groups of azalea and rhododendron, of lilac and 'old' rose, have stolen out of the woodland when nobody was looking and are unsure of their reception; the stalwart lupins in the border also look fearful of being cast out as trespassers. Lord Home would be the last person to banish them, for he is a great plant-lover. Reading my words, Miss Caroline Douglas-Home remarked that her father had in fact planted all these borders himself, there being none outside the walled garden before the family moved here in 1959. At a garden fete in The Hirsel policies, a few days before his seventieth birthday

141

in 1973, I saw him receive, with obvious pleasure, a gift of rose bushes presented by Berwickshire Conservatives.

The naturally undulating character of the land, and the many fine specimen trees already growing there, almost make any additional gardening superfluous. The most famous single tree is the *Liriodendron tulipifera*, the Tulip tree, which was planted in 1742 and still produces some flowers each season. It is in the walled garden. A Spanish chestnut on the Leet bank below the house, and a wire-supported sycamore at one corner of the walled garden, are both believed to be over 400 years old. They must have been young in the heyday of the first Queen Elizabeth, and have already lived through thirty years of the reign of Queen Elizabeth the Second.

Dundock Wood, famous for miles around, is situated at the west end of the Hirsel lake. That ornamental water, home of many water birds, was made over a century ago on an old moss. The six acres now planted with rhododendrons and azaleas was once a mixed wood. It suffered terrible gale damage in the 1890s and had to be cleared. Hundreds of tons of peat were then carted to it from Bonkyl, sixteen miles to the north – a round trip taking twenty-four hours with the horse-drawn carts – and so the soil was made suitable for rhododendrons. In recent years much of the wild *Rhododendron ponticum* in Dundock has been eliminated in favour of new hybrid varieties. Trees to be seen here include good specimens of Scots Pine, Silver Fir, Western Red Cedar, Norway Spruce, and two with the dreadful name of *Cercidiphyllum japonicum*. That lovely 'Katsura' tree takes on the most delicate autumn colouring of crushed strawberry mixed with peach.

This wood is freely open to visitors on foot, but cars must be left outside the gates, preferably in Dundock car park near the junction of A697 and A698. Daffodil time in the latter part of April and rhododendron time in early June are particularly popular with tourists. The Douglas-Homes are very kind to well-behaved visitors on foot, provided that family privacy is respected and the vicinity of Hirsel House avoided. (Those precincts are open only on specific dates in aid of Scotland's Gardens Scheme.) The estate as a whole now consists of about 600 acres of woodland and 2,400 acres of good Merse farmland, growing barley, wheat, and potatoes in the main, while sheep and cattle thrive on various grazings.

The Hirsel is noted for its great abundance and variety of bird life. One hundred and seventy species have been observed here, and ninety-one found breeding. Five warblers; three owls – barn, long-eared and tawny; the great spotted and green woodpeckers and the tree-creeper; the great crested and little grebes; pied and spotted flycatchers; pochard, shoveller, tufted duck and teal; kingfisher, heron, common snipe and kestrel, are just a few of these inhabitants who nest and rear their families on the estate. Boxes on the upper walls of Hirsel House have attracted swifts, who nest in them regularly. In 1973 two ringed as adults turned up for the fifteenth consecutive year. This means that they must have flown about 2,700,000 miles. The late Major Henry Douglas-Home, Lord Home's eldest brother, was very well known as an ornithologist. He compiled a list of 'Birds Seen at the Hirsel'.

Andrew Steele (1811-1888), a bootmaker of Coldstream, wrote for local newspapers and published some verse in a volume called 'Select Productions'. This includes a poem 'The Hirsel Yet for Me', which ends:

> All hail, yon venerable pile.
> Thy hospitable dome;
> May peace and plenty ever smile
> To bless the house of Home!
> And now adieu, thy magic scenes;
> My fondest memory
> Shall ever homage with the lay –
> The Hirsel yet for me!

Evidently this writer did not choose to pronounce the family name as 'Hume'. Many of the older residents of Berwickshire today stick uncompromisingly to Steele's preference, rhyming 'Home' with 'dome'.

7

Castles and Towers

Neidpath Castle

A mile to the west of Peebles, on the A72 road to Lyne and Biggar, this castle stands on a rocky knoll some eighty feet above the Tweed. It began in the fourteenth century as one in a chain of Border defence towers. The land whereon it was built, Jedderfield, at first gave its name to the tower. The 'Castle of Jedwordfelde' is mentioned in a document of 1448. It is not given the name of Neidpath until 1563. The derivation has caused some debate. A suggestion that it means 'turning path', in reference to the twisting approach through Neidpath Gorge, seems reasonable. The fortress has attracted yet a third name, being designated 'Peebles Castle' in some books. As Peebles once had its own royal castle, now demolished, this makes for confusion in the reader's mind.

The massive block of Neidpath, towering up above the Tweed and backed by deep woods, has given those with romantic leanings ample opportunity to take some of the most popular photographs obtainable in the Border country. According to Drummond Gauld, the picturesque fortress was occupied for a time by Professor Adam Ferguson, the historian, whose hospitality Walter Scott enjoyed. Never destined to play a major part in Scotland's history, this castle has certain claims to a place in the annals of war. In 1303 the troops of Sir Simon Frazer of Oliver, whose family owned Neidpath, helped to scatter and defeat three separate 'armies' of Edward I of England at Roslin Moor.

> Three triumphs in a day,
> Three hosts subdued as one,
> Three armies scattered like the spray
> Beneath the common sun.

At a later date, in September 1650, young Lord Yester (after the Battle of Dunbar) garrisoned the castle against Cromwell's forces. Neidpath was not surrendered until December, the last stronghold south of the Forth to hold fast for the King. This same Lord Yester, who became the second Earl of Tweeddale in 1653, made extensive alterations to the old tower. He built the present gateway and on it his crest – a goat's head erased upon a coronet of five points; he planted trees in the policies, and may have extended the old terraced gardens which existed in 1581. Traces may still be seen on the slope above the river.

In 1686 he sold his Peeblesshire estates to William Douglas, first Duke of Queensberry, from whom that peer's second son – William, created first Earl of March by William III – obtained them. He and his successor continued the planting begun by Tweeddale and made further alterations to the tower and the courtyard buildings. The second Earl died in 1731 at an early age, and the third Earl, who became the fourth Duke of Queensberry, gained notoriety as 'Old Q.', also known to Londoners as 'The Star of Piccadilly'. Fashionable life in the English capital during the eighteenth century engrossed the Duke and strained his resources. He let the castle and sold off fine stands of timber in order to raise money. This behaviour led Wordsworth to compose a sonnet in which 'Degenerate Douglas' is soundly reproved for his vandalism.

He did not mend his ways, and the castle was allowed to crumble. The south wall of the west wing collapsed. Old Q. died without leaving issue, and in 1810 the estates passed to the eighth Earl of Wemyss, since when the titles of Wemyss and March have been combined. In 1952 the administration of the estate was undertaken by the Wemyss and March Estates, now made a Discretionary Trust. Neidpath has been open to the public for many years.

The present Earl of Wemyss and March, who is President of The National Trust for Scotland, has been actively directing restoration work at Neidpath since World War II. It is now in a far better state of preservation than many other Tweed Valley towers, including Newark – from which tourists are excluded because it is unsafe – and the remains of Posso, Wrae, Horsburgh and Barns. Neidpath was inhabited continuously until the present century, gradually changing its function and appearance from fortress to country house. It is now an interesting mixture of both, though no longer lived in.

The great hall has been divided horizontally by timbers and flooring, making it a two-storey house. A staircase in the east wall, a chimney and a quantity of pine panelling are some of the seventeenth-century work done during a large scheme of alteration. The larger of the two second-floor bedchambers is said to have been occupied by Mary Queen of Scots in 1563 and by James IV in 1587. The third floor, reached only by the main spiral stair, leads to the south parapet walk, which is roofed. There are traces of some seventeenth-century painting on joists and plaster of the south room. Major repairs made to the roof in 1938 were carried out entirely from timber grown on the estate. Some ancient yews bordering the approach drive on the north are a variety of the common yew which has been named *Taxus baccata neidpathensis* in honour of the place where it was raised.

Readers far outside the Borders and beyond the shores of Britain have been made familiar with this castle by Sir Walter Scott. His poem *The Maid of Neidpath* re-tells a traditional story of young Lady Mary Douglas and her love for the Laird of Tushielaw. Her parents, the Earl and Countess of March, were greatly displeased, and had the wooer sent abroad to cool his ardour. They could not have foreseen the effect of this banishment upon their love-sick daughter, who pined for the young man and became so seriously ill that her mother summoned Tushielaw home in a hurry. Even this remedy failed, for so altered was the girl's appearance, all her youthful bloom gone, that he is said to have passed her by without recognising his Mary, and ridden off without speaking to her. The shock was too much for the ailing girl, who collapsed and died in the arms of her attendant.

More comic than tragic was a fracas of minor domestic nature in the mid-sixteenth century. A dispute arose between the fifth Lord of Yester and his mother, who claimed the contents of two cupboards in an upper room of the castle. After a long series of arguments the cupboard doors were unlocked. Lord Yester's mother cannot have been impressed by the contents. The first cupboard held only 'ane posset top with ane fute of the self of esche (ash), ane litill bikker (beaker) callit ane salt fat with ane fute of esche, ane lame (earthen) can and three paperis of armes of vmquhile Archibald Erle of Angus'. The second cupboard contained 'nihill aliud nisi lie worme wobbis' – nothing but cobwebs.

More valuable treasures – vestments, jewels and precious relics from the Cross Kirk at Peebles – were deposited for safe keeping in the castle at the time of the Reformation. All these articles have long since disappeared. Neidpath is no longer a home. The great rooms lack furnishings. Only the small office of the custodian shows signs of a little comfort and activity. This strong tower, with its whinstone walls of over ten feet in thickness, rises some sixty feet above the courtyard. It is worth a visit, particularly in good, clear weather, when a splendid view of river and countryside may be had from the top.

No love-lorn maids are found at Neidpath now, but visitors are given a reminder of young Tushielaw dashing up to woo his lady when, at the annual March Riding, the Peebles Cornet arrives at the castle gates, attended by a concourse of riders, to be given an official welcome by the Warden. The first in this modern series of March Ridings took place in 1897. The office of 'Warden of Neidpath' was instituted in the 1920s by Dr C. B. Gunn, to commemorate old links between Peebles and this tower. John Buchan (Lord Tweedsmuir) held this office in 1935.

Fast Castle

This impregnable-looking fortress, perched 150 feet above the sea on the cliff edge north of St Abbs, poses several problems to the inquiring mind. How it was ever built in such an inaccessible spot is the first; how anybody managed to capture it is another; the mystery most heard of now is the hidden treasure reputedly sealed up in the ruin, and the curse which operates on those who try to find it. Sir Walter Scott added to these, for he is thought to have taken the place as a model for Wolf's Crag in *The Bride of Lammermoor*. It is almost impossible to persuade people today that in fact Scott himself disclaimed this. In his introduction to *Chronicles of the Canongate* he wrote 'The ironbound coast of Scotland affords upon its headlands and promontories fifty such castles'.

That the fortress is by no means impregnable can be proved without trouble, for it changed hands many times. During one of its periods in English hands, a plan was drawn which shows that the whole rock plateau was then occupied by castle buildings. Within their curtain walls lay two courtyards with a central 'brewe howse' between them. The donjon or keep stood on the east, and there was a range of offices along the north-western verge of the cliff. In one of the yards a crane is shown, with a container swinging over the sea. Provisions are being hoisted up from boats in the small cove down below. The large cave whose entrance lies just above sea level is locally said to house a secret passage connecting with the castle. No entrance has been found; so that makes yet another mystery.

Small wonder the ruins of Fast Castle stir the imagination, perhaps to a greater extent than any other such relic on the Scottish coast. So wild and lonely is this coast, so difficult the access, that there is a real sense of achievement when the goal is reached, even though there are no armed men lying in wait to repel the intruder.

Nobody knows who built the first tower on this site. It was a well-known stronghold by the fourteenth century, and changed hands repeatedly during the long period of Border warfare. In the fifteenth century it was held by Halliburtons, Lumsdens and Homes. Some of the Englishmen involved in the murder of Sir Robert Ker of Caverton were thrown into the Fast dungeon, never to come out. It is not known if they perished from starvation or by more summary means.

After her reception at Lamberton in 1503, Princess Margaret Tudor, the young sister of Henry VIII, is said to have spent a night in this fortress before riding on to meet her betrothed, James IV, at Dalkeith. Some disbelieve the story. It was too good a picture for the romantically-inclined to miss – the girl princess from England, mounted on a white palfrey, attended by richly caparisoned knights with banners – where else should they lodge if not in Berwickshire's impressive sea-girt fortress? She is supposed to have said that there was good cheer, so that every man was content. If they really lodged her in such an eyrie, one would have expected some comment upon the place.

Early in the same century, the third Lord Home, feeling unable to defend the castle against the Duke of Albany, razed it to the ground. His successor rebuilt it soon afterwards, and by 1521 it was again a focal point of Border warfare. While it was under the control of the English Marshal of Berwick, the plan of 1549 already mentioned was prepared on the instructions of the Earl of Rutland. It used to be housed in Belvoir Castle, and may be there still. A strange feature of that plan is the omission of a well. The Scottish historian Hector Boece (1465-1536) wrote of an extraordinary stone, hollowed out and porous as a sponge, which filtered

Fast Castle

sea-water within Fast Castle and so rendered it fit for drinking purposes. Another mystery.

In 1567, soon after Mary Queen of Scots had been incarcerated in Lochleven Castle, Queen Elizabeth's ambassador, Sir Nicholas Throckmorton, came to Fast Castle for a conference with Sir James Melville, Lethington, and the fifth Lord Home. He wrote home to England of 'having been lodgyed at Faux Castle, where I was intretyd very well according to ye state of ye place, whilk ys the more fitte to lodge prisoners in than folks at lybertye, as yt ys very stronge yet very lyttle'. Because the Scots sheltered rebellious subjects – such as the Earls of Westmorland and North-umberland – Queen Elizabeth revenged herself on families who had befriended the fugitives, and Fast Castle was taken by an English force of 2,000 from Berwick, after which it stayed in English occupation until 1573.

On the grounds that it was the rightful property, not of Lord

Home but of his wife, it was then returned to Scotland. Young Logan of Restalrig, Lady Home's son by a former marriage, inherited the property in 1576. Many wild doings are attributed to Restalrig. Assault and murder, theft and treason, conspiracy and rebellion were committed, 'causing his wife to weep' and maintaining a state of perpetual unease in the district. Logan seems to have been one owner who found his castle a safe harbour from which he was not ejected by private enemies or the law.

The strangest event in the history of Fast Castle during Logan ownership is found in the Merchiston Papers. It is an indenture of 1594 between Robert Logan and John Napier, the mathematician and inventor of logarithms. He binds himself to seek out (or prove to be non-existent) a great hoard of gold concealed in a secret vault of the castle. A divining-rod was used, and magical spells, including the sacrifice of a black cock, but so far as is known the exercise proved unproductive. In 1971 another hunt for the hidden treasure took place, with up-to-date metal-divining equipment, but the result was equally disappointing. There is supposed to be a curse on anyone who tries to probe the secret, and when the leader of the most recent attempt died suddenly, local residents shook their heads.

To reach Fast Castle it is necessary to take the A1107 road from Cockburnspath to Coldingham, turning off towards the sea at the corner by Old Cambus Wood, on the narrow road to Dowlaw. The motorist cannot go much beyond the farm of that name. After passing through a gate and continuing by a footpath more or less north for a short distance, the walker then bears away right-handed. It is about a mile to Fast Castle Head. So far, this excursion is within the capabilities of most people, but the final scramble and leap into the ruins on their isolated perch is for the agile and fit, unsuitable for the very young or the elderly.

Duns, Hume and the Vanished Redbraes

Along the southern foothills of Lammermuir, overlooking rich farmlands of the Merse, once stood a chain of castles – including those of Duns, Redbraes near Greenlaw, and Hume – all of which, except for the nineteenth-century reconstruction of Duns as a castellated mansion, are now either uninhabited, ruined, or gone. Nisbet House, sited farther down in the Merse south-east of Duns, is also uninhabited. Duns, which superseded Greenlaw as Berwick-shire's county town, possessed at one time a strong keep, built by Thomas Randolph, Earl of Moray, when he received the lands after the Battle of Bannockburn from Robert the Bruce. It is probable that an older, lesser, defence tower already stood on the site. Randolph's fortress did not withstand the onslaught of Hertford's men in 1545, when the original charters were destroyed in the fire.

Towards the end of the seventeenth century the Hays of Drummelzier inherited the estate and carried out rebuilding of the castle of Duns. In 1820 the present castellated mansion took the place of older structures – outwardly, at least. Within its walls the shell of Randolph's tower still stands. A little to the west are the ruins of Borthwick, probably a watch-tower placed there to protect the castle. The original town of Duns or Dunse also suffered destruction at the hands of Hertford and on other occasions by Bowes, the Governor of Berwick. On higher ground to northward of the present town is a cairn marking the site of the 'Bruntons' – burnt towns – of which no other trace now remains. Duns Castle is not open to the public, although part of the grounds have become a Nature Reserve and may be visited on production of a permit.

The story of Greenlaw also began on a different site from that of the present town. It stood on a green hill on the road to Eccles; now the farm of Old Greenlaw is the only habitation to be seen there. Down in the Blackadder valley the eighteenth-century 'new' town cannot forget that it was once a county town. The domed town hall with its handsome portico serves to remind the visitor that Greenlaw has had its moments. Now somewhat neglected by guide-books and tourist leaflets, this quiet place has considerable charm.

Railway enthusiasts may like to know that in October 1862 Greenlaw had a gala day, when the first sod was cut for the construction of a railway link between Duns and the old North British line at St Boswells. The building of the Tweed Bridge at Leaderfoot was regarded at the time as a marvellous feat of engineering. Lady John Scott of Spottiswoode, however, would have nothing to do with the new line. She persisted in taking main-line trains from Melrose or St Boswells. Now there are no train services nearer than Berwick-upon-Tweed.

Lady John Scott, born Alicia Anne Spottiswoode, married in

1836 Lord John Montague-Douglas-Scott, the second son of Charles, fourth Duke of Buccleuch. He died in 1860, leaving no heir, and in 1870, under her father's will, Alicia resumed her maiden name. But it is as Lady John Scott that she is remembered, and that memory rests almost entirely upon her version of the song 'Annie Laurie', which she is said to have written during a visit to her sister, Lady Home Campbell, at Marchmont House.

Words and music are both adapted from older compositions. The original words are by William Douglas of Fingland, who in 1700 thus honoured the charms of a Miss Laurie of Maxwelton:

> She's backit like a peacock,
> She's breastit like a swan,
> She's jimp aboot the middle,
> Her waist ye weel may span;
> Her waist ye weel may span, she has a rovin' ee,
> And for bonnie Annie Laurie
> I'd lay doon my heid and dee.

The two sisters considered these words to be 'quaint and simple, but too unrefined for modern delicacy', so Alicia set to work and refined them. She also adapted an old tune from 'A Ballad Book' by Charles Sharpe, privately printed in 1824.

> Her brow is like the snowdrift,
> Her neck is like the swan,
> Her face it is the fairest
> That e'er the sun shone on;
> That e'er the sun shone on,
> And dark blue is her ee,
> And for bonny Annie Laurie
> I'd lay me doon and dee.

Alicia's version may have suited the Marchmont drawing-room, and her own image when she made stately expeditions in her private coach with postilions, a style more characteristic of her father's time. He built the eighteenth-century mansion of Spottiswoode, which stood on the site of an earlier family home. Spottiswoodes of Spottiswoode appear in the notorious 'Ragman Roll' of 1296.

On other occasions the Lady Alicia chose to disguise herself in humble clothing, even rags, while roaming the lanes on foot and alone. During these off-beat excursions she made friends with the so-called 'royal line' of Border gypsies, whose tribal headquarters and 'palace' were at Kirk Yetholm – see chapter 8. When their 'queen', Esther Faa Blythe, died in 1883 Alicia sent a wreath of white roses.

She herself lived to be ninety, and her friendship with the gypsies led to a bizarre occurrence at her funeral. A certain 'Prince Robert', supposedly a grandson of the departed queen, insisted on accompanying Alicia on her last journey, from Spottiswoode to the burial ground at Westruther. He climbed into the hearse and lay beside the coffin, at intervals raising a hand in regal salute to crowds lining the road. Alicia Anne Spottiswoode was laid to rest in a grave full of snowdrops.

Less than three miles from Greenlaw stood the old Redbraes Tower, a Home stronghold. Twice rebuilt, it was finally replaced on an adjacent site by the great Adam house of Marchmont. I am indebted to Lady McEwen of Marchmont for an extract from her Presidential address to the Berwickshire Naturalists' Club, given in 1973. The young wife of Lord Polwarth (who was the only son of Hugh, third and last Earl of Marchmont by his second wife), described in a letter to her mother how the newly-built house of Marchmont looked to her in 1772. She had been married three weeks earlier to 'Lord P.', as she called her husband.

> Lord Marchmont's House is, without being fine, a very comfortable good House to live in. . . . All that I have yet seen of Berwickshire is very open Country, seemingly fruitful, especially in Corn, of which the Crops promise extremely well. There is a good deal of plantation about the House, young as yet and not full-grown; the Ascent through them is very pretty.

Robert Chambers in his *Picture of Scotland* (1827) gives a later description: 'The extensive park, most of which is planted, and is approached by an avenue about a mile and a quarter long, and an hundred yards wide, the most imposing thing of the kind I ever saw.' In our time, the great woods of Marchmont screen the house so effectively that it is invisible from Greenlaw.

The story of how Sir Patrick Home of Redbraes was saved by the pluck and endurance of his young daughter Grisell has often been told. During the winter of 1684-5, Home lay hidden in the burial vault below the old church of Polwarth, his life in danger from government forces after the Rye House Plot. Only Grisell was let into the secret of his whereabouts. Every night after dark the girl found her way across the fields on a mile-long walk to the church, carrying whatever provisions she had been able to remove secretly from kitchen or table. In this manner her father was maintained in his ghastly hiding place, until at the end of a month he changed his vault for an underground cell in Redbraes itself. After a narrow escape from dragoons he fled to the continent, to be joined in Holland by his wife and family. His estate was confiscated by the Crown. Following the accession of William of Orange, the position was reversed and the Homes soon reinstated at Redbraes. Grisell later married George Baillie, to become the chatelaine of Mellerstain (see Chapter 6).

Polwarth village, closely bound up with Marchmont, has one of the most interesting little churches in the district. It was rebuilt in the eighteenth century by Sir Patrick Home, who put on the facade a tablet stating that a Christian edifice had stood on the site since 900. Records of a church at Paulworthe which was dedicated to St Mungo in 1242 are extant, and a very ancient stone font has been preserved, together with Lady Grisell Baillie's embroidered pulpit frontal, a funeral bell of 1715 and some old wooden collection ladles. In a churchyard is a tombstone with the date 1699 and an inscription:

> Remember man as thou gost by
> As thou art now so once was I:
> As I am now so most ye be,
> Remember man that ye most dee.

The people of Polwarth were not inhibited by gloomy thoughts, nor were they rendered unhealthy by the swampy nature of the ground. In past centuries nearly every house was provided with a sump-hole, into which rainwater percolated, to be emptied out by the residents at frequent intervals. All the land has long since been given modern drainage.

On the sloping village green are two decaying thorn trees, round about which for some 300 years it was customary for everybody to dance at weddings. Allan Ramsay wrote of this tradition. His verses were sung to the tune called 'Polwarth on the Green'. A more rustic ballad begins with the words:

> Fy let us a' to the bridal,
> For there'll be liltin' there;
> For Jock's to be married to Maggie,
> The lass wi' the gowden hair.

Still following the family of Home, we move on a few miles from Greenlaw, Marchmont and Polwarth to Hume Castle. The village of Hume is reached from Kelso by the road B6364, off which the steep street turns sharply some four miles south of Greenlaw. The huddle of small cottages is dwarfed by the fortress looming above it on a green hillside.

The third Earl of Marchmont, who built Marchmont House, planted its policies with trees, and did much to improve farming on his estate, also constructed the present curtain wall of Hume Castle, with enormous crenellations outdoing any figment of fancy ever seen on a stage. This amazing eighteenth-century 'folly' is visible from great distances – from Berwick Bounds on the east to the Cheviot Hills to southward. The work was carried out with good intent, preserving on that fine site over 600 feet above the Merse the memory of a great and important stronghold. Unfortunately Hume was not restored with the taste that might have been expected from the builder of Marchmont.

An early story of Hume connects it with the death of James II of Scotland, who was accidentally killed when a huge Flemish bombard (called 'The Lion') burst during the siege of Roxburgh Castle in 1460. His Queen, Mary of Gueldres, was staying in Hume at the time. On the day of the accident she set out to visit her husband at Roxburgh, meeting at Stichil a messenger sent with news of the tragedy. The shock is said to have brought about the premature birth of the son who became James III. Ever since that day the spot has been called The Queen's Cairn.

Hume Castle was originally constructed in the thirteenth century by William, grandson of the third Earl of Dunbar. By marrying his cousin Ada, daughter of the fifth Earl of March, William gained control of the Home lands and adopted the name. Their descendant, Sir Alexander Home of Hume Castle, was created a baron in 1473.

The fortress changed hands a number of times between 1547 and 1651, when Cromwell's forces succeeded in destroying it. The story of that event, repeated in a rhyme known to every child in Scotland – later, much altered, it reached England – somehow lost the association with Hume along the way. Few who chanted 'I'm the King of the Castle' in childhood have any idea that it all began in this Berwickshire castle.

When Colonel Fenwick and his troops surrounded it, well equipped with cannon for the assault, the Governor – a Cockburn of Henderland – was requested to surrender the place to Cromwell. This he refused to do, and after a severe battering from the mortars a second opportunity to yield was offered him. Cockburn made reply in the famous jingle:

> I, Willie o' the Wastle,
> Stand firm in my castle;
> And a' the dogs in your toon
> Canna gar me gang doon.

In answer to this defiance Fenwick's men battered the castle to the ground. It remained a heap of stones until the Earl of Marchmont devised his curious reconstruction.

In 1804, when invasion by France seemed imminent, a watchman within the curtain walls of Hume saw what he believed to be a beacon ablaze in Northumberland, and set his own alight. This signal, repeated along the whole chain of Border watchtowers, caused militia and volunteers to muster. Walter Scott played a vigorous part in this assembly, and later wrote of it in *The Antiquary*. The incident, known as the 'False Alarm', soon came to nothing when it was discovered that the English blaze had been accidental.

Smailholm Tower

This plain, square-gabled tower of the early sixteenth century is built of blue whinstone, five storeys high with walls some seven feet thick. The entrance doorway faces south and is round-headed, made of reddish sandstone. It used to be defended by a massive iron yett, with a bolt of three-inch girth. Nine feet within the yett, on the inside of the wall, was an inner door. The apartments on first and second floors have wide fireplaces, garde-robes, and window seats of stone. In the north wall, one small window high up under the bartizan, with access by a narrow turret stair, serves when seen from below to emphasise the fact that this edifice was constructed for business and not for mere aggrandisement or romantic effect. Yet of all the Border towers it is the most picturesque and evocative. However many times it comes into view, the thrill is undiminished. It is hard to tell how much is due to the influence of Sir Walter Scott.

Smailholm Tower

For that author there can be no doubt that an early sojourn beside the tower significantly affected his future life and work. It nearly ended in tragedy. As a sickly infant he was moved from Edinburgh to his grandparents' farm of Sandyknowe at Smailholm, to see if Border air would cure the lameness and malaise from which he suffered after a serious bout of fever, now thought to have been infantile paralysis. In order not to inconvenience the family at the farm, little Wattie was sent down in the care of his nursemaid. Unknown to her employers, this young woman had become infatuated with a worthless fellow in the capital, and, resenting her enforced removal to the country, she planned to vent her spleen on the child. She went so far as to carry him up among the crags, with the intention of killing him and burying the little corpse in the peat moss. Having been deterred by some chance from her monstrous crime, she mentioned her feelings to the old housekeeper at Sandyknowe, and was promptly packed off home to Edinburgh, where she became hopelessly insane.

After this escape from a fate grim enough to provide a chapter in

157

one of his own novels, young Walter Scott began to thrive in his new Border home. Often he was wrapped in the newly-flayed skin of a sheep, a traditional specific for muscular disease, and one which I found still in use not many years ago. An aged shepherd used to carry the helpless bundle out among the rocks by Smailholm Tower, and while the man tended his flock the little boy developed what he later described to his friend Skene as 'the sort of friendship with sheep and lambs which impressed my mind with a degree of affectionate feeling towards them which lasted all my life'. The shepherd in his leisure moments entertained the child with old Border ballads, a congenial process of education continued as time went on by Walter's grandfather, Robert Scott, and by the boy's Aunt Janet.

As his health improved and his body strengthened and grew, Walter gradually managed to stand up, and then to walk and run. When he reached the age of eight he could repeat pages of history and legend by heart. He sang certain old warlike ballads with such gusto that a visiting minister said testily 'One may as well speak in the mouth of a cannon as where that child is'. Probably the handicapped bairn had been spoilt at the farm; but when Sir Walter died, two old farm servants recalled him affectionately as being 'Verra gleg at the uptak', and 'kenned ilka sheep and lamb by the headmark, as weel as ony of us'. It was Walter's greatest delight to ride pick-a-back on the shoulders of women going out to the ewe-milking among the crags behind Sandyknowe.

The scene has changed little since those days. The site is superb. Rocky outcrops and stretches of bogland interspersed with sheep walks and a brown lochan are more suggestive of the untamed West Highlands than of cultivated Border country. The most ardent and up-to-date agriculturist would not attempt to discipline this small remnant of natural wilderness. From these crags there is a vast prospect of Cheviot hills, of the triple peaks of Eildon and of wooded country rolling westwards to the fells of Teviotdale and Liddesdale. To the east lies the rich Merse farmland, and there are glimpses of sea beyond Berwick-upon-Tweed.

In this lonely spot the grim old tower stands firm, as strong as the rock of its foundation, looking fit to withstand another five centuries. Only the outer wall, or barmkin, is in a ruined state. Of the small domestic chapel that once stood within that enclosure there is no trace. Of old, when trouble threatened, flocks and herds were driven for safety to the barmkin, while the human population withdrew into the tower. Its ground floor is roofed with a stone vault as a precaution against fire, should raiders reach the interior. The spiral stair was easy to defend, and so the chief danger would have been caused by smoke, if the enemy set light to bundles of rush and straw and left them smouldering below. It was not uncommon for those taking refuge in otherwise impregnable fortresses to be smoked out like bees from a hive.

When in 1799 Walter Scott learned that Scott of Harden planned to demolish Smailholm Tower, he pleaded with this kinsman not to attempt such a piece of vandalism. A bargain was struck between the two men. If Walter wrote a ballad about Smailholm, Scott of Harden promised to spare the building. *The Eve of St John*, an eerie tale, was spun by Walter Scott to ransom the fortress he had always loved. In *Marmion* he must also have had it in mind –

> Those crags, that mountain tower,
> Which charmed my fancy's wakening hour –

although the 'mountain' is only 637 feet high.

It is of course high enough to give and receive signals warning a chain of such towers along this southern edge of the old kingdom of Scotland. A grassy knoll nearby is still called the 'watchfold', the place where beacon fires were lit. From Hume to Smailholm and Smailholm to Bemersyde the glowing fires spoke, to be taken up by Fatlips above Denholm, by Lanton and Timperdean and many more.

Smailholm Tower is best reached from the B6404 road. It lies about five miles to the north-west of Kelso and is clearly signposted. In 1950 the Earl of Ellesmere, owner of the ancient keep, put it into the care of the Ministry of Works, now the Department of the Environment, under the Secretary of State for Scotland.

For several years the tower has been undergoing restoration of a major kind. It has now been given a car-park and a custodian, a small fee being charged for admission. Opening dates are expected in the future to conform with those of the Border abbeys, but at present Smailholm is not open in winter.

Not far off, on the farmland of Brotherstone, is the 'Coo' or 'Cuthbert' stone, which commemorates the vanished steading of Wrangholm, where the saint was reared. Here he saw the vision of St Aidan, which turned Cuthbert towards the monastic life.

159

Bemersyde Tower

The Haigs of Bemersyde have been in possession of these lands since the thirteenth century, one Petrus de Haga being named in an undated charter which apparently belongs to the years between 1215 and 1220. What kind of dwelling they inhabited is not known, but there would almost certainly have been some small fortalice before the present early sixteenth-century tower was built. It dates from the Act of Parliament of 1535, which required Border chiefs to build strong towers for defence. The present upper storey is a seventeenth-century reconstruction, and the old tower has had later dwellings added at the sides; it is still habitable and in occupation by the family.

Bemersyde stands on a bank above the Tweed, rather more than a mile to northward of Dryburgh Abbey, on the road B6356. From the approach to it one may see also the top of Smailholm Tower, to north-east. Sir Walter Scott loved both of these fortresses. In 1831 he brought J. M. W. Turner to make a sketch of Bemersyde, complete with the ancient 'covin' – 'company' or 'trysting' – tree near the main doorway. Here through the centuries successive lairds had come hospitably to greet their guests. It grows near the site of the original gate in the outer barmkin wall, a first line of defence which had disappeared before Turner made his drawing. The old tree, a Spanish chestnut, is sadly decayed. In its prime it measured fifty feet in height, with a proportionately stout girth of twenty-eight feet. It is reputedly 'as old as the tower itself'.

An attractive garden round about the dwelling leads the eye gently away over sheep pastures, woodlands and sloping green banks to the river below. There is a powerful feeling of monastic calmness about this corner of what used to be the county of Berwickshire, strange to experience within sight of two warlike watchtowers. Perhaps the nearness of Melrose and Dryburgh Abbeys, together with the site of a still older foundation at Old Melrose, has something to do with it.

As a family the Haigs were not given to quiet musing at home. They fought at Stirling Bridge; they went off to the Crusades; they were at Bannockburn, Halidon Hill, and Otterburn; at Piper Dene and Flodden and Ancrum Moor.

At an early stage in their history the de Hagas of Bemersyde received, in return for their benefactions to the abbey of Dryburgh, the right to be buried inside the monastic church of St Mary, near

160

the altar. Their place of interment is in one of the north transept chapels. A wall tablet records (in Latin) that this is the place of burial of the most ancient family of Haig of Bemersyde.

Down below Bemersyde, on the opposite bank of Tweed, is the site of Old Melrose, where in the seventh century monks built their primitive huts and chapel. To this monastery went the young man from Wrangholm, who was to become Saint Cuthbert of Lindisfarne. A less sanctified legend links the monastic life on the south bank with a resident of Bemersyde. A certain monk is said to have formed an illicit attachment to a lady on the estate, which came to the ears of his spiritual superiors. The lady disappeared, and in penance for his fault the monk was required to bathe every day all the year round in a deep pool below the promontory on which the monastic buildings stood. The place is still known as 'Haly Wheel' (Holy Pool), from *Weil*, whirl or eddy.

John Russell, in his book *The Haigs of Bemersyde* published in 1881, describes what happened in the romantic language of late Victorian times.

> This penance he observed even when in winter he had to break the ice for the purpose, keeping silence all the while as to the cause of his extraordinary punishment. After his death a fearful significance was given to these mysterious ablutions for it is said that at midnight, when the moon looks fitfully through driving storm-wrack, and the torrents descend from the hills, and the swollen Tweed chafes angrily between his banks, the figure of a lady is seen to emerge with a wild shriek from the waters of the Haly Wheel, which then divide, one going towards Old Melrose and another towards Bemersyde, between which, with a second piercing shriek, the unhappy lady descends and passes out of sight.

A better-authenticated story relates to a monk named Drythelm, who imposed on himself the voluntary penance of bathing in the river fully clothed in winter, afterwards returning to his duties without changing into dry garments. Possibly some imaginative villager long ago invented the story of illicit amours in connection with Drythelm's self-imposed penance, to entertain the neighbourhood in the long winter evenings.

In monastic times, even the Haig family had to do penance for its failings. A charter of 1260 shows that Petrus de Haga granted 'half a stone of wax annually to the Abbot and Convent of Melros for certain transgressions committed against them by me and mine'. He also gave 'ten salmon, to wit 5 fresh and 5 old (preserved) for ever, to be supplied each year in Lent on the Day of Blessed St Cuthbert – 20th March'. The last witness to this document, his name spelled as 'Thomas Rimor of Ercildun' was none other than the celebrated prophet Thomas Learmonth of Earlston, who in the language of his time 'showed sundry things ere they befell'.

The fifteenth century brought a much more severe penalty to the family. John Haig, great-great-great-grandson of Petrus who gave wax and fish, spent many years of his life feuding with the Abbey and Convent of Melrose, with the result that in 1422 he was excommunicated. The affair centred on some property in an area where Bemersyde land marched with Redpath. The Abbot of Melrose claimed right of cultivation, which Haig disputed. Abbey cattle were killed or driven off, Abbey servants molested. The quarrel dragged on for years before the Church resorted to the dreadful punishment of excommunication.

Even that failed to restrain John Haig, who pursued his course without sign of repentance. So impressed and awed were the local tenantry that a saying became current: 'The Laird of Bemersyde is a living man, who both heard and saw it' – that is, the instrument of excommunication. Haig not only survived, he outlived his adversary, and the next Abbot, John of Fogo, lifted the ban. John Haig was killed fighting with the fourth Earl of Douglas against Earl Percy at Piper Dene in 1436.

His grandson, James, became embroiled in the troubles that followed the rebellion of nobles against James III at Lauder in 1486. He resigned his estates into the hands of the King, who conferred them upon James's son William – the latter having taken care to be on the King's side. Prudent fathers and sons often took different sides, hoping to keep estates in the family whichever side came out victorious. William then took to the popular Border pastime of cattle-reiving, but the spree did not last long. He was killed at Flodden in 1513. His son Robert, also a reiver, was put to the horn (outlawed) by James V, 'for entering to underly the law'. Only Robert's bravery at the Battle of Ancrum Moor in 1544 set the record straight, and he was given an honourable discharge 'of many bygone debts owing to the King'.

The Earl of Hertford, who caused such devastation throughout the Borders, wrecked the abbeys of Melrose and Dryburgh and also Bemersyde Tower, in 1545. Robert's son Andrew, who married Elizabeth McDougall, restored the tower and placed on it a stone commemorating the completion of work in 1581, carved with the initials of himself and his wife and the arms of both families. It is still visible. Andrew's heir, Robert, had an only daughter who married James Haliburton of Dryburgh, and of their union the eldest son was great-grandfather to the wife of Robert Scott of Sandyknowe. The latter is that most celebrated of grandfathers, the man who introduced the infant Walter Scott to the Borders and their lore.

Up to the time of Robert Haig's death in 1602 Bemersyde had been owned by seventeen de Hagas or Haigs. During the next 238 years there were ten more heirs, all in the direct line, ending with three Victorian sisters, who all died unmarried. In 1878 the estate passed to Colonel Balfour Haig of the Clackmannan branch, who seemed likely to be the last of his family to own Bemersyde.

Douglas Haig, the future Field-Marshal (who could trace his descent from Robert Haig, second son of the twelfth Laird of Bemersyde), was taken on a visit to the tower as a boy, and it had become a cherished memory which strengthened with the years. Here, he sometimes thought, would be the ideal place in which to end his days – a dream which had little chance of being fulfilled. As it happened, it came true seven years before his death.

In 1921, when Bemersyde was purchased from Colonel Balfour Haig's legatees and given to the first Earl Haig by the people of Scotland in gratitude for his services in World War I, Field-Marshal Lord Haig became the twenty-ninth Laird. He died in 1928 and was buried at Dryburgh Abbey. The simple headstone is similar to those placed over men who fell on many battlefields during the conflict of 1914-18.

His son, the second Earl Haig, now lives at Bemersyde with his wife and family. Nothing seems materially changed, except that visitors to the tower (which is open to the public once a year), must observe how the sword has been supplanted by the paraphernalia of painting. The second Earl Haig, who is well known as an artist, has a studio at the top of the old fortress. In the words of Thomas the Rhymer:

> Tyde what may betyde,
> Haig shall be Haig of Bemersyde

Hermitage Castle

This great fortress, 'the strength of Liddesdale', stands some twelve miles south of Hawick on a minor road which connects the

A7 Carlisle to Hawick route with the B6399 from Hawick to Newcastleton. This loneliest and grimmest of surviving Border castles is strangely named. Nothing could be further removed from cloistral calm in appearance and history than such a forbidding relic of earlier strife. The rushing hill stream, tributary of the Liddel, which runs beside the road, is now called Hermitage Water. In earlier times, before the advent of twelfth-century monasticism to the region, it was known as Marching Burn. The haughland around it was then Marching Lea. The word 'haugh' sometimes puzzles visitors. It is derived from the Norse *Hagi*, pasture. 'March' here means boundary, and an important one was delineated by the little river, or burn.

In 1180 William, a monk from the Tironensian abbey of Kelso, obtained a grant of land here for a hermitage, together with the chapel of St Mary. The remains of chapel and burial ground lie a short distance upstream from the castle. Several architectural fragments, recovered when in 1900 the Hawick Archaeological Society excavated the site, suggest a thirteenth-century date, although much masonry resembles fourteenth-century work in the castle – whose private chapel this sanctuary was destined to be. The original buildings of the twelfth-century monks have been erased by time.

John of Fordun, a fourteenth-century Scottish chronicler, suggests that in 1242 Scotland and England came to the verge of war because his nation had erected in Liddesdale a certain castle called Hermitage. Whatever the date of its inception, there was certainly a castle here by the end of the thirteenth century, which changed hands as possession of Liddesdale alternated between the two nations. Sir William Douglas, known as the Knight of Liddesdale, captured it in 1338. When he subsequently joined the English, David II granted the castle to William, afterwards first Earl of Douglas, who made sure of his tenure by killing the Knight of Liddesdale somewhere in Ettrick Forest. When the latter's widow married an Englishman (Dacre), Edward III backed the Dacre claim to Hermitage, and they retained it until late in the fourteenth century.

It seems that the oldest part of the surviving remains is probably of Dacre construction. An oblong rectangular block with towers or wings at the four corners, it resembled fortified English manor houses or semi-castellar structures dating from the fourteenth century, of which Danby Castle in the old North Riding of

Hermitage Castle

Yorkshire is a similar example. This 'Dacre' block forms the central mass of the present Hermitage Castle. It seems to have been badly damaged in the Border battles of Richard II, and was later restored and used as the core of a greatly enlarged and strengthened keep, built by the powerful Douglas clan towards the end of the fourteenth century. Later still, rectangular towers were added at the corners of the keep, that at the south west angle being larger than the others. In the sixteenth century the outer walls were pierced in various places with wide-mouthed gun loops, to take the newest form of defence.

The forbidding exterior of the place – parts of it of nineteenth-century reconstruction – at first leads the visitor to expect a more complete and habitable interior. In fact, behind the solid, well-preserved facade there is very little to be seen. The great castle is an empty shell. Remnants of newel stair, and of such domestic details as fireplaces, oven, wells, latrines and drainage may still be found, and a frightful dungeon reached by trapdoor from the prison, situated in the north east tower. Some relics of the Hermitage chapel, including a fourteenth-century grave slab carved with cross and sword, are housed in the western part of the ground floor.

Seen at close quarters, this is a disappointing fortress. Yet its magnificent setting and weird history make it memorable, and the

165

exterior creates an impression of forbidding grandeur. Possibly this would be deeper and more lasting if the interior were left unvisited.

It came into possession of the Hepburn family when James IV put Patrick, Earl of Bothwell, in charge of this vital gateway into Scotland. Like his predecessor, the Earl of Angus, Bothwell proved to be treacherous, indulging in secret diplomacy with England, and in 1540 Liddesdale and the guardian castle were annexed by the Crown. A little later, in 1542, artillery was brought here; gun-loops in the outer walls probably date from then. The Bothwells had still some hold on the castle. James, the fourth Earl, was lying inside badly wounded when Mary Queen of Scots visited him in October 1566. She rode out from Jedburgh and back there in a day, nearly fifty miles over rough moorland tracks to visit her lover.

This royal escapade created much scandal. Queen Mary was taken seriously ill as a result of the ride, and at the end of her tragic reign she was heard to cry 'Would that I had died at Jethart!'

In 1594 the fifth Earl of Bothwell was attainted. By the end of the sixteenth century, Hermitage had passed to the Scotts of Buccleuch. After that it played no part in Border history, and by the eighteenth century it had fallen into a ruinous state. It was repaired in 1820 and again in 1930, when it came into the hands of the Office of Works – now the Department of the Environment. It is open to the public all the year round, the hours being shorter in winter.

Of the legends that centre on this grim place, the most weird relates to the wicked Lord Soulis, who was accompanied by an evil familiar spirit wherever he went. Sir Walter Scott's friend, John Leyden, composed a ballad about it.

> Lord Soulis he sat in Hermitage Castle,
> And beside him Old Redcap sly –
> Now tell me, thou sprite, who art meikle of might,
> The death that I must die?

The spirit says that nothing his enemies can do will be able to overcome Lord Soulis, 'Till threefold ropes of sifted sand around thy body twine:' Seemingly Old Redcap had forgotten the existence of a master wizard, Thomas of Ercildoune, who managed to bind the wicked baron in that miraculous manner. Then it was easy to dispatch him. His end was frightful. They put him in a jacket of lead and boiled him in a brazen cauldron on the Nine Stane Rig.

According to local tradition, the Castle of Hermitage was so weighed down by the evils perpetrated within its walls that they sank partially into the ground. The shell was for long regarded with superstitious terror by inhabitants of the surrounding country. As recently as 1933, a shepherd in the Newcastleton area told the tale of how a tramp made his bed in a recess below the great eastern arch of the castle. He was so plagued by awful nightmares and phantoms that he made off at first blink of day and never went near the place again.

Another story concerns the dungeon, where in the fourteenth century Sir Alexander Ramsay of Dalhousie was thrown by Douglas the Black Knight of Liddesdale, and starved to death. Ramsay prolonged his wretched existence for a short while by eating grains that fell through into his cell from a store above. Modern masons engaged in reconstruction work broke into this vault, and there discovered by the light of torches some human bones, a saddle and rusted sword, all buried in a mouldering pile of oat husks.

The remains of Our Lady's chapel, only 200 yards upstream from the castle, provide a refreshing change of atmosphere. Here all is calm and light. Of the small building, a buttressed single chamber, little is left but some steps up to the chancel and an area of paving. The adjoining graveyard is set within a bank and ditch, and to the west there is a large earthwork. This, it is thought, may mark the site of an earlier castle. If it does, no aura of conflict has survived the advent of the monks.

Even the wild birds seem to regard this place as a sanctuary. A cock chaffinch flitted from perch to perch singing loudly at each stop, within arm's length, as I explored the relics. Below, beside the bubbling Hermitage Water, a dipper cocked an eye without sign of alarm at the human invasion. Over the hilltop rode a young shepherd, mounted on a stout garron and followed by two collies. The horrid image of De Soulis and his gruesome end, and the cruel fate of the Black Knight's prisoner, were erased by the peaceful life of these remote Border hills today.

Floors Castle

Every visitor to Kelso looks at this great chateau-like building from Rennie's bridge over the Tweed and other vantage points in the town; in fact, to view Kelso and not to see Floors is practically impossible. The policies are well wooded and surrounded by a magnificent length of walling – over five miles of it – but in spite of being so enclosed, an open sweep of parkland below the south frontage allows the castle to keep an unimpeded watch over Kelso, while the inhabitants of that cheerful place have their eyes constantly upon Floors. The first plan of which one hears, dated 1721, is commonly ascribed to Sir John Vanbrugh, who in his day was better known as a playwright. If the ascription is correct, this castle is his only building inside Scotland; although, not far off, the Ravensdowne Barracks in Berwick-upon-Tweed are also said to show his influence. He was certainly the architect of much English magnificence, including Blenheim Palace and Castle Howard.

As Professor Colvin pointed out, following some research in the Charter Room during 1965, the attribution of Floors to Vanbrugh is not documented. 'Nothing has been found to support the traditional attribution to Vanbrugh; but, as the Duke was resident in London for so many years, it is possible that he was acquainted with Vanbrugh and obtained a design from him which was worked out in detail by William Adam. On the other hand, Adam's claim to have designed the house himself cannot be lightly disregarded.' Whether Vanbrugh did or did not provide the plan of Floors, it is certain that he died before the construction had been finished. Although it was commissioned by a human peer (the first Duke of Roxburghe), Sir Walter Scott's suggestion that Floors ought to be a kingdom for Oberon and Titania is not inappropriate. Only its massive bulk is somewhat unfairylike. Perhaps Sir Walter contemplated the original castle from Kelso on an autumn day of hazy sunshine, when (even with the Victorian additions) it still manages to look ethereal.

The original house of Floors, a plain dwelling in typical Border style, stood near the present castle. The grander edifice, which may best be described as by William Adam under the influence of Vanbrugh, was envisaged by the fifth Earl and first Duke about seven years after the dukedom was created in 1704. His letters of 1711 refer to provision of 'a better house in Scotland'; but the building of Floors Castle did not begin until 1721. The structure portrayed in William Adam's *Vitruvius Scoticus* is a solid oblong block with towers at the four corners. The early Victorian additions in 'baronial style' were carried out between 1838 and 1849 by W. H. Playfair, an architect who played a part in Edinburgh's Greek

Floors Castle

Revival. He tacked on to Floors a fantastic array of pepper-pot turrets, castellated parapets and decorated water-spouts, described by Laurence Whistler as a 'coral reef of caps and finials'. To my mind they prick the skyline in inescapable reminder of the bristling spears that long ago founded and maintained the fortunes of the House of Ker. All this was done too late for Sir Walter Scott to appraise the effect, although his romantic influence and that of Abbotsford may have been partly responsible.

The Kers are said to be of Scandinavian origin, and a *de Kari*, by tradition, landed with William the Conqueror. The name of Ker appears in Scottish records early in the thirteenth century; one John Ker of Altonburn and the Forest of Ettrick in 1350 put his signature as witness to a charter. From him are descended the two houses, fierce rivals for many generations, of Cessford and Ferniehurst, with the Duke of Roxburghe now head of the former and the Marquess of Lothian (whose seat is Monteviot) of the latter branch. Sir Robert ('Habbie') Ker of Cessford became the first Earl of

Roxburghe in 1616. He took the news of Queen Elizabeth's death to James VI in 1603 and accompanied him to London, afterwards becoming Lord Privy Seal in the reign of Charles I. A century later, John, the fifth Earl of Roxburghe, helped to bring about the Parliamentary Union with England in 1707, three years after he had been created first Earl of Kelso and Duke of Roxburghe. (The final 'e' is retained in the title, although both old Roxburgh and the county have dropped it.)

For well over a century the castle he built was found adequate by his successors. The second Duke, Robert, was given an English peerage with the title of Baron and Earl Ker of Wakefield. His portrait by Allan Ramsay hangs in the dining room at Floors. His son John, who became the third Duke, spent much time at the Court of George III. He is supposed to have been enamoured of Queen Charlotte's elder sister. Unable to marry her, he took refuge in the absorbing occupation of book-collecting, and became world famous as a bibliophile. After his death these rare volumes were sold to defray the expenses of a lengthy law-suit. The men who had between them acquired the collection then formed themselves into the 'Roxburghe Club'.

The fourth Duke, a distant cousin, also left no heir, and after much disputation Sir James Innes in 1812 became the fifth Duke; from that time the family adopted the name of Innes-Ker. He fathered a son late in life, and in 1816 is said to have danced at the ensuing celebrations, footing it in the Highland Fling with the youngest guests in his eighty-first year. A fine portrait by Raeburn hangs over the library chimney-piece. His son, the sixth Duke, had the castle remodelled between 1838 and 1849 by Playfair, and entertained Queen Victoria here. The ninth Duke of Roxburghe was his great-grandson.

His mother, the late Mary, Duchess of Roxburghe, an American by birth, had an expert knowledge of antique furniture, tapestry and china. It was she who collected most of the eighteenth-century French furniture and the tapestries and porcelain now to be seen in the castle, including a splendid Brussels tapestry of the late fifteenth century, representing the Day of Pentecost. This is hanging in the anteroom. The ballroom was repanelled in fairly recent years to take some great Gobelins tapestries of the seventeenth century. The woodwork here was made by a Kelso craftsman, home-grown oak, ash, and elm being used. In this room I particularly liked an old English yellow lac cabinet, and two cream coloured T'ang hares which, although both label and catalogue described them as 'parrots', stood on the yellow cabinet more harmoniously than on the black one, where they were supposed to be. The small needleroom, gorgeously decorated by the late Duchess in crimson and white in the French eighteenth-century manner, contrasts with the cooler scheme in the pine room. Here there is hung a modern painting of Kelso by Raoul Millais, grandson of the famous Victorian artist Sir John Millais, and a portrait of the last Duchess (mother of the tenth Duke) by the younger Millais. From these windows Kelso looks so modest a place that Sir Walter Scott's reference to it as 'the most beautiful *village* in Scotland' comes immediately to mind.

On occasions such as the annual opening day of Floors Castle, (customary in the lifetime of the ninth Duke) when large numbers of people were circulating in one direction, it was difficult to retrace one's steps to take another look at some remarkable exhibit. I did manage to reappraise the Raeburn portrait of the fifth Duchess, regretting that it was not hung in the library with that of the fifth Duke by the same painter. On second thoughts, the Allan Ramsay portraits of the second Duke and Duchess (which flank the Raeburn in the dining room) are most valuable in allowing close comparison of the technique of the two artists. The superiority of Raeburn, particularly in his handling of the flesh, seems very marked; that of the fifth Duchess is amazingly sensitive and tender.

The floral decorations in all these apartments, immense bowls of lilies, carnations, sweet-peas and mixed herbaceous plants, gave an indication of the wealth of bloom to be seen outside in the formal gardens and greenhouses. These are situated to the west of the house and do not at any point take in the beautiful stretch of Tweed. Amid so much that seems designed to impress, it is refreshing to come upon a commonplace modern swimming pool, less ostentatious than many installations to be seen in the 'stockbroker belt' outside London. This asset was presumably made for the pleasure of the ninth Duke's heir, Guy David, Marquess of Bowmont and Cessford (born 1954) and his brother, Lord Robert Anthony Innes-Ker, who is five years younger.

In 1974 the ninth Duke died suddenly, to be succeeded as tenth Duke of Roxburghe by his 20-year-old son, Guy David. He inherited a home of great magnificence. The extraordinary silhouette which its turrets and pinnacles make against the sky astonishes everyone who views it freshly. It has an air of unreality, of ephemeral fantasy that puts the newcomer into the position of a young child who sees a giraffe for the first time. He cannot believe it.

In May 1975 we attended a late evening reception at the castle, following a National Trust for Scotland concert in Kelso at which Yehudi Menuhin was the soloist. Having been taken to the hall by friends who were not going on to the castle, we disengaged from the melee in the car park, stepped straight into a taxi, and arrived at Floors some distance ahead of the other guests.

Coming up the vast sweep of empty drive to that immense pile, with its array of towers, turrets, chimney-stacks and pinnacles like an alpine range pricking the moonlight sky, we found ourselves reduced to the status of matchbox toys or tiny faceless mannikins in a cartoon. For a few seconds we felt incapable of moving through a small doorway at the left-hand side of the central block, which stood open to receive guests, looking like a lamplit mousehole nibbled out of the facade. A duke might easily grow overbearing, we thought, having to keep so arrogant a dwelling in its place all the time. But the tenth Duke, by opening his castle to visitors in summer, does not have to subdue it unaided.

8

Countryside and Village

Border Countryside

E nglish agricultural workers are usually housed in rural villages. In the Scottish Borders, many of the workers' cottages are seen in barrack-like rows close to the farm steadings they serve, and often some distance from church, school and village shops. Owing to the mechanisation of farms and consequent reduction in manpower, many of these homes now stand empty. Even in districts where housing is in short supply, few townspeople care to inhabit them. Although the men can drive to their places of employment, their wives do not take kindly to isolation. The result is that farm cottages are increasingly being refurbished for the use of summer holiday-makers.

Of old, the real villages served as centres for the tradesmen who practised crafts essential to the land and those who lived by agriculture. Joiners, wheelwrights, blacksmiths, stonemasons, thatchers and slaters, mole and rabbit catchers, together with butchers, bakers, grocers, carriers and packmen, made up many a nearly self-supporting community, coupled with those who worked the local sawmills, grain mills and paper mills. Today, except for the general store and post-office, most of those occupations have dwindled and died out. Tailor and shoemaker are no more. Clothing and shoes are bought ready-made. Even repairs to footwear necessitate journeys to the nearest town.

Berwickshire, which is said to possess the largest single area of fertile lowland in Scotland, contains the best arable farms in the Borders. This undulating plain, known as The Merse, extends from the southern edge of Lammermuir to the banks of the River Tweed, its eastern boundary being the North Sea. The richness of this land today, with a wide prospect of grain and root crops, and the developing soft-fruit culture, added to a proportion of dairying, makes it hard to believe that 'Merse' means 'Marsh', and that until the eighteenth-century pioneers drained and improved it, little grew here but broom and whin.

The splendid prospect across this well-farmed land to the blue humps of the Cheviot Hills, which lie beyond the Tweed and are mostly in Northumberland, cannot be matched anywhere else in Britain. A Canadian visitor exclaimed that it was like a huge garden – 'The whole place is just a *garden*!' She had no idea that Berwickshire was so beautiful, and must tell the folks back home to visit it. To my glum comment, that they had better hurry if they wished to see it in undefiled condition, as the Electricity Board planned to run a line of gigantic 400Kv pylons right across the Merse into England, the visitor said 'They must be mad; Scotland would be mad to allow that!' The problem is, how to prevent such insane spoliation by the juggernaut popularly known as 'Progress'.

The agricultural revolution, which began earlier in England, had little effect on the Scottish Borderland until about 1760, although a few enterprising landowners introduced new methods before that date. In Berwickshire as early as 1730 a Swinton of Swinton drained, marled and enclosed his lands, and in 1746 Lord Kames carried out extensive improvements on his estate near by. An Edinburgh lawyer with practical ideas, he introduced turnips and cultivated the potato on ploughland. By 1750 he had begun to sow clover and improved grasses. Fields were marled to remedy lime deficiency, until in 1760 lime became available for the purpose.

Reclaiming the wet Merse land was heavy work. It was not only boggy, it was also full of stones. In some places as much as 1,000 tons per acre had to be removed. The larger stone was used for building dry dykes (walls) – a craft which is still being carried on, albeit by a diminishing number of dykers. A picture of two Selkirk men repairing a dyke in the hills gives some idea of the tough nature of this lonely work, and the skill needed to make walls capable of withstanding gales and blizzards. In order to drain the Merse, channels had to be excavated by hand, there being no mechanical aids at that time. Such drainage boosted land values enormously. It is recorded that some fields bought in 1787 for three pounds an acre, fetched as much as thirty-six pounds an acre after improvement. We do not know how much the labour cost, but eighteenth-century farm workers toiled long hours for a pittance.

The later years of that century brought new implements to

Dry-stane dykers

relieve men from some of the heavier jobs. A local inventor, James Smail, was born in 1740 at Upsettlington, near Ladykirk. He removed to Blackadder Mount in 1763 and put his original mind to the construction of a swing-plough. Deep ploughing, which broke up the subsoil, then began to replace the old-style shallow cultivation. Next came the power-driven thresher. Year by year more capital was invested in farming.

Mr R. L. Forrest of Mersington, who began farming in the Borders just before World War II, has carried mechanisation to lengths then undreamed of. Writing in a farming journal of the 1970s, he described the modern dairy farm as 'a highly sophisticated combination of human stockmanship and engineering technology'. The ration for each cow is computerised, and by pressing buttons whose numbers relate to those stamped on the cows' flanks, the correct ration for each animal is dispensed to the trough in front of the beast during milking.

A Scottish invention of even greater ingenuity provides each cow with an electronic key to its own food locker, in which the correct ration for the day has been placed. This enables the animal to release and eat its computerised food when it feels hungry. Cows find no difficulty in working this system, which suggests – as those of us who have worked with them already knew – that they are highly intelligent creatures.

That invaluable asset – timber – is found for the most part farther west in the Border country. Most farmers in the Merse prefer to clear-fell and sell their trees, and very little replanting is done. In Berwickshire, were it not for the big estates, where in policies surrounding such mansionhouses as The Hirsel, Ayton and Duns Castles, Paxton, Wedderburn, Manderston, Ladykirk and Kimmerghame, the landowners cling to their shelter-belts, lowland Berwickshire might be denuded of trees. The Countryside Commission makes a few grants for tree-planting schemes in villages and picnic areas, these as a rule consisting of small groups of ornamental varieties rather than the traditional long-lived hardwoods.

The Forestry Commission plays a small but useful part in Berwickshire. Young plantations on the eastern shoulder of the Lammermuirs are part of Duns Forest. At Ayton Castle there are some 400 acres of well-managed woodland, and 600 acres on the Duns Castle estate, which contains a Nature Reserve. North of Kelso there are the fine woods – much beech as well as Scots pine – of Mellerstain, now no longer part of Berwickshire. There are also some upland woods on the Marchmont estate near Greenlaw, and solid shelter-belts of conifers protecting farms in Lauderdale up to the 1,000 ft contour. In Roxburghshire, the Floors Castle estate has 1,500 acres of woodland.

In medieval times the great Border monasteries had a disastrous effect on the original forests of Jed and Ettrick. Much of the monastic income derived from exports of wool. As flocks increased, the large numbers of sheep continually grazing and browsing meant that seedling trees were removed and no regeneration could take place. Over a long period these ancient forests were turned into treeless pasture. Most of the Tweedside woods now seen are the outcome of planting during the past two hundred years, with Sir Walter Scott as one of the keenest pioneers in this work.

Between Selkirk and Caddonfoot lies the national forest of Yair Hill, covering 2,300 acres, while a little upstream there are 6,400 acres of the Elibank and Traquair Forests. A more recent project, Cardrona, has 1,800 acres planted in 1935. Timber houses have been provided here for forestry workers. At Glentress, two miles east of Peebles on the A72 road, the Forestry Commission in 1919 began a scheme of afforestation and land settlement in cooperation with the Department of Agriculture. The grouped smallholdings, each of some thirty acres, were designed to give employment to ex-servicemen after World War I. The amenity value of this forest is being developed. There are forest walks skilfully laid out to suit different tastes and capabilities, with seats, picnic areas and an information centre. Eighty-six different kinds of birds have been recorded here, together with fox, otter, badger, roe deer and red squirrel.

Bowhill, the Duke of Buccleuch's Border estate, has already been mentioned. It extends to about 1,400 acres and includes a sawmill and forest nursery. On the upper reaches of the Tweed, a thousand acres of woodland at Dawyck reach up the slopes of Pykestone Hill and Scawd Law to a height of 1,500 feet. Philiphaugh, seat of the Strang-Steel family, brings woodland close to the town of Selkirk. The greatest tracts of forest are found in remote country south east and south west of Hawick. Wauchope Forest, 17,000 acres, forms part of the enormous Border Forest Park, much of which lies on the English side of the Border.

Conservation of historic buildings, apart from the great ruined abbeys in government hands, and inhabited castles and famous houses, such as Abbotsford, Mellerstain and Traquair, has not been pursued with much enthusiasm, owing mainly to lack of finance. Remains of sturdy old tower houses and watchtowers and disused mills are too often used as handy sources of stone for road bottoming and walls. The Department of the Environment has regulations about 'listed' buildings, but is short of cash to help preserve them. Hutton Castle on the Whiteadder is no more than a shell, since Sir William Burrell's art collection and many fittings were removed to be re-housed in a special gallery in Glasgow; Mordington House has been demolished; Nisbet House when last I saw it was uninhabited; Broomhouse was said to be past preserving.

Farther west, conservationist groups have been more success-ful. The remains of the cottage at Foulshiels where Mungo Park was born have been restored; The National Trust for Scotland cares for Turret House in Kelso; Galashiels Arts Club, which purchased Old Gala House in 1949, not only puts the premises to good use as a community centre, but has greatly enhanced it by uncovering a fine painted ceiling of the early seventeenth century. The house belongs to six different periods, with a square tower on the west side dating back, it is thought, to the fifteenth century. The painted ceiling is shown by the caretakers for a small charge.

Older artefacts, if not preserved, have been studied, mapped and recorded. On the western outskirts of Galashiels there is a sign marking the position of the Catrail or Picts Dyke. Professor Veitch interpreted the name as compounded from *Cad*, battle, and *treyle*, to turn, meaning 'battle-turning' or defence. This barrier starts from the broch at Torwoodlee, north-west of Galashiels, and runs regardless of rivers, hilltops and precipices for some fifty miles, crossing the Tweed, Ettrick and Yarrow rivers. It terminates on the slopes of Peel Fell in the Cheviots. The Catrail is a ditch with a double mound, one on either side. Although it is now obliterated in many places, it may often be traced by a lighter shade of grass, or longer-lying snow in winter. On Bartholomew's half-inch 'Tweed-dale' map of 1969, the name Catrail is shown down at Tushielaw on Ettrick Water; but there is not any link between that section and Peel Fell. The Picts Dyke will no doubt cause argument for centuries to come.

The subject of battles long ago takes us across country to a farmhouse called Crosshall near the village of Eccles, where in a field with the gruesome name of Dead Riggs there stands a splendid monument which has received too little notice in books about the Borders. This round-headed cross is nearly fifteen feet high, a monolith of great antiquity and considerable presence. The lack of any inscription makes its date and purpose a matter for conjecture. It is carved with a vigorous design of a male figure, a hound, a double-handed sword and several crosses. It is no doubt a memorial of some bloody battle, as the name of the field suggests.

Eccles was for centuries the home of a large nunnery, whose nominal Prioress after the Reformation disposed of its lands to Alexander Hamilton. Some people assume that the great cross had a connection with the convent. The only link on record is the attempt by an eighteenth-century local landowner to have it moved to the garden of his mansion, Eccles House, which occupies the site of the former nunnery. The workmen who struggled to raise the cross found the shaft going so deep that they were unable to reach its foundations. In the end they abandoned the task.

This magnificent cross, now listed as an Ancient Monument, is well worth a visit. From the A699 road out of Eccles towards Berwick-upon-Tweed, turn left on the minor road just beyond the village and proceed for about a mile in a north-westerly direction.

N

Eccles Cross

The cross stands near an intersection of narrow lanes, within sight of the Crosshall farmhouse.

Another relic which must be visited is the massive Iron Age broch of Edinshall, which stands on the north-east slope of Cockburn Law, four miles north of Duns on the A6112 road.

Commemorative stones of later date include one in the form of a Roman altar, set beside the B6361 road between Leaderfoot and Newstead. It marks the site of a vast Roman camp – Trimontium – built in AD 79 by Agricola. This covered an area three times the size of Chesters on the Roman Wall in Northumbria. A large collection of relics from Trimontium is housed in the National Museum of Antiquities in Edinburgh. Another stone erected in modern times stands at the roadside near Eildon, in the same district. It perpetuates the legend of Thomas the Rhymer, who by the Eildon Tree met the Queen of the Fairies and went off with her for seven long years.

A simple obelisk to the poet James Thomson (1700-1748), author of the long poem 'The Seasons' and of the more popular words sung to 'Rule, Britannia', stands on the green slope of Ferniehill near the village of Ednam where he was born. From it may be seen a taller column – 150 feet high – on Peniel Heugh. This was erected in 1815 and bears the inscription:

To the Duke of Wellington and the British Army, William Kerr VI Marquis of Lothian and his Tenantry, dedicate this monument, XXX June MDCCCXV.

At Denholm in Roxburgh, a village planned in the eighteenth century for a community of hand-weavers, there is a memorial to the scholar, orientalist and poet John Leyden, who was born here in 1775. The monument erected on Denholm village green in 1861 – fifty years after Leyden's death – looks like a humbler edition of the Scott monument in Edinburgh. The single-storeyed thatched cottage of the shepherd who fathered this extraordinarily gifted son has been well preserved and bears a plaque. It stands beside the green.

The mercat (market) cross is a feature of many Border villages and towns. Melrose and Peebles have retained good examples in their town centres, while Duns moved its fine cross from the Market Square in 1816 to make room for a town hall. It was re-erected in 1897 as part of Queen Victoria's Diamond Jubilee celebrations, on a secluded site within the public park.

The villages of Cockburnspath, Coldingham, Ancrum and Swinton all have well-preserved mercat crosses, the two last happily placed on their respective village greens. It is often assumed that such pillars are descendants of the single 'standing stones' of earlier cultures. In medieval times, antique pillars of stone were often inscribed with the Christian cross symbol. The examples mentioned here are mostly of post-reformation date, and are crowned with heraldic devices and sundials, but bear no Christian crosses, in spite of being designated 'mercat crosses'.

When few people were able to read or write, it was customary to set the seal on a bargain or contract by the act of touching the mercat cross. Merchandise used to be displayed round the base, which was usually a flight of shallow stone steps. From these, royal proclamations were cried, burgh officials chosen and named, local news given out and offenders awarded due punishment. Before the Reformation, Saints' Day processions began and ended at the real crosses, and today's Common Riding cavalcades often perpetuate that old custom.

A living monument, in regular use, and a noticeable feature of the lower reaches of the Tweed some ten miles west of Berwick, is the little church of Ladykirk. It stands up above the river, looking down at the village of Norham across in England, with its much larger church and immense ruined castle, poised in alert confidence, a bantam cockerel among turkeys.

It is there as a memorial to the occasion in 1500 when King James IV of Scotland was nearly drowned in a steill (salmon pool) of the river near Norham Ford. In gratitude for his escape the king vowed to build a church in honour of the Virgin Mary 'which will never suffer harm by fire or by flood'. The work was entrusted to Sir Patrick Blackadder, kinsman to the Archibishop of Glasgow, the sum of £483 being paid over to him for 'the Kirk of Steill'.

A good example of the late pointed period of Scottish Gothic architecture, it is cruciform with short transepts and an apsidal east end. The transepts also have apsidal terminations. There is a remarkable barrel-vaulted stone-tiled roof, and many buttresses to cope with its weight. Until the nineteenth century there were no timbers in this building, not even wooden seats, but today the congregation does not sit upon stone benches.

The upper part of the tower was rebuilt in 1743 with a cupola by William Adam. The church is a familiar landmark to residents in east Berwickshire, visible for miles across the open landscape of the

Merse. The old Ladykirk Fair used to be held at a place known as Fairfield, near the farmhouse. From the minister's glebe Sir Walter Scott and J. M. W. Turner obtained a splendid view of Norham Castle, and Turner painted a picture of the scene.

Chirnside

This large village, originally little more than one long street straggling along a windy ridge (highest point some 500 feet above sea-level), is now spilling down the southern slope and increasing its population more rapidly than any other village in Berwickshire. Since 1973 the old-established paper mill, which had become unprofitable and almost defunct, has been rejuvenated by an American group for the production of non-woven paper (used for tea-bags and similar purposes), in place of the high quality woven papers for which it was famed in the past. Council estates are being rapidly extended to house employees who come from all over Britain to work for Dexters, the new owners of Chirnside paper mill.

In spite of Americanisation – an event which has caused some cynic to re-name the place 'Dexterville' – members of old Berwickshire families still make up a fair proportion of the inhabitants. There are people today who carry in their hearts such sentiments as these, expressed by a long-dead native named Robert Mennon:

> Chirsit, dear old Chirsit,
> > the toon of fightin' fame,
> Ne'er conquered by the raiders,
> > oor birthplace and oor hame.
> The toon o' bonnie lassies
> > and men o' richt gude will,
> Wha'd fight and dee for Chirsit,
> > the village on the hill.

Like most patriotic places, it prefers artistic licence to strict historical accuracy. This Border country has been overrun times without number.

During long centuries of strife, Chirnside was ringed by sturdy peel towers and keeps, and to the north it had also the natural protection given by a five-mile stretch of bogland, Billie Mire. This had only one safe crossing, known as 'Causey (Causeway) Bank'. Many a benighted invader must have come to grief in that treacherous area. In a neighbouring bog, south of the Whiteadder, the French knight known as Sieur de la Beauté (sometimes Anthony de la Bastie) was unhorsed in 1517. During the minority of James V, the Duke of Albany appointed the Frenchman Warden of the Eastern Marches, a move so unpopular with the men of the Merse that they waited for an opportunity to despatch their new Warden. A dispute started between Home of Wedderburn and the Sieur de la Beauté, during which the latter had the worst of the encounter. He and his party were put to flight, and the Warden's horse stuck fast in a bog north of Duns. The rider made off on foot, and near Broom House Tower, Home came up with him and using a great Ferrara sword cut his head off at a stroke. The saga of de la Beauté is told with many variations. His real name was D'Arcy. A cairn marked the site of his death in 'De la Beauté's Field'; later on a monument was erected near the place, with the story inscribed upon it.

At one period the causeway over Billie Mire passed near a little knowe, or knoll, noted for the luxuriant growth of yellow broom which crowned it. By old tradition this had been a favourite haunt of the Fairies. When John Knox began his ministry, the little people took to their heels and were never seen again. Who could blame them? The persistence of folk-memory, which has often been remarked on by students of rural life, is exemplified by a story current hereabouts of an old man who, in Victorian days, told Dr Henderson how the Fairies used to come out from an opening in the side of the knowe, all beautifully clad in green, and led by a piper playing music which enchanted those who heard it. He spoke with conviction suggestive of an eye-witness account.

The beautiful but useless Fairies seem to have been less common in the Borders than the more homely and practical Brownies, of which race the Brownie of Bodesbeck was reputed to be the last seen in Ettrick Forest. One night the lady of the house left him a piece of money, placed near his usual dish of milk. Gifts of money or clothing were taken by Brownies as a sign of dismissal. This one was heard wailing 'Farewell to bonny Bodesbeck', and never came to work there again. Dr Henderson of Chirnside recorded a story about the Brownie of Cranshaws in Lammermuir. He took umbrage because someone criticised the way he had mowed a field. He stamped to and fro, carrying away the grain harvest to scatter it over a near-by crag. As he did so he was heard to say:

> It's no weel mowed! It's no weel mowed!
> Then it's neer tae be mowed by me again;
> I'll scatter it ower the Raven's stane,
> And they'll hae some wark ere it's mowed again.

Before the land was drained for agriculture, another great bog stretched away south of Chirnside from Bluestone Ford – now a popular picnic place – to Ninewells House. A causeway known as 'Haud Gate' (keep to the road) crossed this mire from the Allanton road near the sawmill. 'Gate' was originally 'gait', as mentioned in connection with the streets called Marygate and Castlegate in Berwick-upon-Tweed; but ever since Sir Walter Scott used 'gate' that spelling has been accepted. On the north of Chirnside there was once a great cairn, and to this the place owes its name. The Statistical Account of 1799 mentions that the first syllable, 'Chirn', derived from Erse, was then given the pronunciation 'Shirn' by natives. In his *Scenes of Boyhood* the indefatigable Dr Henderson writes that up to the eighteenth century a monument survived on high ground to the north near Harelaw. *Haar* in ancient British meant stone of remembrance; 'hare-stones' were usually monolithic memorials, not piled cairns.

The doctor wrote of Chirnside Church: 'It is as old as the Saxon Heptarchy and the west door may be part of the original.' Most authorities now believe it to be Norman. The building has been considerably mauled by restorers, the last alterations having been effected in 1876, at a time when little respect was paid to the historical aspect of church architecture. A defensive tower at the west end had been removed over a century earlier. The west door, together with a tablet of 1572 inscribed *Helpe the pur*, and a sundial – which is probably older than the Latin inscription dated 1816 – are about all one can discover of interest. Drummond Gauld interprets the motto *Hoc age dum lumen est* as 'Work while it is day'; both inscription and interpretation are common enough in England. Long ago a mason of Chirnside specialised in the fashioning of sundials, and there are a number in the district. His name was Dunbar, but as he did not sign his work it cannot be identified.

The churchyard of Chirnside is visited by many people on account of the grave of Jim Clark, the racing driver, who belonged to a local farming family. He has been given a clock-tower as a monument in the village street, and there is a room exhibiting souvenirs of his remarkable career in Newtown, Duns. Near Chirnside church one may also see a splendid doocot, scheduled as an Ancient Monument by the Department of the Environment. It has a conical roof, with a central aperture, and a dividing ledge at ten feet.

Chirnside, as a barony, had the privilege of an annual Fair, held on the last Thursday in November – a late season which suited the need of arable farmers for its old staple product, the hempen sack used mainly for corn. Creels woven from osiers were also made in the village. Women, bearing these on their backs, used to cart heavy burdens of dung out to the fields. Wintry conditions and a bleak exposure at the site did not deter local people from attending Chirnside Fair, where the entertainment offered latterly by merry-go-round and sideshow vied with stalls for such edible delights as sweetie mice, gingerbread men and Alie Ferguson's treacle toffee. Among more lasting goods on sale were bonnets and hats, haberdashery and Blythe's crockery.

A more regular form of relaxation, the game of quoits, can be traced back in history to the discus throwing of classical times. A pitch was usually between fifteen and twenty yards long, and the quoits were fashioned by the local blacksmith in weights to suit individual requirements. A very stalwart man of 'Chirsit' had one of these iron rings weighing no less than fourteen pounds – double the average. This was a wholly masculine recreation. Women were probably too hard-worked at home to play games, anyhow; but both sexes found time to visit the chalybeate healing spring in Bite-about Wood on quarter-days. This 'Virtue' Well was believed to purge worries as well as diseases of the body. People would walk round it three times *deiseil* (sunwise), throw in a coin, drink of the pure water, and leave a scrap of clothing tied to a bush to symbolise the cares they had cast off.

The philosopher David Hume, who was born in Edinburgh, belonged to the Chirnside family of Ninewells. A later and lesser-known philosopher, the local doctor (George Henderson) already mentioned, also enjoyed gifts as poet and antiquarian and had a good knowledge of natural history. This interesting character was born in 1800 in his father's farmhouse of Little Billie, two miles from the village. The name Billie is the Celtic *baile*, a dwelling-place; local people who believe that no Celtic influences exist hereabouts should think again. George Henderson obtained the Licence of the Royal College of Surgeons in 1829, and thereafter practised in Chirnside until his death in 1864. Only one of his six children grew to manhood, the others having died in infancy. The surviving son Robert, who lived until 1915, spent his days in Chirnside as chemist and Registrar. A. G. Bradley mentions a visit paid to Robert's home, in his book *The Gateway of Scotland*.

Dr Henderson was a founder-member of the Berwickshire Naturalists' Club, and contributed several articles to early volumes of its history. He published *Scenes of Boyhood and Other Poems* in 1840, and *The Popular Rhymes, Sayings and Proverbs of the County of Berwick* in 1856. He left behind unpublished manuscripts and two volumes of commonplace books. These writings are mentioned by Mr William S. Mitchell in Volume XXXIX Part 1 (1971) of the Club's history, and by A. G. Bradley. We have not been told where they are lodged. Another local practitioner of the nineteenth century, Dr McWatt, became an authority on plants, particularly the primrose and primula; his book on the subject may be found in the Duns library. The Edrom Nurseries near Coldingham, one of the most attractive nursery gardens in the country, for many years propagated some of Dr McWatt's plants. My catalogue shows 'Dr McWatt's Cream' offered for sale by this nursery in 1978.

The famous nineteenth-century gardener Robert Fortune was born in 1812, son of a farm worker living in a row of cottages known as Blackadder 'Town' near Chirnside. After school days at Edrom he served his apprenticeship at Kelloe, before moving on to the Royal Botanic Gardens in Edinburgh and then, in 1840, to the Royal Horticultural Society's London Gardens – at Chiswick. He began his plant-hunting under the auspices of that Society, which sent him to Hong Kong in 1843. In 1848 and 1852 he went again to the Far East, for the East India Company, in connection with the introduction of China tea into India. Among many established garden favourites which Fortune brought home to brighten our gardens, the hardy Winter Jasmine is now so familiar that many people regard it as a native of Britain. The old favourite 'Bleeding Heart' (*Dicentra spectabilis*), which was at one time a popular window-plant in cottages, and the 'Japanese Anenome', popular with our grandparents, together with Weigela, Cryptomeria, Winter-flowering Honeysuckle and much else, were collected by Robert Fortune, the boy from Blackadder.

Cockburnspath with Oldhamstocks

If you inquire, as I did, which member of the Cockburn family made a path here, you may be told that the name is a corruption of the earlier Cockbrandspath or Coldbrandspath. My informant could not say what that signified. Perhaps it matters little, seeing that in the Scottish Borders today everyone calls it Co'path. Mr Thomas White, a native who had farmed here all his life and given long and valuable service to his birthplace as well as to the county, told me that in his young days the population was very much larger. The small harbour at the foot of the cliff (Cove) which forms part of the parish, had at that time a thriving fishing industry. From this picturesque hamlet between forty and fifty children trooped up the narrow lane to attend school in Co'path. Cultivation of the arable land was carried out by bands of workers, male and female, who toiled for long hours before the business of agriculture had been mechanised. They too sent large families of children to the school. Now there is only one pupil from Cove at school and numbers from the village are greatly reduced. Because of its position at the northern tip of Berwickshire, youngsters above primary grades have to travel south to Berwick or Eyemouth to continue their schooling, although Dunbar, which is in East Lothian, is less than half the distance away. Under the new regionalisation scheme Co'path might have crossed the line. After much discussion the village elected to stay with Berwickshire and the Borders Region.

It is an attractive village, constructed largely of local pink-grey stone, with a spacious square at its heart and a mercat cross of 1503 carved with the Tudor rose and the thistle – symbols of England and Scotland; for lands around Co'path formed part of the dowry of Queen Margaret, sister of Henry VIII, when she came north to marry Scotland's James IV. There is so much shelter here, given by spreading trees which seem to wrap up the houses against the onslaughts of *haar* and chilly winds off the North Sea, that it requires little effort to imagine oneself down in the kinder climate of Devon or Somerset. This snug, placid character is in marked contrast to the hard-bitten look of most places on a tough coastal region, and the inhabitants seem friendly and relaxed. Included in the parish is the still more venerable village of Oldhamstocks, a few miles inland.

In the early years of this century, the last of the Halls of Dunglass (owner of both Co'path and Cove) had an autocratic way with his tenants, and liked to be his own factor. At one time the fishermen's cottages at Cove were in a sorry state of disrepair, with rain dripping through many a worn-out roof. The occupants decided to write individual letters of complaint to the Laird, all posted at the same time. The Laird at once visited the fishing cove, and toured the cottages inquiring at each how many leaks had been troubling the occupants. With a note of the total in his hand, he then went to the Co'path joiner and delighted that honest craftsman with a large order for oaken tubs. When completed, these were delivered to the homes of the Cove fishermen, to be placed beneath the holes in their roofing.

By far the oldest domestic structure in Co'path is known today as 'Sparrow Castle', and may be found beside a small lane which leads downhill from the post-office. Built by Sir George Douglas in 1547, after his older tower had become uninhabitable, it was subsequently acquired by the King and in 1594 given to John Arnott, Provost of Edinburgh, whose son built the Arnott vault at the east end of the church. Sparrow Castle has outlasted many changes of hand. The Halls of Dunglass were among its former owners – Sir John Hall possessed it in 1694. It fell into disrepair and many of its stones were used for other purposes. In the years of depression after the Great War, what remained of this edifice was used as a hostel for the bands of destitute men who tramped the roads in search of work. In our own time the ancient relic has been bought 'for a song' by a returned exile, restored, and is once again used as a dwelling house.

Other ruins have fared less well. The now roofless chapel of St Helen, built about 1190, was for two centuries a vicarage in the hands of the Prior of Durham. In 1444 it was consigned by Papal mandate to the Priory of Coldingham. David Home ministered here after the Reformation, and the parish ('Old Cambus') was united to Co'path in 1610, St Helen's remaining in use until 1650. Cromwell's troops caused this venerable church savage destruction, and it is now a ruin, where, once a year, a service was held to remind people of its long record of Christian worship. Tower Castle, site of a fortress since the twelfth century, will be found near the Tower

Bridge to seaward of the A1. Until 1435 the tower and surrounding lands belonged to the Earls of March. After that they were vested in the Crown and subsequently formed part of Queen Margaret's dowry.

Co'path has what must be a rare – if not unique – claim to notice in the fact that its approaches cross no fewer than four bridges. The West Road Bridge dates from the late eighteenth century, the Railway Bridge is mid-Victorian (*circa* 1850), the New Road Bridge was built in the 1930s and the Sea Road Bridge is of ancient construction; nobody quite knows how old it is. The house of Dunglass, situated on the Edinburgh side of the Dunglass Burn, is outwith the County of Berwickshire. In his book *The Gateway of Scotland* (1912) A. G. Bradley said that the manuscript of Scott's *Bride of Lammermoor* was kept at Dunglass. It is not there now. The modern house is built on the site of an important castle, originally possessed by the Home family. Sir George Douglas surrendered it in 1547 to Somerset, whose chronicler (Dr Patten) described the Scots garrison as 'Twenty-one sober soldiers, all so apparelled and appointed that I never saw such a bunch of beggars coming out of one house in my life. Yet it would surely have rued any good housewife's heart to have beholden the great unmerciful murder that our men made of a brood of geese, and good laying hens that were slain there that day, which the wives of the town had penned up in holes in the stables and cellars of the castle ere we came'.

Somerset razed the castle; but the Homes erected a bigger one, and entertained James I there on his journeying to England with retinue. During the Covenanters' resistance to Charles I in 1640, Lord Haddington occupied Dunglass. He was blown up with most of his friends by the explosion of the powder magazine. It is thought that an English page-boy, in revenge for slighting remarks made by the Earl about England, ignited the powder. Battles over this stretch of country – where the deep wooded denes, cut by burns running to the sea, formed the last defences of the open road to Edinburgh – have been too numerous to mention here. In some of the denes are splendid oaks, and at Dunglass, beeches of fine stature. Dr Patten described Pease Dean in graphic words:

> So steepe be these banks on eyther side, and so depe to the bottom, that who goeth straight downe shall be in daunger of tumbling, and the commer-up so sure of puffynge and payne; for remedy whereof the travellers that way have used to pass it by paths and footways leading

189

slopwise; of the number of which paths they call it somewhat nicely ye Peaths.

The interesting little fifteenth-century collegiate church of Dunglass, now used only once a year, is situated a mile to the north of Cockburnspath. It may be reached from the main drive (entrance beside a lodge in the hamlet of Bilsdean), and is seen in a peaceful wooded setting above one of the deep denes which so sorely tested invaders in the past.

The present parish church of Co'path, in part pre-Reformation (two gable-ends and most of the tower), was much restored in the nineteenth century. The Arnott vault, built solely for private burial and never part of the church, has a remarkable roof of stone slabs. Also noteworthy is the curious round tower, thirty feet high, which is joined to the west end of the church. With walls only fifteen inches thick, it seems unlikely that it ever served as a stronghold, although it may have been a watchtower. There are also traces of former windows visible in the west gable, and an unusual sundial. From the rear of the pleasant and busy little Cockburnspath Hotel, situated beside the A1, three ogee-shaped windows in the circular tower, two 'eyes' above and a central 'mouth' below, have the appearance of a sinister inhuman face peering over the churchyard wall. This church, originally a chapelry of Oldhamstocks, now has the latter depending on it. The joint parishes cover some thirty-five square miles and are situated in different counties, Oldhamstocks being in East Lothian. Travellers who decide to spend a day, or a week-end or longer, here in Co'path on the way to or from Edinburgh will find much to enjoy.

The small, hidden village of Oldhamstocks is also worth a visit. The name, of Anglo-Saxon origin, means 'a place of old habitation'. It is pronounced with the second syllable accented. Although it seems secluded, it is only a few miles from the A1 with its endless chain of 'long vehicles' and speeding cars, and the main railway line from Newcastle running close to it as Berwickshire gives way to East Lothian. The village has given its name to a burn which flows into that of Dunglass before the swift waters run down to the sea through a splendid wooded gorge. This is one of the comparatively few Scottish villages to have a green at its heart. Ancrum and Denholm in Roxburgh and Gavinton, Swinton and Polwarth in Berwickshire are others in the Border country. Many Scots villages are utilitarian places, a kind of ancient and modern ribbon development, with few concessions to visual pleasure. The

190

discovery of comely examples is all the more delightful by contrast.

In an article published by *The Farmers Weekly* in April 1950 the late Mr Thomas White, JP, of Pathhead gave an interesting account of old days and ways in Oldhamstocks – whose name, although as lengthy as Cockburnspath, has never been abbreviated, it seems. It is an agricultural parish, with rich Dunbar red soil at its north-east end and poorer soil on the rising land which merges into heathy moorland on Lammermuir. Before the fields were enclosed in the latter part of the eighteenth century it was customary to divide the land in strips among the tenantry. Of old, during summer afternoons, it was habitual for farm servants to gather thistles and other weeds from the cornfields to feed work horses during the night – the only green food the poor beasts got while in stables. When the harvest had all been brought home, horses were turned loose on stubble to find what sustenance they could. This was known as 'long halter time'.

After the enclosures were brought about, each farm became a self-contained unit with its own house and offices. A long period of prosperity followed the adoption of a crop rotation similar to that practised in Norfolk. After some years the potato crop increased in size and importance, for it was observed that where this food had been made available to farm workers and their families they were no longer afflicted by ague. Soon Oldhamstocks received a market charter, and then a mercat cross was set up on the village green – where two great fairs were held each year, in July and October. Stock and merchandise from all over East Lothian and the east of Berwickshire were brought to these gatherings. The population of the village (498 in 1791), had increased to 725 by 1820. Among the residents were three wheelwrights, three blacksmiths, seven weavers, five millers, two shoemakers, a tailor and a saddler.

The parish possessed three schools, where extra courses in geometry, book-keeping and navigation were available for the fee of one guinea for each. This, of course, was over and above the usual Three Rs. The ancient church attracted men of considerable learning as ministers. It was well attended. Shepherds from outlying farms looked to their flocks on the way to service, and it was common to see well-trained dogs sitting quietly at their masters' feet in the pews. The chief inn, a hostelry with the strange name of Cromwell's Hall, carried on a thriving trade with drovers, tinkers and pedlars. On fine summer evenings the younger folk danced outside it on the green to the music of local fiddlers.

Little by little the import of cheap foodstuffs – especially meal – upset the economy of this agricultural parish, and farming switched from arable cultivation to permanent leys. As jobs on the land dwindled, the labouring population declined, while mass-produced clothing, footwear, oatmeal and flour put local craftsmen and millers out of business. Only inscribed gravestones now provide us with evidence that so much varied activity went on here in the past. The annual fairs, no longer required, died out. A pathetic remnant of the mercat cross is still preserved in the manse garden to remind us of them. Cromwell's Hall is no more, and the legend that Oliver Cromwell stayed the night here, saying afterwards that he slept as soundly as if he had rested in Abraham's bosom, may be forgotten by the next generation. The good stone-built school has long ceased to accommodate its earlier roll of 154 pupils. Like many another village, Oldhamstocks has turned itself into a mixture of holiday haunt and place of retirement for an ageing population.

The name of one Oldhamstocks family has been perpetuated throughout the musical world. John Broadwood followed his father's trade of joiner in the village until ambition spurred him, at the age of twenty-nine, to leave his birthplace for London. Here in 1761 he obtained work with a Swiss harpsichord-maker, Burkhard Tschudi, at an address in Great Pulteney Street.

Following the best tradition of successful young men, he married the daughter of his employer and in 1773 was taken into partnership. Succeeding Mr Tschudi as sole proprietor in 1782, John, together with his brother Thomas Broadwood and his son James, directed the piano-making firm known since 1807 as Broadwood and Sons. He died in 1812, and in 1854 his descendants gave a belfry and bell to the little church at Oldhamstocks.

Swinton with Simprim and Fogo

Swinton, probably Sweyn's Town in distant centuries, is popularly supposed to derive its name from the herds of swine which used to roam the district. The family of Swinton of Swinton, still resident on its ancestral lands, is one of the oldest in Scotland. It is believed to have acquired property in reward for the service given by Alan de Swinton in hunting down ravenous wild boars and ridding the countryside of their presence. Edulf de Swinton received confirmation of his title to the land from Malcolm Canmore, having helped him to recover the Scottish throne. This charter of 1060 is still possessed by the Swintons.

On Swinton village green the mercat cross of 1769 bears at the top three time-worn sundials and the Swinton coat-of-arms, a wild boar, placed on the north face of the cap. An Inspector of Ancient Monuments told me that it used to be the custom to put the landowner's arms facing the direction of his family seat. As Swinton House is more or less west of the cross, I thought this 'signposting' less than accurate. It was pointed out that another Swinton property, Kimmerghame House, lies northward of the village green. It now seems that the present Swinton House stands on the site of a much older dwelling, so the placing of the arms is debatable. An ancestor, Ernulf Swinton, was knighted by David I in 1140. This was the first recorded knighthood to be bestowed in Scotland. Coming down to more recent times, the Swintons are connected with Sir Walter Scott and with the great family of Home.

Legends of the wild boar are perpetuated in many ways, including the name Swine Wood for a tract of land. The Swine Loch was drained in 1700 and has been forgotten by later generations. Children of the village have told me that the mercat cross marks the spot where Alan de Swinton slew the last boar. That tradition is hard to credit; but the late Brigadier Alan Swinton told me another story of Swinton Green which is easier to believe. Near the site of the present mercat cross there were some antique stones, called 'preaching stones'. Here in the very early days of Christianity, before Swinton had a church, monks from Coldingham Priory used to stand to preach to the assembled people. These relics disappeared before I knew the village, as did the 'tron' where heavy goods were weighed.

The green is so pleasant a feature of this place that it is worth dwelling on. The fine mercat cross, standing more or less in the centre of the wide grassy expanse, is a round column of local stone, with subtly tapered and curved sides (entasis), raised on a square base and reached by three shallow stone steps. To the stranger it is a curious centrepiece for a football ground. Yet the tradition of football on this green is very old, and anyone who tries to stop it does so at his peril. The ancient monument has not so far suffered damage; players have special rules regarding balls that touch it. The very last act of the Middle District Council, offshoot of the Berwickshire County Council (before both came to an end in May 1975) was to provide money for a new set of goal-posts and nets here. At the east end swings and a chute provide entertainment for the younger children. This is a real focus of village life, not just a picnic spot for tourists. A large part of Swinton, including the green, has been designated a Conservation Area, which means that its character will be preserved.

It is the only 'planned village' in Berwickshire, and is based on the rectangular intersection of roads, with a number of houses built in pairs or terraces, mostly of local stone and in simple styles. The late Brigadier Swinton told me that he was once flying from Edinburgh to the South and noticed a comely, well-planned little country place below him. Suddenly he realised that this must be Swinton – his own village. The same informant said that the massive circular base of a tower behind Greenview Garage is not, as most local people think, the remains of a doocot; it is that much rarer construction, a windmill. Unhappily it has been allowed to decay past the point at which it might have been restored. Windmills are uncommon here (as in the rest of Scotland) largely because there is usually plenty of water-power. At Edington there is an operative grain mill, and at Cockburn, between Duns and Abbey St Bathans, the old grain mill on a lovely stretch of the Whiteadder has been excellently preserved by the enterprise of Mrs Prentice, with its original water-wheels and associated grinding wheels intact. The mill building is sometimes shown to garden visitors and to others who are interested in the craftsmanship of the old millwrights.

In this fought-over country of the Berwickshire Merse, it is surprising that Swinton should show so little trace of a castle or tower-house. After the disastrous Battle of Flodden – which took place only a few miles to the south – an Act of 1535 ordered every Scots Borderer possessed of land to the value of £100 to build a 'barmkyn and tower' as refuge for himself and his retainers. The barmkyn was a walled enclosure for cattle. Even in these affairs of life and death an element of class distinction crept in, for Sir Robert Ker let it be known that his fortified house near Jedburgh must have battlements. 'That is the grace of a house and makes it look like a castle, hence so noblest. The other would look like a pele.' The plain pele-tower was for lesser gentry.

There were also 'parsons' peles', fortified houses built for the protection of the priesthood. Chirnside once had a tower beside its church, and traces of a fosse around Swinton church lead one to suppose that an earlier forerunner of the present building may have been a partially fortified tower structure, into which the villagers retired with their priest when the alarm was raised to indicate trouble approaching from the English side of the Tweed.

The present parish church dates from a major restoration of 1729, the north aisle having been added in 1782. In an arched recess beside the pulpit there is a stone effigy, said to be that of the late twelfth-century baron, Alan de Swinton. The original edifice (which may have been eleventh century) was replaced in 1593. That building, supposedly unsafe, proved hard to demolish when the 1729 restoration began, and (says a report of later date) might have stood for ages. In 1098, when Coldingham was founded, King Edgar dedicated the church of Swinton and consigned to the monks upon the altar *Villam totam Swinton cum divisis, sicut Liulf habuit.* The church remained in the hands of Coldingham Priory until the Reformation. In 1296 William de Swinton, vicar, swore fealty to Edward I at Berwick. James Robson, writing in 1893, says that the effigy of Alan de Swinton is 'holding a large clue of yarn, by dexterous use of which in one hand while he used his sword in the other, he despatched a great wild boar in that field at Swinton Hill which still retains the name of Alan's Cairn.'

A list of names of the vicars since 1590 includes that of Edward Jameson, MA, outlawed in 1647 for preaching at conventicles and reinstated in 1687. Swinton and Simprim were united in 1761. The Swinton arms are to be seen on the southern face of the present Swinton church, above the outside stairway to the gallery. This is one of the oldest heraldic stone carvings known in Scotland. The single bell, inscribed with its name of 'Mary', in Latin, dates from 1499 and is of Low Country origin. In 1910, when Sir Robert Lorimer supervised a considerable renovation of the church, he found stone from Swinton quarries so pleasing that he used some in his later work at the Scottish National War Memorial in Edinburgh Castle.

Not far from the parish church, an old cottage in Coldstream road bears a plaque stating that in 1843 it was used as the 'Free Protesting Church of Scotland'. Locally it is known as Fiddlers' Ha'. Perhaps it was the scene of more rollicking groups before 1843. The large Victorian church on the north side of Swinton Green, erected in 1860, was in use until in 1932 union took place with the parish church. Its fine steeple, thought to be dangerous, was removed soon afterwards, leaving a truncated tower which has a sadly cropped look. The building is in use as a community hall. The tower clock, a useful feature of village life, has been expertly maintained by Mr John Paterson. The reputation of this versatile inhabitant has spread far beyond Swinton, for he was a highly skilled craftsman and a maker (among other things) of excellent violins. One of his instruments travelled in 1973 to a Scottish museum in Toronto.

Our tape-recording of John telling the story of how at an early age he became interested in fiddles, and in time taught himself to make and play them, deserves a place in Scotland's archives. When folk in humbler walks of life had to leave school at twelve (with no grants available for technical training or university studies), the man who, after long hours in the fields, managed to acquire specialised knowledge and develop skills like John's must be given honour without reserve. One of the greatest thrills Swinton had to offer us as incomers was the sight of many violins hanging from the rafters of the Paterson cottage, strung up like a collection of hams. John Paterson died in 1980.

Swinton still has its own school – a blessing now denied to many villages. With the addition of children from Ladykirk, the roll stands at about sixty and there are three teachers. In 1973 a scheme for general improvement to the appearance of the place (known as the Swinton Face-Lift) was inaugurated by the Berwickshire Civic Society and carried through by the local community. In order to bring in the children, I devised a competition in the form of a scrap-book about the village, open to all residents under sixteen. Entries came from primary age children and from those who had passed on to the High School at Duns.

One family, all under twelve, managed to scoop three first prizes with entries of more than passing value. The history of the village post-office, with a photograph of the 1914-18 War postwoman (in long tweed skirt, high-necked blouse and buttoned boots), was carefully recorded by Anne Kinghorn, daughter of the present postmistress. Her brother Neill, at the age of nine, had no inhibitions about illustrating his story of local farming with original sketches of tractors and monstrous combine harvesters. He observed that the local stream, the Leet, passes along the north side of the village and is the only river in Berwickshire to run away from the sea, until it joins the Tweed at Coldstream. The youngest member of the clan, wee David, concentrated on Sunday School ('I

John Paterson, violin maker of Swinton

had perfect attendance') and the Primary School. This is sub-standard, an outmoded building of 1876, and David modestly hopes for a modern one 'some time'. Most small children mentioned Sunday School. Diana Gray wrote succinctly, 'It is all about God.'

The enterprise of the Kinghorn family earned the trio a badge from the children's popular 'Blue Peter' programme on T.V. Swinton likes to remember that its first director, Peter Purves, is a descendant of the family which used to run a draper's and tailor's business in Main Street, in what became the butcher's shop. Mrs

Craig still keeps the Purves shop sign. Swinton enjoys another rare distinction, in that the butcher is a charming exponent of that trade – a lady. She does not qualify for the *Guinness Book of Records*, for there have been other women here and there, including a Miss Priestly in Bradford, Yorkshire. But they are rare birds.

In the surrounding country it is worth while to seek out Simprim, where relics of the tiny church may easily be found beside the Coldstream road. It lies nearly opposite a farm with a history going back to 1686. The tall farm building, the 'High Barn' with crow-stepped gables, was used to hide cattle on two floors during troublous times. Herding beasts up the stone stairs must have been an arduous task, but according to tradition it was accomplished. Many of them had been brought from England by Border Reivers. The famous Thomas Boston, Calvinist minister and author of *Fourfold State of Man*, ministered at Simprim from 1699 to 1707. In order to accommodate the crowds that gathered on Sacrament Sundays, it was his custom to transfer the service from kirk to barn.

The curiously-named hamlet of Fogo has a fine seventeenth-century bridge over the Blackadder – whose waters do not suit the salmon, being too dark and peaty for it, although good quality trout and eels are found here. Adder does not refer to the snake-like windings of the stream. It is from the old word for water: *adur*, *avon*, being the same. The 'black' adder is certainly of darker complexion than the 'white' one. Fogo church is an ancient foundation, named in a charter of Malcolm IV, but very much modernised. The farm of Sisterpath, a mile off, retains a memory of the nuns, sisters, whose convent once stood on the site. In the church a 'Harcarse' gallery, with arms (Hog of Harcarse) dating from 1677, relates to an ancient property whose family name died out in this locality centuries ago. Their subsequent history is a surprising one.

Old Harcarse House, much altered, may be found in a little secret lane south-west of the A6112 road between Swinton and Duns. It is an oblong stone building of considerable antiquity, with a square tower at the rear. In the thirteenth century Adam of Harcarres was elected Abbot of Melrose, and one Thomas Harcars became sub-Prior of Arbroath in 1482. The family name appeared in Perth in the fourteenth century, and travelled to Orkney, where it was spelled Hercas, Harkass and Arcas. The current Orkney version is Harcus. The lands of Harcarse in Berwickshire went to

David Home of Wedderburn in 1415, and for a brief period in the sixteenth century they were held by Swintons of Swinton.

There is a local belief that Mary Queen of Scots, on her ride from Jedburgh to Edinburgh in 1566, rested at Harcarse, but of this there is no available record. It belonged to Home of Wedderburn at the time, and Queen Mary certainly stayed at the latter place.

In 1670 Roger Hog purchased the Harcarse lands. He became a Lord of Session with the judicial title of Lord Harcarse. His son, William, had a cloth factory at Harcarse which in 1699-1700 'did make, dress and lit [dye] as much red cloath as did furnish all the Earl of Hyndford's regiment of dragoons'. The last Hog of Harcarse, a lady named Jean, disponed her estate in 1774 to Robertson of Ladykirk. She died unmarried and was buried within the Kirk of Fogo. Robertsons and their descendants, the Askews, owned Harcarse until 1911.

An exciting present-day sequel to all this history took the form of an unexpected visitor from New Zealand. In 1972 Mr Eric Arcus arrived in Berwickshire in search of the home of his ancestors. He was able to prove his descent from the Harcarse family through his great-grandfather, Laurence Arcus, born in 1795. The Lord Lyon regards this branch as entitled to bear arms – another reference to local wild boars, with an oak tree 'proper' for a crest. His family migrated to New Zealand from Shetland (having gone there from Orkney), and members of the clan still live around the Dunrossness area. We residents of Swinton like to think of the old house and lands of Harcarse being talked about in the antipodes, under the Southern Cross.

The Yetholms

The companion villages of Kirk Yetholm and Town Yetholm lie almost on the Border between Scotland and England, where it takes a sharp turn southward from the Tweed and dives into the wild Cheviot Hills. The Bowmont Water, a swift-flowing stream from those hills, separates the two villages and demarcates the distinctive character of each. Here is the very core of what to me is the best south-eastern Border country; open, unspoilt, green, sheep country with few trees, wild but not desolate, a fine stretch for walkers and those who will at least get out of cars to feel the wind in their hair.

Town Yetholm, as its name suggests, is the larger and more built-up of the two villages, dignified with post-office, bank and police station. Kirk Yetholm, which seems more rural and more ancient, has a strange little church, built in the 1830s, whose very dark whinstone walls and narrow, pinnacled tower suggest (when viewed from the right angle) a prick-eared black cat. There is also the unique pink-washed cottage beside the green, which has 'The Palace' inscribed on its front gable. This must be the most miniature palace in Britain, if not in the world.

Until 1902 occupants of the regal but-and-ben were styled 'Kings and Queens' of the Border gypsies, members of the Faa family whose lineage can be traced at least as far back as the fourteenth century. Their 'kingdom' extended beyond the region covered by this book, down west as far as Galloway. In 1540 the gypsy leader, 'Johnne Faw, Lord and Erle of Litill Egipt', was in correspondence with Scotland's monarch, James V.

Yetholm (spelt Jetham in medieval times), was once described as 'inaccessible from without and not to be left from within' – words which are now belied by good motor roads. To the gypsies of old, inaccessibility from without, causing trouble to those authorities who might wish to inquire too closely into their doings, made this place ideal as a winter headquarters. If it became necessary to slip away quietly, the neighbouring Cheviots provided simple enough going for folk accustomed to riding rough over trails known only to themselves.

The sleepily remote air worn now by this, the last parish in Scotland before the road leaves for Wooler in Northumberland, suggests that nothing has ever occurred to excite people, beyond natural patterns of birth and death. The impression is highly deceiving, for the place stands on an ancient highway which for centuries was used by invading forces in both directions. It saw the sad remnants of Scotland's armies after their defeat at Flodden, a battlefield lying only six miles away to the east. Scotland's king, James IV, died fighting here beside some 18,000 of his countrymen. According to local tradition, the bodies of many chieftains were brought back by survivors for interment in Scottish soil. During the nineteenth-century rebuilding of Yetholm's kirk, a stone coffin containing a skeleton of immense size was unearthed six feet below the floor of the old church. Many people regarded this as a relic of the Flodden disaster.

The Reverend John Baird, that energetic minister who – besides

The 'Gipsy Palace' at Kirk Yetholm

having the damp little thatched kirk replaced by one of whinstone –
contrived to build a new manse, and a three-arched stone bridge
spanning the Bowmont Water, managed also to find time for his
gypsy parishioners, and gave considerable thought to the education
of their children. Although these people had settled homes in the
village, they were incurable roamers in the spring and summer
months. Heads were difficult to count, but they were believed to
number between 100 and 140 in Mr Baird's time. During many
centuries of Border life they had nearly always taken partners of
their own race; yet despite so much inbreeding there were few cases
of imbecility. When they were in their winter quarters many of them
would attend the Yetholm Kirk and send their children to Sunday
School.·

In spite of this, the minister felt very dissatisfied with facilities
provided for educating the young gypsies. He prepared a scheme

under which the travellers' offspring would be boarded out in the village and given regular instruction while their parents were on the road. A newly-formed Edinburgh Society which aimed at 'reforming' the Scottish gypsies became closely associated with the zealous Mr Baird's plan, and between them they had the wretched hovel which passed for a school replaced in 1843 by a larger and better building. Being geared to the needs of neglected gypsy children, this has been classed as the earliest 'Ragged School' in all Scotland. Although Baird gained considerable influence over his gypsy parishioners, he was not altogether successful in his attempts to persuade them to take regular employment. On one occasion some rebellious inhabitants showed their resentment by setting the glebe cornstacks on fire. After the minister's death in 1859 no more was heard of the Society for the Reform of the Gypsies.

The dynasty continued to flourish, maintaining its royalty in the little palace until 1902, when Charles Faa Blythe died there, the last of his line. The appearance of his mother, Queen Esther Faa, is known today from many photographs taken by a photographer (Gibson) who conducted a well-known business in Coldstream. In one she is shown with the gypsy sword of state, wearing a long, wide-sleeved scarlet robe and a kind of helmet made from patterned fabric. There is also a picture of the coronation of her son Charles II in 1898. The first resident king, old Will Faa, received the by-name of 'Gley-neckit Wull', owing to a crooked neck. During his long life he had twenty-four children by three wives. Every one of these was given a magnificent christening ceremony, attended by King William wearing his crown and robes. He died in 1784 and was buried with great pomp at Yetholm.

His son, William II, plain 'Will Faa', distinguished himself as a prize-fighter when young. He was also engaged in the profitable business of liquor smuggling, a trade then rife in the Borders. In his later years he became landlord of a Yetholm inn, where he acted the sporting gentleman, wearing a hat covered in fishing flies. He also played football very well, his prowess in the annual contest between married and single men of the parish bringing him more than local fame. Afterwards he and his subjects would eat, drink and dance in the several convenient hostelries until morning. At the age of ninety-six he faded out of this world, never having suffered a day's ill health.

His successor, a brother-in-law named Charlie Blythe, was the intellectual member of this royal line. A diligent student, well

The pony stud, Yetholm

versed in Border ballads, he frequently pitched his tent in summer on the Tweed bank near Abbotsford. There Sir Walter Scott had many a long talk with him, unaware that he spoke with a future King Charles. Much of the information gleaned by the author was used in the Waverley novels, and it is said that a certain Jean Gordon, born in Kirk Yetholm towards the close of the seventeenth century, provided Scott with the model for Meg Merrilies in *Guy Mannering*. Blythe died in Yetholm in 1861 at the age of eighty-three, after a peaceful reign of fourteen years.

The matter of succession could hardly be described as peaceful. Charlie's son David declined the honour, which led to a battle for the vacant throne between his two sisters. The elder, Esther Faa, proved more than a match for the more masculine younger woman, known as 'Black-bearded Nell', and had herself proclaimed Queen. Riding on a pony, she travelled to the Cross of Yetholm, there to be crowned before a large crowd. After the ceremony the procession, led by a piper, made the round of all the local inns, ending with a dance on the green at Kirk Yetholm. Esther's reign lasted from

1861 to 1883, when she died in her palace. Her coffin was covered with her robes of office, and some 1,500 people attended the burial. The flowers included a wreath of white roses from Lady John Scott of Spottiswoode.

Following an interregnum of fifteen years, Charles Faa Blythe was crowned King of the Border Gypsies. This swarthy, vivid character had been a rover for most of his life, but agreed to assume the cares of state and take up settled residence at the age of seventy. The Gypsy Palace was painted up to receive him. His reign lasted only four years, and since his death in 1902 there has been no gypsy monarch in Kirk Yetholm. The former palace, modernised but not outwardly altered in character, is occupied by an incomer who has made a charming little garden round about it.

Nearly opposite, the black-and-white Border Hotel sits snugly on the edge of Kirk Yetholm Green, where the occasional bus from Kelso turns and waits for passengers. On a fine summer's day the tree-shaded grass provides here one of the best picnic sites imaginable, within sight of the great humps of Cheviot and the Scottish end of the long Pennine Way. Walkers coming off it are entitled to claim a free glass of beer each in the hotel bar. There are other, gentler walks within easy reach. A marked footpath alongside the Bowmont Water, entered near the church, is worth exploring even by the casual stroller.

The water running clear and swift, the 'unprofitable gold of the gorse' spread lavishly on either hand, the patches of woodland gently clothing the feet of the hill called Staerough, the songs of thrush and blackbird: above all, the absence of noises made by machinery, combine to create a small paradise for the pedestrian. The Bowmont, a stream of Scottish origin, rises under Windygyle Hill on the northern edge of the Border, runs down past Cocklawfoot, Mowhaugh, Attonburn and Cushat End; thence through the Yetholms into Northumberland, clinging to the boundary of the National Park as far as Kirknewton and eventually joining the River Till a little to the north of Wooler. Having ventured thus far into England, the Bowmont Water (now swelling the Till) doubles back on an almost parallel course to join the Tweed below Coldstream. Here that noble river forms the Border down as far as Gainslaw, where the County of the Borough and Town of Berwick-upon-Tweed has appropriated the lowest reaches (and lands to the north of them) in England's name.

If the exterior of Yetholm's kirk provokes startled comment, owing to its blackness (one writer has called it 'dour – with the warning voice of John Knox issuing from its porch'), the interior is all sweetness and light. The neat rows of pale-coloured pews, the wall panelling, all wood stripped clean of sticky varnish stain, the many large windows of clear glass which allow so much light to fill the uncluttered space, provide a suitable setting for that artless old hymn composed long ago by Puritans in America:

> 'Tis the gift to be simple, 'tis the gift to be free,
> 'Tis the gift to come down where you ought to be;
> And when we find ourselves in the place just right,
> It will be in the valley of love and delight.

Appendix

Seasons and times when admission may be obtained are shown here as guides. They are subject to change and should be verified at tourist centres or by application to the owners or curators of properties. Because of inflation, charges are not quoted. Ruined abbeys and uninhabited castles are generally inexpensive.

Abbeys
(ruined)

Melrose, Kelso and Dryburgh Abbeys
(Department of the Environment)

April 1st to September 30th
Weekdays   9.30 am to 7 pm
Sundays   2 pm to 7 pm

October 1st to March 31st
Weekdays   9.30 am to 4 pm
Sundays   2 pm to 4 pm

Jedburgh Abbey

Times as above, except closed all day Friday and on Thursday afternoon.

Art Galleries

Berwick-upon-Tweed
Library building, Marygate

Weekdays in summer
Tel. Berwick-upon-Tweed 7320

Hawick, Scott Art Gallery
Wilton Lodge
Tel. Hawick 3457

April to November
Weekdays   10 am to 5 pm
Sundays   2 pm to 5 pm

Winter
Weekdays   10 am to 4 pm
Closed on Sundays

Castles and Towers
(uninhabited)

Hermitage Castle, Hawick
(Department of the Environment)

April 1st to September 30th
Weekdays   9.30 am to 7 pm
Sundays   2 pm to 7 pm

October 1st to March 31st
Weekdays   9.30 am to 4 pm
Sundays   2 pm to 4 pm

Neidpath Castle, Peebles
(The Lord Wemyss Trust)

Open April 15th to mid-October
Monday to Saturday
10 am to 1 pm and 2 pm to 6 pm
Sunday
1 pm to 6 pm

Curator: Tel. Peebles 20333

Smailholm Tower, Melrose
(Department of the Environment)

April 1st to September 30th
Weekdays   9.30 am to 7 pm
Sundays   2 pm to 7 pm

Car park at foot of tower, which is signposted on B6404

Great Houses
(inhabited)

Abbotsford, Melrose
(Mrs P. Maxwell-Scott, O.B.E.)

Situated on B6360 road west of Melrose on the south bank of River Tweed. House open from late March through October.
Weekdays 10 am to 5 pm
and on Sunday afternoons

Teashop open April through September. Facilities for disabled visitors in wheelchairs.

Tel. Galashiels 2043

Bowhill, Selkirk
(The Duke of Buccleuch)

Situated off the A708 road, 3 miles west of Selkirk.
House open from Easter to late September several days each week.
Weekdays 12.30 pm to 5 pm
Sundays   2 pm to 6 pm

Afternoon teas, gift shop, adventure play area, nature trails, riding centre and pony trekking.

Buccleuch Recreational Enterprises Ltd., Bowhill, Selkirk.
Facilities for the handicapped in wheelchairs. Disabled drivers may drive right up to the house.

Tel. Selkirk 20732.

Floors Castle, Kelso
(The Duke of Roxburghe)

Castle open to the public over Easter week-end and thereafter on five days each week from early May through September.
Open 11 am to 5.30 pm, last admission to the castle at 4.45 pm.
Closed on Saturdays and Mondays, except for Bank Holidays.
Entrance to the castle is by the main gates at the end of Roxburghe Street, Kelso. The car park is a few minutes' walk away from the frontage, but disabled drivers may drive right up to the castle, if application is made at the ticket booth.
Most of the apartments are on one level, leading one from another. The restaurant, sited in an attractive courtyard, may be reached from inside the castle by a stair, or from outside by a short path.

Further particulars from the Factor, Roxburghe Estates Office, Kelso, Roxburghshire. Tel. Kelso 3333.

Floors Garden Centre. With its own car park, refreshment room, gift shop and toilet facilities, this forms a separate complex.
To reach this centre, take the A6089 northerly towards Nenthorn, past its junction with B6364, after which the Garden Centre signs are well displayed. Admission is free, and the Centre is open all the year round, seven days a week. Tel. Kelso 2530.

Manderston, Duns
(Mr Adrian Palmer)

House and grounds open mid-May to late September, Thursdays and Sundays, also Bank Holiday Mondays in May and September. Open 2 pm to 5.30 pm.
Also at other times of the year by special appointment. Parties at reduced rates. Admission charges for the garden, stables and marble dairy are half the combined house-and-gardens rate.
The entrance for visitors is situated off the A6105, a short distance down the turning marked Buxley. The car park is some way from the house, but disabled drivers may drive right up to the forecourt if application is made at the ticket booth. Be sure to ask which part of the forecourt may be used, to avoid having to shift the car. There is a flight of steps up to the door and the apartments shown are on two floors.

Further details from The Secretary, Manderston, Duns, Berwickshire, Tel. Duns 3450.

Mellerstain, Gordon
(Lord Binning)

Signposted on the A6089 road between Gordon and Nenthorn, a mile to westward of the main road.
House and garden open for Easter week-end and from May 1st until September 30th. Daily 1.30 pm to 5.30 pm (except Saturdays).
No admission after 5 pm.

207

Further particulars from the Curator, Mellerstain, Berwickshire. Tel. Gordon 225.

Monteviot, Jedburgh
(The Marquis of Lothian)

House and garden open on Wednesdays only, May to November 1.30 pm to 5.30 pm.
Woodland Centre (Harestanes) usually as above. For special parties, apply to Lothian Estates Office, Jedburgh 2201, where details of the Visitors' Centre at Harestanes may be obtained.

Thirlestane Castle, Lauder
(Captain the Hon. Gerald Maitland-Carew)

Open at Whitsun 1983 and through September, on Saturdays, Sundays, Wednesdays and Thursdays.

Border Country Life Museum
(Attached to the castle)

Opening in Summer 1983 until October, and at week-ends throughout the year.

Inquiries:
Castle: Tel. Lauder 254
Museum: Tel. Lauder 560

Traquair, Innerleithen
(Mr Peter Maxwell Stuart)

Approached by a turning off A72 road, B709, near the Traquair Arms Hotel in Innerleithen.
House and grounds open daily, from Easter Saturday to October 25th 1.30 pm to 5.30 pm, except in July and August, when they open at 10.30 am. No admission after 5 pm. Separate admission charges for grounds and house. Car park close to house and tea-room. Tickets for admission to house to be obtained from the gift shop on left within courtyard gates. Cloak-rooms in the same wing.
A leaflet describing a tour of the grounds – woodland walks, maze, etc. – may be had from the shop.

Further details from Maxwell Stuart, Tel. Innerleithen 830323 or from tea-room. Tel. Innerleithen 830777 where bookings for parties are taken. Several craft workshops may be visited in the grounds.

Grounds

Dawyck Aboretum, Peebles
(Royal Botanic Garden, Edinburgh)

Open April to September, daily 10 am to 5 pm.
Turn south off A72 west of Peebles, taking B712. No animals admitted. In winter, visitors may be admitted on special application.

Duns Castle Nature Reserve, Duns
(Mr G. H. Hay)

Usually open to visitors on foot. Details from Scottish Wildlife Trust, 26 Johnstone Terrace, Edinburgh. Tel. 031-226 4602.

Harestanes Woodland Centre, Roxburghshire
(The Marquis of Lothian)

See Monteviot, under 'Great Houses'.

The Hirsel, Coldstream
(Lord Home of the Hirsel, K.T.)

Open to visitors on foot – cars are left either in the Dundock Wood car park or at the Information Centre at the east end of the lake. The Centre is reached off the A698, turning into The Hirsel by Coldstream Lodge.

Leaflets, *The Hirsel,* and *Birds seen at The Hirsel,* may be had from the Information Centre or by post (send stamped envelope) from The Estate Office, The Hirsel, Coldstream, TD12 4LP.

St Abbs Nature Reserve
(National Trust for Scotland)

Turn left off B6438 half a mile before St Abbs.
Parking is being made outside the reserve. Inside, there is restricted parking (twelve vehicles) close to the lighthouse. For this a fee is charged, except

to the disabled, pensioners, members of the Wildlife Trust and the National Trust for Scotland.

Open all the year round, closed at dusk. People on foot admitted free of charge. Tel. Warden Coldingham 443.

Information Centre
(National Trust for Scotland)

Priorwood, Melrose

Shop, information office and garden with picnic area. Garden specialises in flowers for drying, with arrangements on sale.

May 1 to end October,
Monday to Saturday 10 am to 6 pm
Sundays 1.30 pm to 5.30 pm

Month of April, and end October to December 24th,
Monday to Friday 10 am to 1 pm and 2 pm to 5.30 pm
Saturday 10 am to 5.30 pm

Museums

Berwick-upon-Tweed

Museum in Library building – see times shown for Art Gallery.
Town Hall and old prison – by arrangement with the custodian.
Tel. Berwick-upon-Tweed 7433.

K.O.S.B. Museum, Ravensdowne Barracks. Open all the year round except on Sundays.
Hours: 9 am to 12 noon, 1 pm to 4.30 pm Monday to Friday
Saturday mornings only.

Coldstream, Market Square

Mid-May to mid-September.

Duns, Jim Clark Room,
44 Newtown Duns

Open Easter to October. For special visits at other times, Tel. Duns 2331 extension 30.

Eyemouth – Maritime Museum

Open Easter week-end and first week-end in May, then May 7th to October 30th on weekdays, Sunday afternoons only.
Tel. Eyemouth 50678.

Hawick Museum – see Scott Art Gallery, Wilton Lodge, for times.

Jedburgh Castle – old prison

Open early April to end September 10 am to 12 noon and 1 pm to 5 pm weekdays and Saturdays.
Sundays 1 pm to 5 pm.

Jedburgh, Mary Queen of Scots House

Open mid-March to mid-October.
Every day 10 am to 12.30 pm and 1 pm to 5.30 pm.

Peebles Museum

Open Monday, Tuesday, Thursday & Friday 9 am to 7 pm.
Wednesday 9 am to 5.30 pm.
Closed on Saturday

Selkirk, Sir Walter Scott's courtroom

Ettrick & Lauderdale District Council.
Tel. Selkirk 20096 or Selkirk 21382 (caretaker).
Open only on application.

Lauder, Thirlestane Castle

Border Country Life Museum opening Summer 1983.
Details given under Thirlestane Castle.

Walkerburn, Clan Royal Museum of Textiles

Open April 1st to October 30th.
Weekdays 9.30 am to 5 pm.
Sundays 2 pm to 6 pm.
Other months, special times arranged for parties.
Tel. Walkerburn 281.